Final Report of the Forty-first Antarctic Treaty Consultative Meeting

ANTARCTIC TREATY
CONSULTATIVE MEETING

Final Report of the Forty-first Antarctic Treaty Consultative Meeting

Buenos Aires, Argentina
13 - 18 May 2018

Volume I

Secretariat of the Antarctic Treaty
Buenos Aires
2018

Published by:

Secretariat of the Antarctic Treaty
Secrétariat du Traité sur l' Antarctique
Секретариат Договора об Антарктике
Secretaría del Tratado Antártico

Maipú 757, Piso 4
C1006ACI Ciudad Autónoma
Buenos Aires - Argentina
Tel: +54 11 4320 4260
Fax: +54 11 4320 4253

This book is also available from: *www.ats.aq* (digital version)
and online-purchased copies.

ISSN 2346-9897
ISBN (vol. I): 978-987-4024-67-1
ISBN (complete work): 978-987-4024-63-3

Contents

VOLUME I

VOLUME II

PART II. MEASURES, DECISIONS AND RESOLUTIONS (Cont.)

4. Management Plans

3. List of Participants

Consultative Parties

Non-Consultative Parties

Observers, Experts and Guests

Host Country Secretariat

Antarctic Treaty Secretariat

Acronyms and Abbreviations

ACAP	Agreement on the Conservation of Albatrosses and Petrels
ACBR	Antarctic Conservation Biogeographic Region
ASMA	Antarctic Specially Managed Area
ASOC	Antarctic and Southern Ocean Coalition
ASPA	Antarctic Specially Protected Area
ATS	Antarctic Treaty System or Antarctic Treaty Secretariat
ATCM	Antarctic Treaty Consultative Meeting
ATME	Antarctic Treaty Meeting of Experts
BP	Background Paper
CCAMLR	Convention on the Conservation of Antarctic Marine Living Resources and/or Commission for the Conservation of Antarctic Marine Living Resources
CCAS	Convention for the Conservation of Antarctic Seals
CCRWP	Climate Change Response Work Programme
CEE	Comprehensive Environmental Evaluation
CEP	Committee for Environmental Protection
COMNAP	Council of Managers of National Antarctic Programs
EIA	Environmental Impact Assessment
EIES	Electronic Information Exchange System
HSM	Historic Site and Monument
IAATO	International Association of Antarctica Tour Operators
IBA	Important Bird Area
ICAO	International Civil Aviation Organization
ICG	Intersessional Contact Group
IEE	Initial Environmental Evaluation
IGP&I Clubs	International Group of Protection and Indemnity Clubs
IHO	International Hydrographic Organization
IMO	International Maritime Organization
IOC	Intergovernmental Oceanographic Commission
IOPC Funds	International Oil Pollution Compensation Funds
IP	Information Paper
IPCC	Intergovernmental Panel on Climate Change
IUCN	International Union for Conservation of Nature

MARPOL	International Convention for the Prevention of Pollution from Ships
MPA	Marine Protected Area
RCC	Rescue Coordination Centre
SAR	Search and Rescue
SCAR	Scientific Committee on Antarctic Research
SC-CAMLR	Scientific Committee of CCAMLR
SGCCR	Subsidiary Group on Climate Change Response
SGMP	Subsidiary Group on Management Plans
SOLAS	International Convention for the Safety of Life at Sea
SOOS	Southern Ocean Observing System
SP	Secretariat Paper
UAV/RPAS	Unmanned Aerial Vehicle / Remotely Piloted Aircraft System
UNEP	United Nations Environment Programme
UNFCCC	United Nations Framework Convention on Climate Change
WMO	World Meteorological Organization
WP	Working Paper
WTO	World Tourism Organization

PART I
Final Report

1. Final Report

Final Report of the Forty-first Antarctic Treaty Consultative Meeting

Buenos Aires, Argentina, 16-18 May 2018

(1)   Pursuant to Article IX of the Antarctic Treaty, Representatives of the Consultative Parties (Argentina, Australia, Belgium, Brazil, Bulgaria, Chile, China, the Czech Republic, Ecuador, Finland, France, Germany, India, Italy, Japan, the Republic of Korea, the Netherlands, New Zealand, Norway, Peru, Poland, the Russian Federation, South Africa, Spain, Sweden, Ukraine, the United Kingdom of Great Britain and Northern Ireland, the United States of America, and Uruguay) met in Buenos Aires from 16 to 18 May 2018, for the purpose of exchanging information, holding consultations and considering and recommending to their Governments measures in furtherance of the principles and objectives of the Treaty.

(2)   The Meeting was also attended by delegations from the following Contracting Parties to the Antarctic Treaty which were not Consultative Parties: Belarus, Canada, Colombia, Malaysia, Portugal, Romania, Switzerland, Turkey and Venezuela.

(3)   In accordance with Rules 2 and 31 of the Rules of Procedure, Observers from the Commission for the Conservation of Antarctic Marine Living Resources (CCAMLR), the Scientific Committee on Antarctic Research (SCAR), and the Council of Managers of National Antarctic Programs (COMNAP) attended the meeting.

(4)   In accordance with Rule 39 of the Rules of Procedure, Experts from the following international organisations and non-governmental organisations attended the Meeting: the Antarctic and Southern Ocean Coalition (ASOC), the Secretariat of the Agreement on the Conservation of Albatrosses and Petrels (ACAP), the International Association of Antarctica Tour Operators (IAATO), and the World Meteorological Organization (WMO).

(5)   The Host Country Argentina fulfilled its information requirements towards the Contracting Parties, Observers and Experts through Secretariat Circulars, letters and a dedicated website.

Item 1: Opening of the Meeting

(6)   The Meeting was officially opened on 16 May 2018. On behalf of the Host Government, in accordance with Rules 5 and 6 of the Rules of Procedure, the Head of the Host Country Secretariat, Juan Antonio Barreto, called the Meeting to order and proposed the candidacy of Ambassador María Teresa Kralikas as Chair of ATCM XLI. The proposal was accepted.

(7)   The Chair warmly welcomed all Parties, Observers and Experts to Argentina. The Chair highlighted Argentina's historic commitment to Antarctica and the Antarctic Treaty System. She noted the unusual circumstances that led to this condensed ATCM XLI–CEP XXI, and thanked the Delegation of Argentina and the Antarctic Treaty Secretariat for organising the meetings in such a short time frame. The Chair emphasised that this was not a normal or ordinary meeting, and should not be seen as setting a precedent for future meetings. She wished the delegates well in their deliberations and expressed hope for a fruitful meeting.

(8)   Delegates observed a minute of silence in honour of the passing of Vice Commodore Carlos Rolando (Argentina), Shri Subhajit Sen (India), frigate captain Javier Montojo Salazar (Spain), and Ship Operations Manager Mr Bigboy Joseph (South Africa). Delegates also honoured Dr José Valencia, a leading Chilean Antarctic ornithologist, and General Jorge Edgar Leal, who led Argentina's first land expedition to the South Pole and established Esperanza Station.

(9)   His Excellency Jorge Faurie, Argentine Minister of Foreign Affairs and Worship, joined the Meeting and warmly welcomed all delegates to Buenos Aires. In noting the honour Argentina felt in hosting the Meeting, he recognised the enormous efforts of the Argentine Ministry of Foreign Affairs, the Host Country Secretariat, and the Antarctic Treaty Secretariat in organising the Meeting at such short notice. His Excellency recalled Argentina's long and uninterrupted presence in Antarctica, and emphasised Argentina's continued commitment to the objectives and principles of the Antarctic Treaty System.

(10)   He underlined how the Treaty was the fruit of ambitious diplomatic achievements in its success over almost 60 years. As one of the 12 original

signatories to the Antarctic Treaty, whose membership had increased to 53, he noted Argentina's continuing commitment to strengthening the objectives of peace, science, international cooperation and environmental conservation in the region. Highlighting Argentina's involvement in all aspects of the Antarctic Treaty System by scientists, logistical staff, and diplomats, he described Argentina as one of the leaders in addressing the whole range of issues facing Antarctica. Recognising that the increase in Antarctic tourism has potential for generating economic growth yet also environmental impacts that may not be desirable, he underscored the importance of the advice from the Committee for Environmental Protection, as a fundamental pillar of the Antarctic Treaty System. Celebrating international cooperation, he also recalled the more than 20 cooperative agreements signed between Argentina and other Parties, including with the United Kingdom and Uruguay on the margins of this ATCM.

(11)   Conscious of the key role of Argentina's Antarctic gateway city and port of Ushuaia, he noted the arrangements put in place for those transiting through Argentina to undertake Antarctic research. He also noted the role of Argentina as a Member of CCAMLR, and its proposal of a Marine Protected Area (MPA) in the Western Antarctic Peninsula and the Southern Scotia Arc in collaboration with Chile. He further underscored that Argentina sees the role of CCAMLR as vital to the protection of the global environment and economic sustainability of activities in the region, and that Meetings such as this demonstrated that the Parties could manage new issues whilst maintaining a commitment to the original Treaty principles. In closing, he emphasised that all Parties had to always work together to maintain peace and collaboration at the core of all Antarctic activities for the next generations. He wished all Parties a fruitful meeting. The full remarks of his Excellency Jorge Faurie can be found in Volume II, Part III.1.

(12)   The Hon. Ségolène Royal, Ambassador for the Arctic and Antarctic Poles of France, made a speech on climate impacts in Antarctica and the role of Antarctica in the climate system.

Item 2: Appointment of Officers

(13)   Dr Martin Smolek, Head of Delegation of the Czech Republic, Host Country of ATCM XLII, was elected Vice-chair. In accordance with Rule 7 of the Rules of Procedure, Mr Albert Lluberas Bonaba, Executive Secretary of the Antarctic Treaty Secretariat, acted as Secretary to the Meeting. Mr Juan

Antonio Barreto, head of the Host Country Secretariat, acted as Deputy Secretary. Mr Ewan McIvor of Australia continued to act as Chair of the Committee for Environmental Protection. The Chair noted that Mr McIvor concluded his chairmanship of the CEP this year and thanked him for the work he had done. She further noted that Ms Birgit Njåstad of Norway had been elected the next CEP Chair.

(14) Noting the shorter timeframe for the Meeting, the Chair indicated that the ATCM would be conducted in plenary and that the Chairs of each Working Group would chair the discussions on the agenda items allocated to their Working Group within the plenary sessions. Agenda items on Policy, Legal and Institutional Issues were chaired by Ms Therese Johansen from Norway, and agenda items on Operations, Science and Tourism were chaired by Professor Dame Jane Francis from the United Kingdom and Mr Máximo Gowland from Argentina.

Item 3: Adoption of the Agenda

(15) The following Agenda was adopted:

1. Opening of the Meeting
2. Appointment of Officers
3. Adoption of the Agenda
4. Operation of the Antarctic Treaty System:
    a) Reports by Parties, Observers and Experts
    b) Venezuela's request to become a Consultative Party
    c) Urgent matters related to the Secretariat and Financial Issues
5. Biological Prospecting in Antarctica
6. Inspections under the Antarctic Treaty and the Environment Protocol
7. Tourism and Non-governmental Activities in the Antarctic Treaty Area
    a) Trends and patterns
    b) Environmental impacts
8. Multi-year Strategic Work Plan
9. Report of the Committee for Environmental Protection
10. Preparation of ATCM XLII
11. Any Other Business

12. Adoption of the Final Report

13. Close of the Meeting

(16)   The Meeting adopted the following allocation of agenda items:

- Plenary: Items 1, 2, 3, 4a, 9, 10, 11, 12, 13
- Working Group 1: Items 4b, 4c, and 5
- Working Group 2: Items 6 and 7
- Working Group 1 and 2: Item 8

(17)   The Meeting also decided to allocate draft instruments arising out of the work of the Committee for Environmental Protection and the Working Groups to a legal drafting group for consideration of their legal and institutional aspects.

Item 4a: Operation of the Antarctic Treaty System: Reports by Parties, Observers and Experts

(18)   Pursuant to Recommendation XIII-2, the Meeting noted reports from depositary governments and secretariats. In the light of the limited time available the Chair reported that the Information Papers would be taken as presented and highlighted that:

- Turkey had ratified the Environment Protocol, which entered into force for Turkey on 27 October 2017 (IP 6);
- Ukraine had reported that it had approved Measure 4 (2004), Measure 1 (2005) and Measure 15 (2009) (IP 16);
- Australia as depositary government of the Convention on the Conservation of Antarctic Marine Living Resources (CCAMLR) had received no new accessions to the Convention since ATCM XL (IP 39);
- the United Kingdom, as depositary government for the Convention for the Conservation of Antarctic Seals (CCAS), had not received any requests to accede to the Convention, or any instruments of accession since ATCM XL (IP 1 rev. 1);
- Australia, as depositary government for the Agreement on the Conservation of Albatrosses and Petrels (ACAP), had reported that there had been no new accessions to the Agreement since ATCM XL (IP 38);

- The Council of Managers of National Antarctic Programs (COMNAP), in its annual report, had reported it was celebrating its 30th anniversary (IP 11); and

- CCAMLR had also presented its annual report (IP 40).

(19) The United States informed the Meeting that Ukraine's announcement of its approval of Measure 4 (2004), Measure 1 (2005) and Measure 15 (2009) had not yet reached the depositary and was not yet officially recorded. It further explained that, once it had received the announcement through the formal depositary channels, it would communicate the approval to all Antarctic Treaty Parties.

(20) In recognition of its 60th anniversary, the Chair invited SCAR to address the Parties.

(21) SCAR reported on its history and the exceptional and extraordinary contribution of its members and their scientists during the last six decades. SCAR reminded the meeting that it was a body of the International Council for Science that facilitated science in, from and about Antarctica and the Southern Ocean, and provided advice to the Antarctic Treaty Parties, to other bodies of the Antarctic Treaty System, and to other organisations. SCAR noted that in 1957, the International Council of Scientific Unions established a Committee and asked it to prepare a plan for the scientific exploration of Antarctica. SCAR held its first meeting from 3 to 5 February 1958 in The Hague, the Netherlands. Since then the scope of activity and membership of SCAR had grown significantly. SCAR acknowledged the productive working relationships with the Parties to the Antarctic Treaty, the Committee for Environmental Protection, other bodies of the Antarctic Treaty System, Observers, Experts, and civil society. Finally, SCAR noted that it looked forward to further collaboration with the Parties, especially as it addressed the significant science challenges and global responsibilities facing the Antarctic community.

(22) The Meeting congratulated SCAR on its 60th anniversary and COMNAP on its 30th anniversary. In noting IP 11, several Parties thanked COMNAP for developing the COMNAP Antarctic Station Catalogue, which was a useful and well-developed tool that had increased efficiency.

(23) The Meeting took as read the papers submitted pursuant to Recommendation XIII-2:

- IP 1 rev. 1 *Report by the Depositary Government for the Convention for the Conservation of Antarctic Seals (CCAS) in Accordance with Recommendation XIII-2, Paragraph 2(D)* (United Kingdom). The

United Kingdom, in its capacity as Depositary of the Convention for the Conservation of Antarctic Seals (CCAS), reported that it had not received any requests to accede to the Convention, or any instruments of accession since ATCM XL.

- IP 6 *Report of the Depositary Government of the Antarctic Treaty and its Protocol in accordance with Recommendation XIII-2* (United States). The United States, in its capacity as Depositary Government of the Antarctic Treaty and its Environment Protocol, reported that there was one accession to the Protocol in the past year: Turkey had deposited its instrument of accession to the Protocol on 27 September 2017. The Protocol had entered into force for Turkey on 27 October 2017. It noted that there were currently 53 Parties to the Treaty and 40 Parties to the Protocol.

- IP 11 *Annual Report for 2017/18 of the Council of Managers of National Antarctic Programs (COMNAP)* (COMNAP). The paper highlighted that COMNAP's 30th anniversary would occur in September of 2018. It noted that COMNAP's membership now included 30 national Antarctic programmes and four observer programmes, which was the highest number in COMNAP history. It stated that the inaugural COMNAP Medal was awarded to co-recipients Patrice Godon (formerly IPEV) and Henry Valentine (formerly SANAP). It informed the Meeting that COMNAP's 29th Annual General Meeting (AGM) (2017) was held in Brno, the Czech Republic, hosted by Masaryk University, and included focussed sessions on safety/air activity, crisis management (social perspective), and shipping/Polar Code, and a workshop on energy and technology innovations. It noted that COMNAP's 30th AGM and the 18th Symposium would take place in Garmisch-Partenkirchen, Germany in June of 2018 and would be hosted by the Alfred Wegener Institute. The AGM would include focussed discussions on telemedicine, preventing harassment, marine science support, facilitation of internationally collaborative science and an environmental session.

- IP 26 *The Scientific Committee on Antarctic Research* (SCAR) Annual Report 2017/18 to the Antarctic Treaty Consultative Meeting XLI (SCAR). This paper noted that SCAR was in the process of developing a new suite of Scientific Research Programmes. SCAR indicated that this was an opportunity to examine ways in which to include the science priorities being discussed by the Parties into SCAR's Scientific Research Programme. The paper informed the Meeting that the XXXV SCAR Delegates Meeting and Open Science Conference would take place from 15 to 26 June 2018 in Davos, Switzerland. The meeting would be held in conjunction with the Arctic Science Summit Week 2018 and the Business Meetings of the International Arctic Science Committee (IASC) and would be known as Polar2018 *Where the Poles Come Together*. SCAR reported some recent developments within its organisation, in particular that: Dr Chandrika Nath would become the new Executive Director in July 2018; SCAR's parent body, the International Council for Science (ICSU), had merged with the International Social Science Council (ISSC) to form the International Science Council (ISC); and SCAR would hold its XXVI Delegates meeting and Open Science Conference in Hobart, Australia in 2020.

- IP 38 *Report of the Depositary Government for the Agreement on the Conservation of Albatrosses and Petrels (ACAP)* (Australia). Australia, in its capacity as depositary for ACAP, reported that there had been no new accessions to the Agreement since ATCM XL, and that there were 13 Parties to the Agreement.

- IP 39 *Report of the Depositary Government for the Convention on the Conservation of Antarctic Marine Living Resources (CCAMLR)* (Australia). Australia, in its capacity as depositary for CCAMLR, reported that there had been no new accessions to the Convention since ATCM XL. It noted that there were currently 36 Parties to the Convention.

- IP 40 *Report by the CCAMLR Observer to the Forty First Antarctic Treaty Consultative Meeting* (CCAMLR). This paper provided a summary of the outcomes of the 36th Annual Meeting of CCAMLR which was held in Hobart, Australia, from 16 to 27 October 2017. It was chaired by Dr Monde Mayekiso (South Africa). Twenty-three Members, two Acceding States, two State Observers and nine Observers from non-government organisations participated. Key outcomes of interest to the ATCM included current endeavours to renew the arrangement for the release of CCAMLR vessel monitoring system (VMS) data to support search and rescue (SAR) efforts in the CAMLR Convention Area. It reported on the harvest of toothfish and krill under CCAMLR-regulated fisheries in the 2017/18 season, and continuing work in relation to MPAs. It highlighted the ongoing work to plan MPAs in the Antarctic Peninsula region and the Weddell Sea and progress towards developing research and monitoring in the Ross region MPA and the South Orkney Islands southern shelf MPA. It informed the Meeting that there had been a significant sea ice loss event from the Larsen C Ice Shelf in Statistical Subarea 48.5 on 12 July 2017. The

Commission endorsed the Scientific Committee recommendation that the initial Stage 1 Special Area for Scientific Study, as provided for in Conservation Measure 24-04, should be extended to a Stage 2 Special Area. This was designated for a period of ten years. It noted that the Commission, its subsidiary bodies and the Scientific Committee, had considered the Report of the Second Performance Review (PR2). Key recommendations that had received support at CCAMLR-XXXVI included: continued efforts to examine revenue generation options and reduce costs, work to strengthen capacity building efforts, and the establishment of a Commission Bureau and a Scientific Committee Bureau. It informed the Meeting that the report was publicly available on the Commission's website.

(24)   In relation to Article III-2 of the Antarctic Treaty, the Meeting noted the reports submitted from other international organisations under this agenda item. The Chair noted that these Information Papers would also be taken as presented:

- IP 47 *WMO Annual Report 2017-2018* (WMO). This paper described WMO's activities during the period since ATCM XL. It explained that the WMO Polar and High Mountain regions priority activity was to promote and coordinate relevant observations, research and services carried out in the Antarctic, Arctic and high mountain regions by nations and by groups of nations. It informed the Meeting that the Global Cryosphere Watch (GCW) was foundational to WMO's polar initiatives and its observing component was one of the four essential observing systems under the WMO Integrated Global Observing Systems, which also included the Antarctic Observing Network (AntON), maintained by WMO and SCAR. WMO noted that the Year of Polar Prediction (YOPP) covered the period 2017-2019 and that a special Observing Period was planned in Antarctica from 16 November 2018 to 15 February 2019 (IP 48). WMO notified the Meeting that it was developing the concept of an Antarctic Polar Regional Climate Centre (PRCC) Network based on the lessons learned from the Arctic PRCC Network, and that a scoping workshop was provisionally planned for May 2019. Both the ATCM and CEP would be invited to send representatives to this workshop. WMO highlighted that the World Climate Research Programme, which WMO co-sponsored, was currently drafting new Strategic and Implementation plans. The climate of the polar regions was a key aspect of these plans. WMO also referenced the launch of the WMO-SCAR Fellowship Program for early career scientists (IP 44).

- IP 56 *Liability Annex: Financial Security* (IGP&I Clubs). This paper reported that the 13 principal underwriting associations comprising the IGP&I Clubs provided third party liability insurance cover for approximately 90% of the world's ocean-going tonnage, including many of the vessels that operated in the Antarctic. It informed the Meeting that the IG was continuing to analyse the issues raised in ATCM XL - IP 87 and would welcome a further opportunity to participate in the next ATCM in 2019 to assist in the implementation and application of Annex VI.

- IP 57 *ASOC Report to the ATCM* (ASOC). This paper briefly described ASOC's work over the past year and outlined some key issues for this ATCM. It noted that during the last year, ASOC and its member groups' representatives had participated actively in intersessional discussions in the ATCM and CEP forums, as well as in other international meetings. ASOC indicated that its priority issues for the ATCM were expanding the protected areas network; increasing the efficacy of the climate change response work programme (CCRWP); improving the follow up to Comprehensive Environmental Evaluations (CEEs); responding to the projected growth in Antarctic tourism; harmonising ASPAs and ASMAs with CCAMLR MPAs; and developing guidance on marine mammal avoidance by vessels. ASOC noted that over the past year it had engaged with CCAMLR and many partners, including IAATO, SCAR, the Coalition of Legal Toothfish Operators (COLTO), and the Antarctic Wildlife Research Fund (AWR), to work broadly towards identifying strengths and weaknesses existing in the Antarctic Treaty System procedures and practices, while suggesting solutions to these gaps.

- IP 70 *Report of the International Association of Antarctica Tour Operators 2017-18* (IAATO). This paper reaffirmed IAATO's mission to advocate and promote environmentally safe and responsible visitation to the Antarctic Treaty area, and welcomed opportunities for collaboration with other organisations. It noted that since 2010, IAATO had represented almost all passenger vessels operating in Antarctic waters under the International Convention for the Safety of Life at Sea (SOLAS). The paper further reported on IAATO activities during the 2017-18 season. It reported that during the 2017-18 Antarctic tourism season, the total number of visitors who travelled with IAATO Operators was 51,707. This represented an increase of 17% compared to the previous season as well as a new high, having passed the previous peak of the 2007-8 season (46,265). It was noted that recent work and activities included: the launch of a SCAR/IAATO two-year collaborative research project to develop a Systematic Conservation Plan for the Antarctic Peninsula; investment in the assessment of field staff, recognising the importance of their role in enforcing Treaty agreements and IAATO standards and guidelines; and work with COMNAP and the United States Automated Flight Following System to improve air safety. It was further noted that, during the 2017-18 season, IAATO Operators cost-effectively or freely transported 211 scientific, support and conservation staff, and their equipment and supplies between stations, field sites and gateway ports.

- IP 73 rev. 1 *Statement by the Secretariat for the Agreement on the Conservation of Albatrosses and Petrels (ACAP)* (ACAP). The paper confirmed the commitment of ACAP to collaborate with the Antarctic Treaty and related agreements in the implementation of actions to improve the conservation status of species of interest and their habitats. ACAP reported on the Sixth Session of ACAP's Meeting of its Parties between 7 and 11 May in Skukuza, South Africa, which involved the reviewing, developing and updating of conservation guidelines on biosecurity, eradication of introduced species, surveys and sample collections, as well as advice on best practice to mitigate the incidental mortality of seabirds in fisheries. The importance of the Antarctic Treaty area to ACAP was emphasised, as nearly all of the species currently listed under ACAP either breed or forage in this area. ACAP hoped the two-way relationship with the Antarctic Treaty and its related agreements would continue.

(25) The following papers were also submitted under this agenda item, and taken as presented:

- IP 16 *Ukraine's Approval of Measure 4 (2004), Measure 1 (2005), and Measure 15 (2009)* (Ukraine). This paper reported that Ukraine had approved three Measures: Measure 4 (2004) *Insurance and contingency planning for tourism and non-governmental activities in the Antarctic Treaty area*, Measure 1 (2005) *Annex VI to the Protocol on Environmental Protection to the Antarctic Treaty: Liability arising from environmental emergencies*, and Measure 15 (2009) *Landing of persons from passenger vessels in the Antarctic Treaty area*. It noted that the legislation to implement these measures, the Decision of the Government of Ukraine No. 441 *On Implementation of the Measures approved by the Antarctic Treaty Consultative Meeting*, had entered into force on 21 June 2017.

- SP 3 *List of Measures with status "not yet effective"*. This paper reported that, according to the information in the ATS database, there were several Measures that were not yet effective.

(26) Argentina introduced WP 8 *Typology of Consultative Meetings: the need for further definitions*. Reflecting on the special circumstances surrounding the organisation of ATCM XLI, Argentina described to the Parties the process by which, at very short notice, it had organised the meeting. Argentina reported that, as part of this process, it had consulted with Parties on the meeting format, work plan structure and whether or not ATCM XLI and CEP XXI should be considered special meetings. This process had highlighted the fact that there were no specific rules of procedure for Antarctic Treaty Meetings of Experts, Special Consultative Meetings, or funding the ATCM or CEP when such extraordinary circumstances occur. Argentina recommended that Parties consider discussing intersessionally the need for better anticipation of the organisational aspects of ATCMs and the potential incorporation of specific issues into the Rules of Procedure.

(27) The Meeting thanked Argentina for its paper, and expressed its sincere gratitude to Argentina and the Secretariat for taking on the responsibility of organising and hosting ATCM XLI under unique and challenging circumstances. Many Parties showed strong support for WP 8 and recognised the value of intersessional discussions to capitalise on lessons learned from Argentina's experience and ensure appropriate mechanisms were in place for the future. Many Parties expressed their interest in participating in intersessional discussions on this matter.

(28) While noting the importance of discussing and seeking to improve the organisational aspects of ATCMs, some Parties believed that the circumstances surrounding ATCM XLI presented a unique exception that was unlikely to arise often. These Parties emphasised a cautious approach so as not to set a precedent or encourage Parties to forgo their responsibilities under the Antarctic Treaty. It was also noted that the existing Rules of Procedure applied equally to an ATCM or a Special Consultative Meeting.

(29) Ecuador extended its apologies that, due to the adoption of Ecuador's Decree 135, it was unable to host ATCM XLI. It thanked Argentina for taking on the responsibility of hosting the ATCM XLI and reaffirmed its commitment to the principles of the Treaty.

(30) The Meeting agreed to establish an ICG on Organisational Aspects of the ATCM, and agreed to the following terms of reference:

1. to examine the implications and lessons learned from the organisation of ATCM XLI and CEP XXI, including:
   - Impact on ATCM and CEP matters as they relate to ensuring efficient governance of Antarctica or the maintenance of the Antarctic Treaty System;
   - Impact on the Secretariat's resources.

2. To consider options for how best to manage future scenarios where, because of exceptional circumstances, the organisation of the ATCM and CEP does not follow existing practice of rotation through the Consultative Parties, (unless rotation exchange has been previously arranged) including, for example:
   - The usefulness of the submission of an IP by the Host Country of the next ATCM during the previous meeting, and the contents of it;
   - Anticipation, regularity and deadlines for the submission of (informal) progress reports by the Host Country to the Antarctic Treaty Secretariat regarding the organisation of the ATCM;
   - Consider the merits of creating a guarantee fund (possibly with special contribution by the next ATCM host country) to bear the cost of any extraordinary expenses assumed by the ATS required by the organisation of an ATCM in a country other than the one originally agreed;
   - Any possible implications for ATCM or CEP Rules of Procedure;
   - Any possible guidance for handling any future such scenarios; and
   - Except in cases of *force majeure*, the possibility of measures taken with regard to the Parties not abiding by the commitment to organise the ATCM (e.g. payment of an extra fee to compensate for unforeseen expenses, losing rights on the next two ATCMs, etc.).

(31) It was further agreed that:
   - The exchange of information would be open only to Consultative Parties;
   - The Secretariat would develop a forum for the e-debate and would provide assistance to the ICG; and
   - Argentina would act as convenor and report to ATCM XLII on progress made in the ICG.

Item 4b: Operation of the Antarctic Treaty System: Venezuela's request to become a Consultative Party

(32) Venezuela informed the Meeting that, following Decision 2 (2017), it had submitted a new request to become a Consultative Party to the depositary government of the Antarctic Treaty. Venezuela noted that it had progressed its research activities in the Antarctic and increased its bilateral agreements in South America, demonstrating its commitment to international cooperation. It reported that, over the last decade, Venezuela had contributed to scientific knowledge of the Antarctic area and indicated it was committed to increasing scientific and logistical activities in the future. It had created an Antarctic studies centre that concentrated on climate change, microbiology, and ecology, and had become an associate member of SCAR in 2014 and an observer in COMNAP. It also noted its contribution to education and outreach through its dissemination of information to schools and the public.

(33) The Meeting considered Venezuela's request in light of the requirements set out in the Antarctic Treaty and the Guidelines contained in Decision 2 (2017). Several Parties noted Venezuela's progress in the development of its Antarctic research programme. Several Parties noted that Venezuela's Antarctic programme was still emerging and in need of further development before meeting the requirements to become a Consultative Party. There was therefore no consensus to grant Consultative Party status at this time.

(34) The Meeting encouraged Venezuela to continue developing and strengthening its scientific programme in Antarctica in collaboration with other interested Parties.

Item 4c: Operation of the Antarctic Treaty System: Urgent matters related to the Secretariat and financial issues

(35) The Executive Secretary introduced SP 4 rev. 1 *Secretariat Report 2017/18*, detailing the Secretariat's activities in the Financial Year 2017/18 (1 April 2017 to 31 March 2018).

(36) The Executive Secretary updated the Meeting on issues related to coordination and contact services, information technologies, publication of the Final Report of ATCM XL, public information, and personnel and financial matters. The Antarctic Treaty Secretariat demonstrated two proposed new designs to the Antarctic Treaty Secretariat website. Both designs sought to

improve the ease with which delegates and the general public could access information on the website and to improve the aesthetics of the website.

(37) The Meeting thanked the Antarctic Treaty Secretariat for its work to update and improve the website. It noted that both options presented seemed to address the identified issues with the current website design.

(38) A new version of the contacts database was also demonstrated. In this version, the same password could be used to access all password-protected parts of the website.

(39) The Executive Secretary introduced SP 5 rev. 1 *Secretariat Programme 2018/19*. This outlined the activities proposed for the Secretariat in the Financial Year 2018-19 (1 April 2018 to 31 March 2019). The Executive Secretary highlighted that much of the proposed programme related to: improvements to the website; collaboration with COMNAP to reduce duplication and increase compatibility across their databases; and providing support for host countries of upcoming ATCM and CEP meetings.

(40) The Executive Secretary advised the Meeting that the last contract with the auditor (Sindicatura General de la Nación - SIGEN) had ended and that he would negotiate a new contract in the coming year to cover the financial years 2018-21.

(41) The Executive Secretary also introduced SP 6 *Five Year Forward Budget Profile 2019/20 - 2023/24*, which provided the Secretariat's budget profile for the period 2019-2024. Whilst noting the continued increase in cost adjustments in US dollar terms, the budget profile anticipated a zero nominal increase in contributions until 2023/24. The Executive Secretary further noted that many outstanding dues had been paid, significantly reducing the debts owed to the Secretariat, and that the costs associated with ATCM XLI and CEP XXI were lower than in previous years due to the unusual nature of this shorter meeting. However, the change of venue from Ecuador to Argentina resulted in a net cost to the Secretariat of approximately USD 110,000.

(42) Japan noted that it supported the use of the general fund to organise ATCM XLI and CEP XXI and appreciated the use of the fund for such emergency cases. Japan also noted that this expenditure contributed to reduce the amount of the fund, which had otherwise been shown to gradually increase.

(43) The Executive Secretary introduced SP 7 *Human Resources Policy for the Secretariat of the Antarctic Treaty*. It recalled Decision 3 (2003) that defines matters related to human resources through the Staff Regulations. The

Executive Secretary noted several issues in relation to these Staff Regulations, and invited the Parties to consider the matters raised in the paper.

(44) The Meeting thanked the Executive Secretary for providing this helpful introduction to Human Resource policy for the Antarctic Treaty Secretariat staff. It requested that the Secretariat develop a more detailed proposal specifically regarding performance evaluation, career development and progression, and retirement ages, which could be discussed informally by the Parties during the intersessional period. The Meeting further suggested that the Secretariat consider whether the staff regulations already in place at the CCAMLR secretariat could be seen as a model. Argentina agreed to lead the informal discussions on the ATCM discussion forum.

(45) The Meeting agreed on the need for further discussion on revisions to the Electronic Information Exchange System (EIES) and included this item in the Multi-year Strategic Work Plan.

(46) The Meeting noted that due to the abridged nature of this meeting, the issue of liability and the progress towards ratifying Annex VI were not included on the agenda this year. The Meeting agreed to extend an invitation to the International Group of Protection and Indemnity Clubs (IGP&I Clubs), the International Maritime Organisation (IMO) and the International Oil Pollution Compensation Funds (IOPC Funds) to participate in the liability discussions at ATCM XLII.

(47) Following further discussion, the Meeting adopted Decision 1 (2018) *Secretariat Report, Programme and Budget* and Decision 2 (2018) *Renewal of the Contract of the Secretariat's External Auditor*.

Item 5: Biological Prospecting in Antarctica

(48) Argentina introduced WP 25 *Biological prospecting in Antarctica – the need for improved information and consideration by the ATCM*, prepared jointly with Chile, France and Norway. It recalled that, at ATCM XL, the Meeting had agreed on the need for further discussion of this topic at ATCM XLI and had included biological prospecting in the Multi-year Strategic Work Plan.

(49) The Netherlands presented IP 29 *Biological Prospecting in the Antarctic Treaty Area*. This paper provided an update on status and trends in biological prospecting in the Antarctic Treaty area, and an overview of relevant discussions within Antarctic Treaty System bodies. The Netherlands highlighted the various Antarctic Treaty area-related

pharmaceutical, industrial and krill-related patents already in existence. The paper also considered issues relating to reporting, access to specimens, commercialisation and definitions, and provided updates on recent policy developments in other international fora. The paper provided arguments for the ATCM to take the lead on the question of biological prospecting in the Antarctic Treaty area and recalled that the Antarctic Treaty System has a tradition of addressing matters in a proactive manner, anticipating issues and developing responses to them before they arise.

(50) The Meeting thanked the authors of WP 25 and IP 29. Many Parties noted the importance of the issue of biological prospecting to the Antarctic Treaty System, as reflected in its status as a longstanding ATCM agenda item.

(51) The United States, while expressing appreciation for these papers, indicated that it had strong doubts about what the ATCM can meaningfully accomplish in debating many aspects of this issue. In the view of the United States, the basic question of what we are worried about remains unanswered. The US Government does not fund "bioprospecting" in Antarctica, based on any reasonable definition of that term. Moreover, this term remains internationally undefined. In the view of the United States, it is necessary to consider the context related to the negotiations at the UN of a new legally-binding instrument related to biodiversity beyond national jurisdiction (BBNJ). In the view of the United States, some areas in the Southern Ocean might be covered by a new BBNJ instrument and the United States would like the discussions on BBNJ to play out further before the ATCM sends any signals that marine genetic resources within either the Antarctic Treaty area or the CAMLR Convention Area should be excluded from BBNJ.

(52) Most delegations expressed the view that the Antarctic Treaty system must continue to address the issue of bioprospecting, regardless of the BBNJ issue, in light of its inherent competence regarding all activities in Antarctica. The need for the ATCM to exercise its responsibilities was emphasised. Some delegations highlighted aspects of collection and use of biological organisms, conservation and the possible implications of patenting on the free availability of scientific observations and results, as provided in Article III of the Antarctic Treaty. Most delegations supported the establishment of the ICG as proposed by WP 25.

(53) ASOC thanked the authors of WP 25 and IP 29, noting that they clearly illustrated the extent of biological prospecting activities related to Antarctica and further underscored the need for the ATCM to be proactive on this issue. ASOC considered that there was a need for greater clarity and transparency

on how biological prospecting activities took place in Antarctica, and how these affected directly or indirectly the Antarctic environment and other Antarctic values. ASOC encouraged Parties to support further discussions on this issue and to implement the exchange of information requirements of Resolution 7 (2005) and Resolution 6 (2013).

(54) Brazil introduced WP 27 *An enhanced definition of Bioprospection in Antarctica*. Recalling ATCM XXXVII - WP 12, and noting the complexity of natural resource exploration in Antarctica, Brazil proposed that Parties discuss a working definition of bioprospecting of Antarctic organisms and the use of bioprospecting as a source of biotechnological bioproducts.

(55) The Meeting thanked Brazil for its paper. While several Parties welcomed the proposal to work towards a practical definition of biological prospecting in Antarctica, some raised concerns that the definition proposed in WP 27 was too narrow in scope and that it may not be productive to reopen the matter. Brazil indicated its willingness to address its proposal contained in WP 27 in the framework of the discussions proposed in WP 25 should they be established.

(56) The Meeting recalled Resolutions 7 (2005), 9 (2009), and 6 (2013), agreed to continue its work on the collection and use of biological material next year at ATCM XLII, and noted that the agenda item was included in the Multi-year Strategic Work Plan.

(57) While encouraging Parties to submit relevant Working Papers to continue this work, the Meeting agreed on the following:

- To hold an informal intersessional exchange of information by Consultative Parties through the ATCM Forum on activities taking place regarding the collection and use of biological material in Antarctica and their possible implications on the free availability of scientific observations and results as provided in Article III of the Antarctic Treaty.

- To request SCAR to present at ATCM XLII an update to its report contained in WP 2 *Biological prospecting in the Antarctic region: a conservative overview of current research* presented at ATCM XXXIII.

(58) SCAR welcomed the request and confirmed its willingness to contribute to the work of the ATCM.

(59) The following paper was also submitted under this item, and taken as presented:

- IP 32 rev. 1 *Diversity, resilience and applicative potential of microcosm from Antarctic icy habitats* (Romania). It provided the results of biological prospecting studies conducted on King George Island in 2015-16 by researchers from Romania's National Institute for Research and Development for Biological Science and Korea's Polar Research Institute.

Item 6: Inspections under the Antarctic Treaty and the Environment Protocol

(60) Norway introduced WP 26 *Summary of findings and reflections on trends from the Inspections undertaken by Norway under Article VII of the Antarctic Treaty and Article 14 of the Environmental Protocol*. The inspections were carried out from 9 to 17 February 2018 on seven installations: four scientific research stations (Halley VI, Neumayer III, SANAE IV and Princess Elisabeth Antarctica), one field station/logistical support base/e-base (SANAP summer station) and two installations that provide support functions to national Antarctic programmes (Novo Airbase and Airfield, and Perseus Runway). Norway reported that the inspection team was given complete freedom of access to all areas of the stations and installations visited, and that no weapons, military activity, or nuclear material or disposals were observed during the inspection at any of the installations. It noted that, as far as the inspection team could discern, permits and authorisation were in place for all installations and that safety and emergency procedures and facilities at most installations seemed to be of satisfactory standard, with some exceptions noted in the report. It also noted that there was a continuing shift towards more complex technological systems that, to a much greater extent than before, could be operated remotely. Norway noted that this provides new and exciting opportunities with regard to, for example, operation efficiency, standalone operations and remote data collection. It also noted that it may pose some risks, making stations more vulnerable and reliant on specialised personnel, as well as being vulnerable to cyber risks. It highlighted that, overall, the inspection team was impressed by the high standards and level of technological innovation at the stations, and encouraged Parties to continue to share information on best practices in this regard.

(61) Norway reported that the inspection team also reflected on the general developments and trends observed in Antarctica during the inspection. Some of these reflections included: the need for exchanging information and best practices between national programmes, operators and personnel at Antarctic stations, especially in relation to the greening of stations, and technological solutions for research and observation efforts in Antarctica; the potential for better coordination among stations and data sharing; ensuring the availability of relevant information about ownership and

management structures for all operations in Antarctica; Search and Rescue and safety issues that could result from increased air traffic in the region; and the timing for conducting inspections. Norway noted that a lesson learned had been that conducting inspections at a time when many stations were very busy closing down after the summer season and when there was a high level of traffic activity may not be ideal. Nonetheless, it emphasised that the inspection team was received warmly in all stations and thanked the inspected Parties for such a positive outcome.

(62) Parties whose stations had been inspected thanked Norway for its report and the professionalism with which the inspections had been undertaken. The inspected Parties noted their commitment to addressing the recommendations raised in the report.

(63) The Meeting congratulated Norway for its successful inspections and for the high quality of the inspection report. Parties confirmed the importance of the inspection regime to the Antarctic Treaty, and acknowledged the expense and logistical efforts required to undertake inspections.

(64) Many Parties noted particularly important points arising from the report, including: the increase of air traffic in Antarctica; search and rescue competency and availability; the importance of long observational time series; the increased use of advanced technologies and renewable energy; the availability of contact information for individual stations; information exchange; and science coordination.

(65) In noting the comments on air safety contained in the inspection report, IAATO highlighted a need for further review of flight safety issues, particularly with the potential for increased air traffic, and associated SAR implications. IAATO encouraged all Parties to ensure their aircraft had aircraft tracking devices and were linked to an Antarctic-wide real time monitoring system. IAATO thanked COMNAP for moving the Antarctic Flight Information Manual (AFIM) into an electronic format (e-AFIM) which had improved updating efficiency. In both live flight tracking and e-AFIM, IAATO operators and other flight operators were being encouraged to participate fully.

(66) COMNAP emphasised the national Antarctic programmes' commitment to sharing information on technologies to increase energy efficiency through the COMNAP Environmental Expert Group and noted that in addition to information exchange, funding is often required for implementation of technologies. On the issue of search and rescue, COMNAP noted that it was tasked with producing

the Antarctic Flight Information Manual, and reminded Parties that it stood ready to accept new or updated information on air operations. COMNAP also referred to its IP 4, which described an upcoming SAR workshop in New Zealand.

(67)   ASOC thanked Norway for WP 26 and noted its view that inspections were important to provide information about developments from both governmental and non-governmental activities in inland and remote areas, and in addition, helped to ensure transparency and compliance with the Antarctic Treaty and its Protocol. ASOC noted that the report identified some interesting trends worth following up in the future, in particular concerning the increase in air traffic, including from tourism.

(68)   The Secretariat introduced SP 8 *Inspections Database developments and mapping system*, and recalled the report and recommendations of the ICG on Inspections in Antarctica (ATCM XL - WP 40). In response to Parties' requests, the Secretariat presented developments made to the ATS Inspections Database including a new "List of Facilities" which allowed users to easily obtain the inspection-related information for each facility and to produce customised listings, including a list of the stations that had never been inspected. The Secretariat also demonstrated improvements to the display of recommendations, clarifications and follow-up to inspection reports.

(69)   The Secretariat also explained the process followed in selecting a geographical information system and informed the Meeting that it had managed to obtain the right to use a geographical information system software at a nominal fee. It noted that the same tool could be used to show other geographical information already stored in the Secretariat databases.

(70)   The Meeting thanked the Secretariat for further developing this useful tool and for its detailed report.

(71)   ASOC also thanked the Secretariat for its outline of recent developments in the Inspections Database and mapping system, which it regarded as an extremely useful tool for environmental management.

(72)   The following papers were also submitted under this item:

- BP 1 *Follow-up to the Recommendations of the Inspections at the Eco-Nelson Facility* (Czech Republic).
- BP 23 *Follow-up to the Recommendations of the Inspection at the Johann Gregor Mendel Czech Antarctic Station* (Czech Republic).

Item 7a: Tourism and Non-governmental Activities in the Antarctic Treaty Area: Trends and patterns

(73)   IAATO presented IP 71 *IAATO Overview of Antarctic Tourism: 2017-18 Season and Preliminary Estimates for 2018-19 Season*. The paper presented data collected from IAATO Operator Post Visit Report Forms for the 2017-18 season but without non-IAATO visits. IAATO's membership continued to incorporate the vast majority of private-sector tour operators, including all commercial SOLAS ship operators. All IAATO operators submitted Environmental Impact Assessments or equivalent operational documents to their appropriate national authority. Antarctic tourism continued to be primarily focused on traditional commercial ship-borne tourism in the Antarctic Peninsula, which accounted for over 95% of all landed activity. In the 2017-18 season, 42,576 people landed in Antarctica, including those from IAATO land-based operators, which surpassed the previous season. IAATO noted that this was in part due to vessels being operated with higher passenger capacity and that the industry was benefitting from strong world economic growth. Additional site-specific information was highlighted in IP 72, submitted by IAATO. IAATO's estimates for the 2018-19 season indicated that passenger numbers would rise to circa 55,764 individuals, in line with global trends of travel growth to remote and high latitude places. More than 100 different nationalities were represented by tourists who visited the Antarctic during the 2017-18 season. The highest proportion of nationalities travelled from the USA (33%), China (16%), and Australia (11%), followed by Germany, the UK, Canada, France, Switzerland and the Netherlands, with all other nationalities contributing a combined 14%. IAATO reported that their ban on the recreational use of RPAS in wildlife rich coastal regions remained in force for the 2018-19 season. IAATO confirmed that it remained committed to providing comprehensive information annually to the CEP and ATCM on its operators' activities.

(74)   The Meeting thanked IAATO for its paper, which provided Parties with a useful overview of tourism trends, both at a broad and a detailed scale. It agreed that this information provided Parties with a sound basis for their deliberations on Antarctic tourism and highlighted where Parties' attention should be directed with respect to tourism management.

(75)   Parties agreed that the trend of increasing tourist numbers and diversification of tourism activities warranted their attention. Australia expressed the view that it was important not only to observe such trends but also to consider the implications of tourism growth. Argentina also highlighted the challenges

that the presence of non-IAATO operators implied for the coordination of operations, both to the collection of accurate tourism statistics and to compliance with ATCM tourism measures, also indicating the need of Parties to define clear strategies on how to deal with non-IAATO operators considering its inclusion in the Multi-year Strategic Work Plan.

(76) Several Parties made reference to IP 53, submitted by the Russian Federation, which outlined some of the problems in preventing and taking action against unauthorised activities in Antarctica. To illustrate its point, the Russian Federation reported on an incident in the 2017-18 Antarctic season whereby the crew and passengers of a Maltese flagged vessel, captained by a Russian skipper, were observed violating multiple ATCM measures and visitor guidelines. The Russian Federation reported that it only became aware of this unauthorised activity when notified by IAATO of the violations, which were captured in videos and images by the yacht's crew and passengers, and posted online.

(77) Parties expressed their deep concern at the incident reported by the Russian Federation, noting that the presence of unauthorised activities in Antarctica was a serious matter requiring their attention and action.

(78) The Meeting noted the complex nature of regulating vessels, individuals and activities that were not authorised by Treaty Parties. It stressed the importance of continued and strengthened information exchange between Parties to ensure they were well informed in a timely manner about Antarctic activities being planned and carried out by their citizens and entities. It noted the valuable and ongoing work being undertaken by the Competent Authorities Contact Group, underlined the need to upload information about authorised tourism activities as promptly as possible to the EIES, and encouraged Parties to further engage in the Contact Group.

(79) While noting the importance of enhanced information exchange, some Parties expressed the view that more proactive action was required to deter unauthorised yacht visits to Antarctica. Argentina underscored both flag state responsibility and that of the nationality of the vessel captain or owner, further indicating that the Port State is not entitled to prevent vessels from departing ports with Antarctica as their possible destination, insofar as they are in compliance with international law. The United Kingdom suggested that an ATCM discussion on yachts would be extremely timely particularly in light of the number of unauthorised yachts as highlighted in IP 55. New Zealand highlighted that several unauthorised yachts in Antarctica were repeat offenders and encouraged Parties to ensure each had appropriate legislation in place in

order to be able to take action against such cases. Noting that unauthorised operators were often viewed in a positive light by the general public, Belgium suggested that Parties also engage with media outlets to raise public awareness about the negative impacts of these activities.

(80) SCAR recalled ATCM XL - IP 166, which it co-authored with IAATO, on their intentions to undertake a collaborative effort to develop a systematic conservation plan for the Antarctic Peninsula, particularly with a view to managing the long-term sustainability of Antarctic tourism. SCAR informed the Meeting that this work was progressing.

(81) France highlighted that many ideas had already been raised in previous WPs and ATCMs and could provide a good basis to work further on these issues. France expressed its willingness to collect and update those ideas with the aim to move forward at the next ATCM.

(82) The following papers were submitted under this item, and taken as presented:

- IP 53 *On regulation of yachting in Antarctic waters* (Russian Federation). It recalled a proposal made by the Russian Federation at ATCM XL for the preparation of blacklists of motor-sailing yachts that violate the main provisions of the Environment Protocol during their voyages. The paper noted events that occurred during the Antarctic season 2017/18 and proposed that Parties reconsider the proposal made at ATCM XL or find a new agreed decision on this matter.

- IP 55 *Data Collection and Reporting on Yachting Activity in Antarctica in 2017-18* (United Kingdom, Argentina, Chile and IAATO). The paper consolidated information from the proponents relating to yachts sighted in Antarctica, or indicating an intention to travel to Antarctica, during the 2017-18 season.

- IP 63 *Report on Antarctic tourist flows and cruise ships operating in Ushuaia during the 2017/2018 Austral summer season* (Argentina). It provided information about the flows of passengers and vessels that visited Antarctica during the 2017-18 Austral summer season, operating from the port of Ushuaia. It also presented data collected on the number of voyages that took place, passengers and their nationalities, average number of crew per vessel, expedition staff, and vessel registry.

- IP 72 *Report on IAATO Operator Use of Antarctic Peninsula Landing Sites and ATCM Visitor Site Guidelines, 2017-2018 Season* (IAATO). It provided information on the landings undertaken in the Antarctic Peninsula region by IAATO vessels, primarily focussed on traditional commercial ship-borne tourism, which accounted for over 95% of all landed tourism activity. A total of 41,417 passengers had made landings, surpassing the previous season. IAATO reported that despite the increase of activities, only two sites had received an average of more than two visits per day throughout the season; and operations therefore remained well within individual site guideline visitation capacities. It noted that all of the most-visited sites were covered by site specific management plans; and that the IAATO Ship Scheduler effectively managed all their ship visits following ATCM, IAATO and national programme Site Guidelines.

Item 7b: Tourism and Non-governmental Activities in the Antarctic Treaty Area: Environmental impacts

(83) The United Kingdom introduced WP 22 *A Practical Approach to Antarctic Tourism Management*, prepared jointly with the United States. It reported that, overall, tourism had a positive impact, particularly when it was managed appropriately to ensure that it had no more than a minor or transitory impact on the environment. It further noted that tourism should: have no negative impact on national Antarctic programmes; fully comply, both in practice and in spirit, with the rules of the Antarctic Treaty and the Environment Protocol; and create Ambassadors for Antarctica. It reviewed the implementation of Resolution 7 (2009) and concluded that Antarctic tourism was generally very well managed with minimal impacts, but noted that significant challenges in relation to the management of tourism remained to be addressed by the ATCM, including the impact of unauthorised tourism and the wider growth in tourism numbers and the types of tourist activity. The United Kingdom emphasised that significant Measures agreed by the ATCM and designed to regulate and improve the management of tourism were not yet in force including: Measure 4 (2004), Measure 1 (2005) and Measure 15 (2009).

(84) The proponents recommended that Parties: make further efforts to collaborate over authorisations, ensure domestic implementation of existing rules and undertake appropriate prosecutions; encourage Parties to support scientific research on tourism impacts and request that the CEP continue its work to explore the long-term impacts of tourism on the environment; ensure that all Measures adopted by the Antarctic Treaty were approved domestically; and consider the implications for the Antarctic Treaty System of tourism growth and the growth in non-IAATO registered operators.

(85)   The Meeting thanked the United Kingdom and the United States for their joint paper and reiterated its commitment to adopting a strategic approach to tourism management, noting that when managed well, tourism had a positive impact on Antarctica. Parties expressed their broad support for the recommendations contained in WP 22. The Meeting noted that the 60th anniversary of the Antarctic Treaty in 2019 could help focus efforts to develop a strategic approach to tourism, and motivate Parties to implement ATCM Measures designed to regulate and improve the management of tourism that were not yet in force.

(86)   The Netherlands underlined the importance of the issues identified in WP 22 and asked for special attention to cumulative impacts on the Antarctic environment. In that context it underlined the importance of attention to impacts on the wilderness values of Antarctica. It noted that these values are explicitly mentioned in Article 3 of the Protocol and in the *General Principles of Antarctic Tourism* (Resolution 7 (2009)).

(87)   The Meeting welcomed both the Netherlands' announcement that it plans to hold an informal workshop during the intersessional period to discuss tourism management, and China's announcement that it had made progress in developing domestic regulations to manage Chinese tourism to Antarctica.

(88)   The Meeting noted several key issues raised by Parties in the course of the discussion, including:

- concern about the increasing pressures on the environment, in particular regarding the pressures on landing sites and on search and rescue resources, presented by the anticipated growth in volume of tourism, in terms of both the number of vessels and number of visitors, and in high-risk adventure tourism activities;
- the need to consider cumulative impacts when assessing tourism activities including those unauthorised or of non-IAATO members;
- the desire to maintain wilderness values;
- the importance of providing national authorities with the correct legal instruments and tools to respond to unregulated or unauthorised activities in the Antarctic;
- the need to find additional mechanisms to improve the monitoring of tourism;
- the need to consider the implications of potential SAR burdens on national programmes and personnel associated with increased activities in Antarctica;

- a further consideration of the understanding of the terms non-permanent, semi-permanent and permanent in light of the EIA provisions of the Environment Protocol;

- the desirability of improving communications, in particular the speed of communication, between Parties regarding tourism issues, noting that the Competent Authorities Forum was helpful, but potentially not sufficient, in this regard; and

- the desirability of developing an interactive mapping tool on the ATS website (based on the Geographical Information tool demonstrated for the inspections database) that could help illustrate visitation over time for sites covered by Site Guidelines.

(89) ASOC presented IP 61 *Anticipated growth of Antarctic tourism: Effects on existing regulation* (ASOC). Noting that polar tourism was expected to grow, ASOC raised the matter of how the current Antarctic tourism regulatory system would respond to growth and provided a first attempt to answer this question. It recommended that the Meeting: review the current regulatory and management system for tourism to ensure adequate resilience and effectiveness in the future, including the adoption and/or review of Site Guidelines; consider ways to improve the assessment and monitoring of cumulative impacts, particularly at the most visited sites and on a regional basis; and continue to expand the network of ASPAs and ASMAs taking into consideration tourism growth on a regional basis. ASOC further noted that with projected increases in visitor numbers and other measures of tourism growth, and a continued focus of visitation at particular sites, it will be necessary for the ATCM to develop a more targeted look at visited sites to ensure that activities have a minimal impact.

(90) The following papers were also submitted under this item, and taken as presented:

- IP 14 *Notification of the presence of an unauthorized sailing vessel in the Antarctic, with a non-indigenous species on board* (France). It reported on a French sailing vessel with a hen on board that entered the Antarctic Treaty area in February 2018 without the authorisation of any competent national authority. It stated that the competent French authority began the administrative procedures set out in its national legislation and highlighted the need for Parties to continue working to prevent and sanction this type of incident. It stressed that illegal activities in the Antarctic were a threat to the environment and to the safety of operators and recommended that the Parties continue to work on these issues in line with the priorities relating to tourism in the Multi-year Strategic Work Plan.

- IP 41 *Expedition by the Windrose of Amsterdam yacht, December 2017* (Spain). It reported that the *Windrose of Amsterdam* sailed in the Antarctic Peninsula area in December 2017 without the authorisation of any competent national authority and with several Spanish nationals on board. It pointed out that the incident had increased Spain's concern regarding the legal framework applicable to such vessels and noted that in addition to sailing in the Antarctic Treaty area without authorisation, these vessels did so under the flags of countries that were not Parties to the Treaty. It highlighted the fact that the competent jurisdiction with respect to such activities was undefined and needed to be addressed.

Item 8: Multi-year Strategic Work Plan

(91) The Meeting considered the Multi-year Strategic Work Plan adopted at ATCM XL (attached to SP 1 rev. 1). It considered how to take each priority item forward in the coming years, and whether to delete current priorities and add new priorities.

(92) Following discussion, the Meeting updated the Multi-year Strategic Work Plan and adopted Decision 3 (2018) *Multi-year Strategic Work Plan for the Antarctic Treaty Consultative Meeting*.

(93) The following papers were submitted under this item, and taken as presented:

- IP 13 *Korea's 3rd Basic Plan for the Promotion of Research Activities in Antarctica (2017-2022)* (Republic of Korea). It reported on Korea's Third Basic Plan, which was initiated in 2017 and included Korea's vision to "become a leading nation of Antarctic research, which contributes to the resolution of the global changes faced by humanity." The paper noted that Korea's major goals were: the expansion of Antarctic research projects related to global issues such as climate change; the conservation of the ecological system; the advancement of Korea's research support basis; and the enhancement of Korea's leadership in terms of Antarctic governance and scientific research.

- IP 37 *Future Antarctic Science Challenges* (Australia). This paper provided a progress report on informal intersessional discussions on future Antarctic science challenges initiated at ATCM XL. The paper reported that the intersessional discussions had promoted a useful exchange of information on Antarctic science objectives, key research questions, geographic areas of focus, and existing international collaboration. Australia noted that it intended to continue the informal discussions through the next intersessional period and to provide a report for consideration at ATCM XLII.

Item 9: Report of the Committee for Environmental Protection

(94) Mr Ewan McIvor, Chair of the Committee for Environmental Protection, introduced the report of CEP XXI. The CEP had considered 30 Working Papers. In addition, 40 Information Papers, 3 Secretariat Papers and 4 Background Papers had been submitted under CEP agenda items. The Chair of the CEP highlighted the items on which the CEP had agreed specific advice to the ATCM, but encouraged Parties to review all parts of the CEP Report.

Opening of the Meeting (CEP Agenda Item 1)

(95) The Chair of CEP advised that the CEP had welcomed Switzerland and Turkey as new Members.

Draft Comprehensive Environmental Evaluations (CEP Agenda Item 3)

(96) The Chair of the CEP reported that the Committee had discussed the draft Comprehensive Environmental Evaluation (CEE) circulated by China for the proposed construction and operation of a new Chinese research station in the area of Victoria Land, Antarctica, the report of the open-ended ICG led by the United States to review the draft CEE, and two Information Papers submitted by China presenting further information in response to points raised by the ICG. The Committee had welcomed the improvements made to the original draft CEE circulated in 2014, including in response to comments made by Members at that time. The Committee had welcomed China's commitment to further consider in the final CEE the points raised by the ICG and comments expressed by Members during the meeting.

(97) The Committee had agreed to advise the ATCM that the draft CEE generally conformed to the requirements of Article 3 of Annex I to the Protocol. If China decided to proceed with the proposed activity, the final CEE could be strengthened through the inclusion of additional information and clarification on a number of aspects which were outlined in the CEP and ICG reports, and

summarised in the Committee's advice to the ATCM. China was encouraged to consider the detailed comments provided by ICG participants summarised in the ICG report, and issues raised during CEP XXI as summarised in the CEP report. The information provided in the draft CEE supported the conclusion that the impact of the construction of the station would be likely to be more than minor or transitory, and that the draft CEE was well-written and logically organised, although some minor adjustments could strengthen the document further.

(98)   New Zealand thanked China for the draft CEE, noting the significant work involved in its preparation, and looked forward to collaborating closely with China in the Ross Sea region. China expressed its willingness to cooperate with New Zealand in every respect.

(99)   The Chair of the CEP reported that the Committee had also discussed the draft Comprehensive Environmental Evaluation circulated by the United Kingdom for the proposed Rothera wharf reconstruction and coastal stabilisation, and the report of the open-ended ICG led by Norway to review the draft CEE. The Committee had highlighted the very comprehensive nature and high quality of the draft CEE, and welcomed the United Kingdom's continued refinement of the proposal, to further reduce the environmental impact of the proposed activities. The Committee had welcomed the United Kingdom's commitment to fully address in the final CEE the points raised by the ICG and in discussion during the meeting.

(100) The Committee had agreed to advise the ATCM that the draft CEE largely and broadly conformed to the requirements of Article 3 of Annex I to the Protocol on Environmental Protection to the Antarctic Treaty. If the United Kingdom decided to proceed with the proposed activity, there were some aspects for which additional information or clarification could be provided in the final CEE to enhance its comprehensiveness, noting the considerable detail already provided on the impacts and mitigation associated with all aspects of the activity which were outlined in the CEP and ICG reports and summarised in the Committee's advice to the ATCM. The United Kingdom was encouraged to consider the detailed comments provided by ICG participants, as well as the summary of the main issues as put forward in the ICG report, and issues raised during CEP XXI as summarised in the final report. The information provided in the draft CEE supported the conclusion that the impacts of some activities within the project would have a greater than minor or transitory impact, and that this level of EIA had been appropriate for this project. The draft CEE was thorough, systematic, clear,

well structured, and well presented, although it had been noted that some minor adjustments could be considered to strengthen the document even further.

(101) The Meeting thanked the CEP for its work. It was acknowledged that the preparation of CEEs was a substantial amount of work, and the Meeting noted the spirit of collaboration and cooperation in regard to the development of the proposals.

Management Plans (CEP Agenda Item 4)

(102) The CEP Chair reported that the Committee had considered six revised management plans for Antarctic Specially Protected Areas (ASPAs), and had agreed to forward each of the revised management plans to the ATCM for approval by means of a Measure.

(103) Accepting the CEP's advice, the Meeting adopted the following Measures on ASPAs and ASMAs:

- Measure 1 (2018) *Antarctic Specially Protected Area ASPA No. 108 (Green Island, Berthelot Islands, Antarctic Peninsula): Revised Management Plan.*

- Measure 2 (2018) *Antarctic Specially Protected Area ASPA No. 117 (Avian Island, Marguerite Bay, Antarctic Peninsula): Revised Management Plan.*

- Measure 3 (2018) *Antarctic Specially Protected Area ASPA No. 132 (Potter Peninsula, King George Island, (Isla 25 de Mayo), South Shetland Islands): Revised Management Plan.*

- Measure 4 (2018) *Antarctic Specially Protected Area ASPA No. 147 (Ablation Valley and Ganymede Heights, Alexander Island): Revised Management Plan.*

- Measure 5 (2018) *Antarctic Specially Protected Area ASPA No. 170 (Marion Nunataks, Charcot Island, Antarctic Peninsula): Revised Management Plan.*

- Measure 6 (2018) *Antarctic Specially Protected Area ASPA No. 172 (Lower Taylor Glacier and Blood Falls, McMurdo Dry Valleys, Victoria Land): Revised Management Plan.*

(104) The Committee had agreed to advise the ATCM that five-yearly reviews of the following ASPAs had been conducted in accordance with Article 6.3 of

Annex V to the Protocol, and that the existing management plans remained in force with the next reviews to be initiated in 2023:

1. ASPA 137 North-West White Island, McMurdo Sound
2. ASPA 138 Linnaeus Terrace, Asgard Range, Victoria Land
3. ASPA 156 Lewis Bay, Mount Erebus, Ross Island

(105) The CEP Chair also invited Parties to refer to the outcome of the Committee's discussions on other matters addressed under this agenda item, in particular in relation to:

- The prior assessment of proposed new ASPAs at the Léonie Islands, Ryder Bay, Antarctic Peninsula, and at Inexpressible Island.

- The report on the status of ASPA 144 Chile Bay (Discovery Bay) by Chile, and its possible delisting in light of guidance/criteria for delisting ASPAs that are under development.

(106) Concerning the issue of the establishment of the ASPA at Inexpressible Island, Italy reaffirmed, as it had affirmed during the CEP, its will to participate as a co-proponent with China to this initiative, considering the Italian scientific activities carried out for three decades in the area and still in progress. Recalling the principles expressed in the Antarctic Treaty and in the Protocol on Environmental Protection to the Antarctic Treaty on the establishment of cooperative working relations and on the promotion of co-operative programmes concerning the protection of the Antarctic environment and dependent and associated ecosystems, Italy strongly believed that working together on this proposal would be the only right way to start a fruitful collaboration and cooperation with current and future neighbouring countries in the area. Italy therefore reaffirmed its will in participating as a co-proponent to this proposal.

(107) China expressed its appreciation for the work that Italy had conducted in the area over the past several decades. China emphasised that it did not feel there were any obstacles for international cooperation in the preparation for the potential ASPA and welcomed Italy to work together with it on the proposal.

Site Guidelines (CEP Agenda Item 5)

(108) The Chair of CEP advised that the Committee had considered papers presenting seven revised Site Guidelines and three new Site Guidelines. The Committee had agreed to forward revised site guidelines for Brown Bluff,

Devil Island, Half Moon Island, Paulet Island, Pendulum Cove, Telefon Bay, and Whalers Bay to the ATCM for adoption. The Committee had also agreed to forward new Site Guidelines for Astrolabe Island; Georges Point, Rongé Island; and Portal Point for adoption.

(109) The Meeting considered and approved the seven revised Site Guidelines and three new Site Guidelines by adopting Resolution 1 (2018) *Site Guidelines for Visitors*.

(110) The Chair of CEP also referred the Meeting to the outcomes of other discussions under this agenda item, in particular in relation to:

- Further work on the development of a formal checklist to aid the future review of Site Guidelines, and on the development of an online repository of pictures from sites with Site Guidelines to aid in ongoing monitoring and formal site review.

- The anticipated growth of Antarctic tourism, and the consideration of actions to address the environmental implications of increasing numbers of tourists visiting landing sites.

(111) The Meeting welcomed the work of the CEP on the development of Site Guidelines, particularly in those sites experiencing increasing numbers of tourists. The United Kingdom was thanked for supporting the site visits for the purposes of considering new and revised Site Guidelines.

Inspection Reports (CEP Agenda Item 6)

(112) The Chair of CEP noted that, under this agenda item, the Committee had considered the environment-related elements of a report on inspections conducted by Norway in February 2018. It had welcomed the generally positive findings of the inspection team regarding environmental matters.

Reports from Subsidiary Bodies and Intersessional Contact Groups (CEP Agenda Item 7)

(113) The Chair of the CEP advised that the Committee had considered a report by Norway and the United Kingdom on the work of the ICG to develop guidance for conservation approaches for the management of Antarctic heritage objects. The Committee had endorsed the *Guidelines for the assessment and management of Heritage in Antarctica*, and agreed to forward to the ATCM for adoption a draft Resolution encouraging the use of the guidelines.

(114) The Committee had also endorsed a revision to the Guide to the presentation of Working Papers containing proposals for Antarctic Specially Protected Areas, Antarctic Specially Managed Areas or Historic Sites and Monuments, to reflect the Guidelines for the assessment and management of Heritage in Antarctica, which provide guidance with regard to required information for the purpose of listing Historic Sites and Monuments (HSM), and had agreed to forward to the ATCM for adoption a draft Resolution on updating the Guide.

(115) The Committee had also recalled its advice to ATCM XXXVIII that future proposals for new designations of HSM should be put on hold until further guidance had been established regarding assessment and management of Antarctic heritage. The Committee had agreed to advise the ATCM that, with the adoption of the Guidelines for the assessment and management of Heritage in Antarctica, proposals for new designations of HSM could again proceed as appropriate.

(116) The Meeting thanked the CEP for its work on the management of Antarctic Historic Sites and Monuments. The United Kingdom noted that in the lead up to significant anniversaries of historical achievements, Parties should be encouraged to consider proposing relevant sites for HSMs.

(117) Accepting the CEP's advice, the Meeting adopted Resolution 2 (2018) *Guidelines for the assessment and management of Heritage in Antarctica* and Resolution 3 (2018) *Revised Guide to the presentation of Working Papers containing proposals for Antarctic Specially Protected Areas, Antarctic Specially Managed Areas or Historic Sites and Monuments*, to reflect the Guidelines for the assessment and management of Heritage in Antarctica.

(118) The Committee had also agreed that there would be value in giving further consideration to several overarching issues identified by the ICG, in particular: the format of the HSM list; legal issues associated with ownership and potential removal for *ex situ* conservation, noting that this may require guidance from the ATCM; involvement of heritage expertise when assessing options for heritage management; and the possible need for EIA documentation as part of new HSM proposals.

(119) The CEP Chair advised that the Committee had considered a report by Germany on the work of the ICG established at CEP XX to develop guidelines on the environmental aspects of the use of Remotely Piloted Aircraft Systems (RPAS) in Antarctica. The Committee had endorsed the Environmental guidelines for the operation of Remotely Piloted Aircraft Systems (RPAS)

in Antarctica and had agreed to forward to the ATCM for adoption a draft Resolution encouraging the use and further development of the guidelines.

(120) The Committee had noted the importance of reviewing and revising the guidelines, as appropriate, to reflect the current state of scientific knowledge of the environmental impacts and benefits of RPAS, and had encouraged support for further related research. It had also agreed that it would be appropriate to keep under consideration the outcomes of any relevant RPAS-related discussion in the ATCM, including regarding circumstances under which recreational uses of RPAS should or should not be allowed.

(121) The Meeting welcomed the CEP's work to develop the RPAS guidelines. It was noted that the Antarctic Environments Portal could serve as a repository for information regarding the use and impact of RPAS, and that in reviewing and revising the guidelines in due course, the CEP could work with COMNAP and SCAR to develop consolidated best practice guidance for the use of RPAS in Antarctica.

(122) Some delegations expressed the view that it would be desirable to codify IAATO's moratorium on the use of RPAS for recreational purposes in wildlife-rich coastal areas in the Antarctic, and requested the CEP and ATCM to keep the guidelines under review with specific attention to the use of RPAS for recreational purposes.

(123) Accepting the CEP's advice, the Meeting adopted Resolution 4 (2018) *Environmental guidelines for the operation of Remotely Piloted Aircraft Systems (RPAS) in Antarctica*.

(124) The CEP Chair also reported that the Committee had adopted a work plan for the Subsidiary Group on Management Plans (SGMP) for 2018/19.

Five-Year Plan (CEP Agenda Item 8)

(125) The Chair of the CEP noted that the Committee had considered a paper presenting *SCAR's Environmental Code of Conduct for Terrestrial Scientific Field Research in Antarctica*. The Committee had endorsed SCAR's *Environmental Code of Conduct for Terrestrial Scientific Field Research in Antarctica*, and agreed to forward to the ATCM for adoption a draft Resolution on encouraging its dissemination and use.

(126) Accepting the CEP's advice, the Meeting adopted Resolution 5 (2018) *SCAR's Environmental Code of Conduct for Terrestrial Scientific Field Research in Antarctica*.

(127) The Chair of the CEP also noted that the Committee had considered a paper by the CEP Chair, which followed on from discussions at CEP XX on ways to ensure the CEP can remain well placed to support Parties' efforts to comprehensively protect the Antarctic environment.

(128) In accordance with Article 12(k) of the Environment Protocol, and noting the ATCM Multi-year Strategic Work Plan priority relating to strategic science priorities, the Committee had agreed to advise the ATCM that it had incorporated a list of CEP science needs into the CEP Five-year Work Plan, and that it had agreed to regularly review and revise these science needs as appropriate.

(129) The Chair of the CEP further noted that the Committee had also recognised that modest funding could assist it to undertake priority work to develop high quality and timely advice and recommendations in line with its functions under Article 12 of the Environment Protocol, and that it had agreed to seek advice from the ATCM on possible opportunities for obtaining such funding. In this regard, the Committee had noted that WP 17 presented a possible process for consideration of funding proposals that could assist to ensure that any funding proposals were structured and targeted to agreed priorities.

(130) The CEP Chair advised that the Committee had not anticipated that there would be a large number of requests for funding, and had recognised the previous and ongoing generous support of Members and Observers.

(131) The Meeting expressed its willingness to consider future proposals for funding to assist the CEP to undertake priority work, on a case-by-case basis.

(132) The Chair of the CEP noted that the Committee had strongly supported a proposal to convene a joint SCAR/CEP workshop on further developing the Antarctic protected area system, agreed to terms of reference for the workshop, and warmly welcomed the offer by the Czech Republic to host the workshop in Prague prior to CEP XXII.

(133) The Chair of the CEP also noted that the CEP had updated its Five-year Work Plan to incorporate actions that arose during the meeting.

General Matters (CEP Agenda Item 10)

(134) The CEP Chair invited the Meeting to refer to the outcomes of discussions on matters addressed under this agenda item, in particular in relation to:

- Discussions in the ATCM and CEP on papers relating to climate change.

- A proposal to establish an ICG to support harmonisation of marine protection initiatives across the Antarctic Treaty System.

- A report by China on informal intersessional discussions on developing a draft Code of Conduct for the Exploration and Research in Dome A in Antarctica.

- The protection of the wreck of Sir Ernest Shackleton's vessel *Endurance*, should it be located, under the terms of Resolution 5 (2001).

- Colombia's announcement that it is in the process of ratifying the Protocol.

Election of officers (CEP Agenda Item 11)

(135) The CEP Chair noted that the Committee had re-elected Patricia Ortúzar (Argentina) to serve a second two-year term as CEP Vice-chair, elected Birgit Njåstad (Norway) as CEP Chair, and agreed to appoint CEP Vice-chair, Kevin Hughes (United Kingdom) as convener of the Subsidiary Group on Climate Change Response (SGCCR).

(136) The Meeting thanked Ewan McIvor for his excellent leadership of the CEP over the past four years and expressed appreciation for the professionalism with which the CEP had been conducted.

(137) The Meeting congratulated Birgit Njåstad for her election as new CEP Chair, and Patricia Ortúzar for her re-election as Vice-chair.

Preparation for Next Meeting (CEP Agenda Item 12)

(138) The Chair of the CEP noted that the Committee had adopted a Preliminary Agenda for CEP XXII.

(139) The Meeting thanked Mr McIvor for his comprehensive report on the work of the CEP, and thanked the rapporteurs, interpreters and translators for their work.

Item 10: Preparation of ATCM XLII

a. Date and place

(140) The Meeting welcomed the kind invitation of the Government of the Czech Republic to host ATCM XLII in Prague, from 1 to 11 July 2019.

(141) For future planning, the Meeting took note of the following likely timetable of upcoming ATCMs:

- 2020 Finland.
- 2021 France.

b. Invitation of International and Non-governmental Organisations

(142) In accordance with established practice, the Meeting agreed that the following organisations having scientific or technical interest in Antarctica should be invited to send experts to attend ATCM XLII: ACAP, ASOC, IAATO, the International Civil Aviation Organization (ICAO), IGP&I Clubs, IHO, IMO, IOC, IOPC Funds, IPCC, the International Union for the Conservation of Nature (IUCN), UNEP, UNFCCC, WMO and the World Tourism Organization (WTO).

c. Preparation of the Agenda for ATCM XLII

(143) The Meeting approved the Preliminary Agenda for ATCM XLII (see Appendix 1).

(144) The Czech Republic introduced WP 24 *Declaration on the occasion of the 60 years of Antarctic Treaty*, which proposed that a Declaration by Consultative Parties be made at ATCM XLII to commemorate the 60 years since the signing of the Treaty. It was suggested that the drafting of the 'Prague Declaration' should occur on the ATS Online Forum.

(145) The Meeting thanked the Czech Republic and expressed strong support for this proposal. The Meeting noted that the Prague Declaration presented an important opportunity for Parties to reaffirm and make visible to the public the principles of the Antarctic Treaty and its continued strength, importance and relevance. It was also an opportunity to highlight the achievements of the Antarctic Treaty System and its remarkable ability to evolve and adapt to the challenges arising over the past 60 years. Many Parties expressed their interest in participating in the drafting of the declaration, and noted the value in receiving input from Consultative and non-Consultative Parties, as well as Experts and Observers.

(146) The Meeting agreed that it was also important that the Prague Declaration highlight the many changes that have taken place in Antarctica over the past 60 years. It requested SCAR's participation in the drafting of the declaration,

to ensure that it reflected and drew the public's attention to the importance of Antarctic science and the relevance of Antarctica to the rest of the world. It was noted that the logistic support of Antarctic science had also undergone great changes over the last 60 years and that COMNAP's input would be valuable in this regard.

(147) SCAR expressed its willingness to contribute to the declaration in the context of how Antarctic science had changed over the past 60 years.

(148) The Czech Republic thanked the Parties for their expressions of support. It encouraged Consultative Parties and Observers to contribute to the drafting of the Prague Declaration via the ATS Online Forum.

(149) France recalled that the Secretariat had received a note (Ref: DG/2/18/419) from Audrey Azoulay, Director-General of UNESCO, regarding the *Protecting Ice Memory* initiative. France explained that the initiative was a Franco-Italian collaboration launched in 2015 designed to develop an ice core repository in Antarctica. The project involved preserving ice cores from selected glaciers worldwide so that a sufficient amount of high-quality ice may be available for future scientists to carry out research and make discoveries. France, supported by Italy, stressed that all stages of the project in Antarctica would be carried out in compliance with the Antarctic Treaty and its Environment Protocol. They encouraged Parties to participate in informal intersessional discussions, lead by France and Italy, on the initiative and looked forward to providing an update to Parties at ATCM XLII.

(150) The Meeting thanked France and Italy for bringing this matter to its attention. It noted the significance of this project and many Parties expressed their interest in participating. It welcomed France and Italy's comment that all Antarctic aspects of the *Protecting Ice Memory* initiative would be conducted in compliance with the Antarctic Treaty and its Environment Protocol.

(151) The Meeting agreed to send a letter in response to the note sent by Ms Azoulay to the Secretariat. It further agreed that the letter would read as follows:

> Dear Director General,
>
> I have the pleasure to acknowledge the receipt of your letter of March 14, 2018 which has been communicated to the Antarctic Treaty Consultative Parties. Thank you for providing updated information as to the substance and status of the "Protecting Ice Memory" project.

I would like to take this opportunity to highlight the special legal status of Antarctica, as set out in the Antarctic Treaty of 1959 and other documents of the Antarctic Treaty System (ATS), and to recall that the ATS is the competent framework to address the issues related to Antarctica. The ATS has established duly elaborated procedures with regard thereto which comprise *inter alia* an environmental impact assessment under the Protocol on Environmental Protection to the Antarctic Treaty.

Informal discussion about the project in the context of relevant measures to be taken in accordance with the Antarctic Treaty and the Protocol on Environmental Protection to the Antarctic Treaty will take place among Parties ahead of XLII ATCM and XXII CEP which will take place from 1 to 11 July 2019 and will be reported to the ATCM consequently.

Executive Secretary

Secretariat of the Antarctic Treaty

d. Organisation of ATCM XLII

(152) According to Rule 11 of the Rules of Procedure, the Meeting decided to propose the same Working Groups for ATCM XLII as originally planned for this meeting. The Meeting agreed to appoint Ms Therese Johansen from Norway as Chair for Working Group 1 for 2019. It also agreed to appoint Professor Dame Jane Francis from the United Kingdom and Mr Máximo Gowland from Argentina as co-Chairs for Working Group 2 in 2019.

e. The SCAR Lecture

(153) Taking into account the valuable series of lectures given by SCAR at a number of ATCMs, the Meeting decided to invite SCAR to give another lecture on scientific issues relevant to ATCM XLII.

Item 11: Any Other Business

(154) Argentina, noting its status as an Antarctic gateway country, referred to IP 65 and briefly updated the Meeting on the progress it had made in streamlining its migration visa process for international scientists and technical personnel transiting through Argentine ports of entry to work in Antarctica. It highlighted that individuals linked to national Antarctic programmes or universities with Antarctic programmes would now qualify

for one year visas. Argentina anticipated that this increase in visa length would eliminate most of the problems associated with Antarctic personnel seeming to overstay their Argentine visas while working in Antarctica.

(155) Belarus thanked Argentina for its efforts in smoothening the migration process and indicated that Belarusian experts had recently had positive experiences transiting through Argentina. It thanked Argentina and all Antarctic gateway countries for facilitating access to Antarctica. It also thanked the many national Antarctic programmes and COMNAP for assisting their returning Antarctic personnel when problems arose. It commended the Antarctic community for its willingness to offer assistance when asked.

(156) Colombia referred to IP 21 and BPs 14-22 and thanked the Parties who had cooperated with it and facilitated its Antarctic activities. It also thanked Argentina for preparing IP 65 and streamlining its migration process.

(157) The following papers were submitted under this item, and taken as presented:

- IP 2 *Future Antarctic Science Challenges – Ukrainian Perspective* (Ukraine). Recalling the promotion of identifying priority research areas in ATCM XL, the paper presented Ukraine's vision for their future Antarctic research activities. It reiterated the need for all Parties to provide information on their research priorities, and for Parties to decide when and how the Meeting would receive, prioritise and implement scientific recommendations in the following years. Ukraine indicated that it was willing to participate in international research consortia on the subject, and would be ready to take part in further discussion on the research priorities of other Parties.

- IP 4 *COMNAP Search and Rescue (SAR) Workshop IV* (COMNAP). Noting Resolution 4 (2013) *Improved Collaboration on Search and Rescue (SAR) in Antarctica*, the paper reported that the next COMNAP SAR Workshop (Workshop IV) would take place in New Zealand from 14 to 17 May 2019. The workshop would be co-hosted by Rescue Coordination Centre New Zealand, Maritime New Zealand, and Antarctica New Zealand.

- IP 7 *Information on the activities of the Republic of Belarus in the Antarctic Treaty area: X Belarusian Antarctic Expedition 2017-2018* (Belarus). This paper reported on the activities of the Republic of Belarus in the Antarctic Treaty area in 2017-2018, which includes amongst others scientific research in five activity areas, and the installation of the Belarusian Scientific Station infrastructure during the X Belarusian Antarctic Expedition of 2017-2018.

- IP 18 *Brazilian XXXVI Antarctic Operations* (Brazil). This paper reported on the Antarctic Brazilian activities between October 2017 and April 2018, which involved 24 scientific research projects with 260 researchers, specialised in areas such as oceanography, glaciology, geology and climate change.

- IP 19 *Reconstruction of Brazil Comandante Ferraz Antarctic Station* (Brazil). This paper provided an update of the information presented on the reconstruction of the Comandante Ferraz Antarctic Station (EACF). It noted that the initial schedule was readjusted in order to take into account delays in manufacturing and pre-assembling. Three of the four planned stages had been completed.

- IP 20 *Turkish Antarctic Science Program Application to COMNAP* (Turkey). This paper provided a brief report on the Turkish Antarctic Science Program and its relationship with COMNAP.

- IP 21 *Avances y proyección del Programa Antártico Colombiano-PAC* (Colombia). This paper reported on the progress and achievements of Colombia's Antarctic activities during the previous year, and on the approval of the Environment Protocol by the Colombian parliament. It reported that this instrument of ratification would soon be sent to the Depositary Government of the Antarctic Treaty.

- IP 34 *Fatal accident during convoy operation at Indian Barrier, Maitri Station, East Antarctica* (India). This paper reported on the death of Subhajit Sen, aged 23 years, a student participant of XXXVII Indian Scientific Expedition to Antarctica (ISEA), as the result of a vehicle accident on 26 March 2018.

- IP 43 *COMNAP Antarctic Remotely Piloted Aircraft Systems (RPAS) Operator's Handbook* (COMNAP). The paper presented the current edition of the handbook first introduced in ATCM XXXIX (2016). COMNAP encouraged those national Antarctic programmes deploying RPAS in the Antarctic to develop their own site-specific, use-specific and RPA type-specific guidelines, and highlighted that many countries had developed national procedures related to RPAS use. The paper noted that COMNAP's RPA Working Group continued to keep the handbook under review and would respond to new states of knowledge on safety, rapidly increasing technology and other aspects of RPAS operation in the Antarctic area.

- IP 51 *Preparation for putting into operation the Perseus runway in the vicinity of the Romnaes Mount (Queen Maud Land)* (Russian

Federation). This paper reported that, on 25 May 2017, the Federal Service for Hydrometeorology and Environmental Monitoring of Russia issued an official permit to the Russian 'ALCI NORD' Company for maintenance of the seasonal runway in the vicinity of the Romnaes Mount (Queen Maud Land). It noted that these maintenance activities began in December 2017.

- IP 65 *Gateways to Antarctica: facilitation of access to Antarctica for purposes of scientific and technical activities in the framework of the Antarctic Treaty* (Argentina). The paper recalled discussions at ATCM XXXIX and ATCM XL relating to the facilitation of access to Antarctica for purposes of scientific and technical activities. Argentina reported that it had established a new regulation for those visiting Antarctica to obtain a transitory visa which would allow for a stay in Argentina of up to one year with multiple entry/exits.

- IP 68 *Current cooperation of Romania with Argentina in Antarctica* (Romania). This paper reported on the development of the cooperation between Romania and Argentina. It described the new cooperation proposal submitted by Romania to Argentina in February 2018, including the scientific results regarding investigation of aquatic virus-like particles (VLP) presence in Deception Island, based on the RONARE Expedition in March 2017 performed with logistic support from Argentina, and presenting the future plans for the two new projects proposed in the field of marine & terrestrial aquatic ecology, and extreme human medicine. Romania thanked Argentina for the logistic and scientific support provided during the expedition.

- IP 69 *Japan's Antarctic Research Highlights 2017-18* (Japan). This paper reported on three topics: a ground-based ice radar survey and shallow ice core drilling conducted to search for intact million-year ice layers near the Japanese Antarctic station Dome Fuji; hot-water drilling carried out to get access to the water underneath the ice in the terminus region of Langhovde Glacier to understand ocean-glacier interactions under a changing environment; and the tracking of Weddell seals from April to September to study the effects of climate change in the Antarctic.

(158) The following papers were also submitted under this agenda item:

- BP 2 *Libro-juego: No al cambio climático - #EmpiezoPorMí* (Venezuela).

- BP 3 *Libro Un viaje al sexto continente: La Antártida* (Venezuela).

- BP 4 *Exposición pictórica: De Mérida a la Antártida, Una mirada desde la pintura* (Venezuela).

- BP 5 *Exposición:"Venezuela en la Antártida"* (Venezuela).

- BP 6 *Turkish Antarctic Expedition (TAE - II) 2017-2018* (Turkey).

- BP 7 *Highlights of the Turkish Antarctic Science Program 2018-2022* (Turkey).

- BP 8 *Children's book: Celebrating Antarctica translated into Turkish* (Turkey).

- BP 9 *SCAR awarded visiting professor from Korean Polar Research Institute (KOPRI) to Turkish Polar Research Center (PolReC) for 2017* (Turkey).

- BP 10 *Scientific Collaboration in Antarctica* (Turkey).

- BP 12 *Estado cartografía náutica internacional Antártica editada y publicada por Chile* (Chile).

- BP 13 *Experiencias de Chile en la Antártica, respecto a la obtención de un panorama de superficie confiable y actualizado en función de actividades de Búsqueda y Salvamento Marítimo y/o Evacuaciones Médicas* (Chile).

- BP 14 *IV Expedición Científica de Colombia a la Antártica "Almirante Tono"* (Colombia).

- BP 15 *Actualización de la Agenda Científica Antártica de Colombia 2014-2035* (Colombia).

- BP 16 *V Expedición Científica de Colombia a la Antártica "Almirante Campos"* (Colombia).

- BP 17 *Aspectos operacionales relevantes en el desarrollo de expediciones científicas de Colombia en la Antártida* (Colombia).

- BP 18 *Cooperación Internacional del Programa Antártico Colombiano 2014-2018* (Colombia).

- BP 19 *Aportes de Colombia al estudio de tardígrados y bacterias asociadas provenientes de la Antártica* (Colombia).

- BP 20 *La Historia de Tiempo Presente y su implementación como estrategia para la difusión del Programa Antártico Colombiano* (Colombia).

- BP 21 *Coordinación de Colombia con Chile y Reino Unido para la generación de cartografía náutica en la Antártica* (Colombia).

- BP 22 *Campaña de Educación y Cultura: "Todos Somos Antártica"* (Colombia).

- BP 24 *Scientific and Science-related Cooperation with the Consultative Parties and the Wider Antarctic Community* (Republic of Korea).

- BP 25 *Cartografía Aeronáutica Antártica* (Chile).

- BP 26 *The first experience of Ukraine-Latvia Scientific Collaboration in Antarctica* (Ukraine).

- BP 27 *Progress of Ukraine on the fulfilment of the State Antarctic Research Program for 2011-2020* (Ukraine).

- BP 28 *Campaña Antártica Ecuatoriana 2017-2018 (ECUANTAR XXII)* (Ecuador).

- BP 29 *Fortalecimiento de las capacidades para la Estación Científica "Pedro Vicente Maldonado"* (Ecuador).

- BP 30 *Incremento de la seguridad antártica en la Estación Maldonado* (Ecuador).

- BP 31 *Jornadas Antárticas 2017* (Ecuador).

- BP 32 *Circulación Costera en la Ensenada Guayaquil-Isla Greenwich, Verano Austral 2017-2018* (Ecuador).

- BP 33 *Evidencias geológicas sobre cambios climáticos y antropización en la Isla Greenwich* (Ecuador).

- BP 36 *Campaña Antártica ANTAR XXV Verano austral 2017-2018* (Peru).

Item 12: Adoption of the Final Report

(159) The Meeting adopted the Final Report of the 41st Antarctic Treaty Consultative Meeting. The Chair of the Meeting, Ambassador María Teresa Kralikas, made closing remarks.

Item 13: Close of the Meeting

(160) The Meeting was closed on Friday, 18 May 2018 at 17:24.

2. CEP XXI Report

Table of Contents

Report of the Twenty-first Meeting of the Committee for Environmental Protection (CEP XXI)

Buenos Aires, Argentina, 13-15 May 2018

(1)   Pursuant to Article 11 of the Protocol on Environmental Protection to the Antarctic Treaty, Representatives of the Parties to the Protocol (Argentina, Australia, Belarus, Belgium, Brazil, Bulgaria, Canada, Chile, China, the Czech Republic, Ecuador, Finland, France, Germany, India, Italy, Japan, Malaysia, Netherlands, New Zealand, Norway, Peru, Poland, Portugal, the Republic of Korea, Romania, the Russian Federation, South Africa, Spain, Sweden, Switzerland, Turkey, Ukraine, the United Kingdom, the United States, Uruguay, and Venezuela) met in Buenos Aires, Argentina, from 13 to 15 May 2018, for the purpose of providing advice and formulating recommendations to the Parties in connection with the implementation of the Protocol.

(2)   In accordance with Rule 4 of the CEP Rules of Procedure, the meeting was also attended by representatives of the following Observers:

- A Contracting Party to the Antarctic Treaty which is not a Party to the Protocol: Colombia;
- the Scientific Committee on Antarctic Research (SCAR), the Scientific Committee for the Conservation of Antarctic Marine Living Resources (SC-CAMLR), and the Council of Managers of National Antarctic Programs (COMNAP); and
- scientific, environmental and technical organisations: the Antarctic and Southern Ocean Coalition (ASOC), the International Association of Antarctica Tour Operators (IAATO), and the World Meteorological Organization (WMO).

Item 1: Opening of the Meeting

(3)   The CEP Chair, Ewan McIvor (Australia), opened the meeting on Sunday 13 May 2018 and thanked Argentina for organising and hosting the meeting in Buenos Aires.

(4)   The Chair highlighted that 2018 marked 20 years since the entry into force of the Protocol, and noted the increasingly important role played by the Committee in supporting the Parties' efforts to comprehensively protect the Antarctic environment.

(5)   On behalf of the Committee, the Chair welcomed Switzerland and Turkey as new Members, following their accession to the Protocol on 1 June 2017 and 27 October 2017, respectively. The Chair noted that the CEP now comprised 40 Members.

(6)   The Chair summarised the work undertaken during the intersessional period (IP 67 *Committee for Environmental Protection (CEP): summary of activities during the 2017/18 intersessional period*). He highlighted the significant progress made on actions arising from CEP XX and noted that, due to the abbreviated format of this meeting, some items had been deferred for further consideration at CEP XXII.

Item 2: Adoption of the Agenda

(7)   The Committee adopted the following agenda and confirmed the allocation of 30 Working Papers (WP), 40 Information Papers (IP), 3 Secretariat Papers (SP) and 4 Background Papers (BP) to the agenda items:

1. Opening of the Meeting

2. Adoption of the Agenda

3. Draft Comprehensive Environmental Evaluations

4. Management Plans

5. Site Guidelines

6. Inspection Reports

7. Reports from Subsidiary Bodies and Intersessional Contact Groups

8. Five-Year Work Plan

9. Cooperation with Other Organisations

10. General Matters

11. Election of Officers

12. Preparation for the Next Meeting

13. Adoption of the Report

14. Closing of the Meeting

Item 3: Draft Comprehensive Environmental Evaluations

(8)   China introduced WP 13 *The Draft Comprehensive Environmental Evaluation for the Proposed Construction and Operation of a New Chinese Research Station, Victoria Land, Antarctica*. The paper presented a non-technical summary of a new draft CEE, which had taken into consideration the comments and suggestions raised during the Committee's discussions of an earlier draft CEE at CEP XVIII (2014). China also referred to IP 23 rev. 1 *The Initial Responses to the Comments on the second Draft CEE for the construction and operation of the New Chinese Research Station, Victoria Land, Antarctica*, and IP 25 *The Updated Draft Comprehensive Environmental Evaluation for the construction and operation of the New Chinese Research Station, Victoria Land, Antarctica*.

(9)   In a presentation that gave an overview of the proposed construction and operation of the proposed new research station, China highlighted its plans to minimise vehicle use, employ low-emission technologies and renewable energy resources, limit the footprint of the station, strictly implement the Non-native Species Manual, recycle water, and develop a waste management plan. It also noted that the location for the proposed station had been moved two kilometres to the south of the preferred location identified in the 2014 draft CEE, to avoid any potential impact to the Adélie penguin colony, and that it planned to propose an ASPA to ensure the protection of the colony. Through the EIA process, China had concluded that the benefit derived from scientific research and monitoring activities and the opportunities for international collaboration with the support of the new Chinese Antarctic station would outweigh the more than minor and transitory impact of the construction and operation of the station on the Antarctic environment, and fully justified the proposed activity proceeding.

(10)   The United States introduced WP 28 *Report of the Intersessional Open-ended Contact Group Established to Consider the Draft CEE for the "Proposed Construction and Operation of a New Chinese Research Station, Victoria Land, Antarctica"*. The United States noted that participants had commented favourably on several aspects of the draft CEE, as detailed in the ICG report. The ICG felt that the CEE was generally clear, well-structured and

well-presented and generally conformed to the requirements of Article 3 of Annex I to the Protocol.

(11) The United States reported that some ICG participants made suggestions to further strengthen the document by providing additional information on specific topics. It highlighted that several ICG participants recommended that the proponents address cumulative impacts resulting from the terrestrial as well as maritime activities of the German, Italian and Korean stations which were in close proximity to the proposed Chinese station. It noted that there were questions related to the assumption that some materials were pre-staged, and whether an Initial Environmental Evaluation (IEE) had been carried out in relation to the activities conducted prior to the projected first building season (2018-19). The ICG advised that the information contained in the draft CEE supported the proponent's conclusion that the construction and operation of the proposed new Chinese station was likely to have more than a minor or transitory impact on the environment. The ICG advised that, should China decide to proceed with the proposed activity, the final CEE could be strengthened through the inclusion of additional information and clarification on a number of aspects, as outlined in WP 28. The ICG encouraged China to consider the detailed comments provided by ICG participants as well as its summary in the ICG report.

(12) The Committee thanked China both for preparing the draft CEE and for its comprehensive overview presentation during the meeting. The Committee welcomed the improvements made to the original draft CEE circulated in 2014, including its response to comments made by Members at that time. It also thanked China for providing further details regarding the proposed activity, and its initial responses to comments raised by the ICG. The Committee also thanked Polly Penhale from the United States for her excellent work as ICG convener, and expressed its general support for the findings and conclusions of the ICG.

(13) China thanked the ICG participants for their work on reviewing the draft CEE and commended Polly Penhale from the United States for her excellent work in convening and coordinating the discussions. China noted that it had already responded to all of the suggestions put forward by the ICG one by one, through the information and update provided in IP 23 rev. 1 and IP 25. China recalled discussions during CEP XVII when the Committee had concluded that the draft CEE generally conformed to the Protocol and emphasised that since then it had improved the draft and had added new information.

(14) Members welcomed China's initial responses to the comments raised in the ICG, and China's commitment to expanding the use of renewable energy and other measures to minimise the impact of the construction and operation of the proposed station, including moving the station further away from the Adélie penguin colony. Several Members with facilities and activities in Terra Nova Bay and the broader Ross Sea region expressed their willingness to collaborate with China on science and logistics, and also on the development of the proposed ASPA on Inexpressible Island.

(15) Members also highlighted points that could be given further consideration during the preparation of the final CEE, should China decide to proceed with the proposed activity, including:

- consideration of the results of past and ongoing scientific activities conducted by other nations at Inexpressible Island and in the surrounding area;

- further consideration of alternatives to construction of a new station, including the no-action alternative and sharing of existing facilities;

- further consideration of non-native species risks;

- consideration of cumulative impacts associated with the activities of multiple national programmes in Terra Nova Bay and the broader Ross Sea region;

- further details to enhance the description of the initial environmental reference state, including details of microbial and terrestrial invertebrate communities; and

- details regarding the environmental assessment of activities, related to the proposed new station, that had already been undertaken at Inexpressible Island.

(16) In response to these comments, China advised that:

- it acknowledged that several stations in the area were contributing to important scientific research, and believed that the proposed new station would make a further significant contribution to Antarctic science, particularly in relation to climate change research and marine observing systems;

- regarding concerns about potential cumulative impacts and non-native species risks, it would fully comply with the Protocol and take serious consideration of all relevant CEP/ATCM guidelines, with a view to improving the environmental protection measures in the final CEE; and

- it looked forward to enhancing international cooperation within the Antarctic community.

(17) Noting and recognising the assessment made and the conclusion reached by the proponent on the need to establish a separate station in this area of the Ross Sea region in which there already are a number of other stations, Norway took the opportunity to reemphasise the core issue flagged in earlier and ongoing discussions in both the Committee and in the ATCM regarding the need and the desire for enhanced logistical cooperation and joint operations to increase efficiency and decrease environmental impacts. Norway encouraged Parties to continue to consider opportunities for such cooperation.

(18) The Committee welcomed China's commitment to further consider in the final CEE the points raised by the ICG and comments expressed by Members during the meeting.

CEP advice to the ATCM on the draft Comprehensive Environmental Evaluation prepared by China for 'Proposed construction and operation of a New Chinese Research Station, Victoria Land, Antarctica'

(19) The Committee discussed in detail the draft Comprehensive Environmental Evaluation (CEE) prepared by China for 'Proposed Construction and Operation of a New Chinese Research Station, Victoria Land, Antarctica' (WP 13). The Committee discussed the report by the United States of the ICG established to consider the draft CEE in accordance with the Procedures for Intersessional CEP Consideration of Draft CEEs (WP 28), and information provided by China in an initial response to the ICG comments (IP 23 rev. 1 and IP 25). The Committee also discussed additional information provided by China in response to issues raised during the meeting.

(20) Having reviewed the draft CEE, the CEP advised the ATCM that:

1) The draft CEE generally conformed to the requirements of Article 3 of Annex I to the Protocol on Environmental Protection to the Antarctic Treaty.

2) If China decided to proceed with the proposed activity, the final CEE could be strengthened through the inclusion of additional information and clarification on a number of aspects. In particular, the ATCM's attention was drawn to the suggestions that further details could be provided regarding:

    i. Description, impacts, and mitigation of the full range of activities associated with the building of the station proper, including:

aircraft operations; the ice runway and associated facilities; construction of the proposed wharf; wind and solar power installations; scientific field installations and activities; sourcing and processing of local rock; marine noise; waste management; and fuel transport, handling, and storage;

    ii. Mitigation measures related to non-native species, fuel management and energy production, and potential disturbance and impact to both terrestrial and near-shore marine fauna and flora and nearby HSMs; and

    iii. The potential for cumulative impacts of operational and scientific research activities in proximity to other national programmes.

3) China was encouraged to consider the detailed comments provided by ICG participants as well as the summary of the main issues summarised in the ICG report, and issues raised during CEP XXI as summarised in the final report.

4) The information provided in the draft CEE supported the conclusion that the impacts of some activities within the project would have a more than minor or transitory impact, and that this level of EIA had been appropriate for this project.

5) The draft CEE was well-written and logically organised, although some minor adjustments could strengthen the document even further.

(21) The United Kingdom introduced WP 19 *Draft Comprehensive Environmental Evaluation (CEE) for the Proposed Rothera Wharf Reconstruction and Coastal Stabilisation*, which presented a non-technical summary of a draft CEE carried out by the British Antarctic Survey in accordance with Annex I of the Protocol, and approved and endorsed by the United Kingdom Government. The United Kingdom explained that the reconstruction of the wharf at Rothera Station was part of broader station modernisation plans, and was required to accommodate the new icebreaker, the *RRS Sir David Attenborough*. The proposed coastal stabilisation was required to ensure the safety of operations at the station. The draft CEE described the various construction and support activities proposed over two seasons (2018-20) and included the local sourcing of rock from a temporary quarry within the existing station footprint. It was emphasised that mitigation of impacts of the construction would include measures to avoid the introduction of non-native species, and procedures to avoid pollution from spills and other disturbances to marine mammals. It was further noted that, in progressing

the plans for the wharf construction, less impact than originally expected was likely to occur, in particular due to the reduced requirements for blasting and coastal stabilisation. The draft CEE concluded that the significant science and operational advantage that would be gained from the reconstruction of the Rothera wharf justified the greater than minor or transitory impact expected from some of the proposed activities.

(22) Norway introduced WP 23 *Report of the intersessional open-ended contact group established to consider the draft CEE for the "Rothera Wharf Reconstruction and Coastal Stabilisation"*. The ICG advised the CEP that the draft CEE largely and broadly conformed to the requirements of Article 3 of Annex I to the Protocol, and was thorough, systematic, clear, well structured, and well presented. Norway noted that ICG participants had commented favourably on several aspects of the draft CEE, as detailed in the ICG report. It noted minor adjustments could be considered to strengthen the document by including more details on *inter alia* further precautions to avoid non-native species risks; potential damage by icebergs; the effects of underwater noise on marine fauna; and the effect of the construction on sewerage works.

(23) The ICG further concluded that the draft CEE had identified environmental impacts of the activity in a structured and transparent manner, and, where necessary, had suggested methods to mitigate impacts of the construction. The ICG nevertheless raised some issues that would benefit from additional attention, including: impacts of dust and the monitoring of the emperor penguin colony in ASPA 107. It advised that the information provided in the draft CEE supported the conclusion that the impacts of some activities within the project would have a greater than minor or transitory impact. The ICG suggested that, if the United Kingdom decided to proceed with the proposed activity, there were some aspects for which the inclusion of additional information or clarification could be provided in the final CEE to enhance its comprehensiveness, as outlined in WP 23.

(24) The Committee thanked the United Kingdom for its very comprehensive and high-quality draft CEE, and for its informative presentation to the meeting, which had usefully highlighted further updates and details in response to comments made during the ICG. The Committee welcomed the United Kingdom's continued refinement of the proposal to further reduce environmental impact of the proposed activities, as well as the United Kingdom's initial responses to comments raised during the ICG on matters such as non-native species risks, water use, iceberg impacts, sewage treatment, cumulative impacts and clarity of maps/figures, as outlined in the presentation.

(25) The Committee also thanked Birgit Njåstad from Norway for convening the ICG, expressed its support for the ICG's conclusions and recommendations, and highlighted the very comprehensive nature and high quality of the draft CEE.

(26) During the meeting Members raised points that could be given further consideration during the preparation of the final CEE, should the United Kingdom decide to proceed with the proposed activity, including:

- possible challenges with the proposed programme and timing of the construction activity due to the ice conditions in the area;

- providing further details of the possible cumulative impacts of the proposed activities in light of the planned broader modernisation of Rothera Station;

- giving further details of possible alternative mechanisms for station resupply, such as the use of smaller boats or helicopters; and

- analysis of noise impacts on land of the proposed activities, taking into account the noise associated with existing activities undertaken at Rothera Station.

(27) It was noted that the proposed pre- and post-activity environmental monitoring in ASPA 129 could be useful as a good model for the Committee's broader interests when considering approaches to the monitoring of natural values in ASPAs. Members also looked forward to learning more about the United Kingdom's experience with managing the underwater noise aspects of the activity, and the effectiveness of the mitigation measures outlined in the draft CEE.

(28) The United Kingdom thanked Birgit Njåstad for convening the ICG, and also thanked the ICG participants for their comments. In response to further comments and questions raised by Members during the discussion, the United Kingdom advised that:

- it had thoroughly considered the possible challenges associated with ice conditions in the area when developing the construction programme/ timing for the project;

- it recognised the need for environmental monitoring to support the CEE, and indicated that the proposed monitoring in nearby ASPA 129 would be relatively straightforward due to that Area's close proximity to the station;

- it would need to further develop the broader plans for modernisation of Rothera before presenting an environmental assessment for those activities, but that an update would be included in the final CEE;

- its Antarctic programme logistics depended on ship-based resupply, but that it would include further description of alternatives in the final CEE;

- it would be pleased to report back to the Committee on its experience regarding underwater noise aspects of the activity, and that it was aware of the need to consider an analysis of potential noise on land in conjunction with existing activities at Rothera; and

- it would also be pleased to report back to the Committee on the effectiveness of the CEE, noting that it undertakes follow-up of all environmental impact assessments.

(29) The Committee welcomed the United Kingdom's commitment to fully address in the final CEE the points raised by the ICG and in discussion during the meeting.

CEP advice to the ATCM on draft Comprehensive Environmental Evaluation prepared by United Kingdom for the 'Proposed Rothera Wharf Reconstruction and Coastal Stabilisation'

(30) The Committee discussed in detail the draft Comprehensive Environmental Evaluation (CEE) prepared by the United Kingdom for 'Proposed Rothera Wharf Reconstruction and Coastal Stabilisation' (WP 19). The Committee discussed the report by Norway of the ICG established to consider the draft CEE in accordance with the Procedures for Intersessional CEP Consideration of Draft CEEs (WP 23). The Committee also discussed additional information provided by the United Kingdom in response to the ICG comments and issues raised during the meeting.

(31) Having reviewed the draft CEE, the CEP advised the ATCM that:

1) The draft CEE largely and broadly conformed to the requirements of Article 3 of Annex I to the Protocol on Environmental Protection to the Antarctic Treaty.

2) If the United Kingdom decided to proceed with the proposed activity, there were some aspects for which additional information or clarification could be provided in the final CEE to enhance its comprehensiveness, as outlined in this ICG report. In particular, and noting the considerable detail already provided on the impacts and mitigation associated with all aspects of the activity, the Committee's attention was drawn to the suggestions that some further consideration could be provided regarding:

    i. additional aspects regarding impacts and mitigation relating to underwater and land-based noise;

    ii. additional aspects regarding impacts and mitigation relating to dust; and

    iii. cumulative impact relating to potential future activity and increased future traffic in the area.

3) The United Kingdom was furthermore encouraged to consider the detailed comments provided by ICG participants, as well as the summary of the main issues as put forward in the ICG report, and issues raised during CEP XXI as summarised in the final report.

4) The information provided in the draft CEE supported the conclusion that the impacts of some activities within the project would have a greater than minor or transitory impact, and that this level of EIA had been appropriate for this project.

5) The draft CEE was thorough, systematic, clear, well structured, and well presented, although some minor adjustments could be considered to strengthen the document even further.

(32) ASOC presented IP 62 *Follow-Up of Comprehensive Environmental Evaluations*. It recalled that Resolution 2 (1997) encouraged Members to anticipate and carry out follow-up for CEEs. ASOC also noted that CEE follow-up was implied in monitoring requirements under Annex V, EIA guidelines and in the inspection checklist for stations. ASOC highlighted that, in practice, there had been a very limited follow-up of CEEs and considered it timely to undertake this in order to identify and communicate the environmental performance of activities subject to CEE. It recalled a good example of a successful CEE follow-up in 2007 where, at the invitation of Antarctica New Zealand, an independent environmental audit was conducted by the British Antarctic Survey and the Australian Antarctic Division on the ANDRILL McMurdo Sound project. ASOC recommended that: those Members that had submitted final CEEs in the recent past submit reports in accordance with Resolution 2 (1997); CEE documents include follow-up plans; and observations on CEE follow-up be included in inspection reports where applicable.

(33) Belarus supported ASOC's recommendations and emphasised that the EIA follow-up process should be continuous.

(34) The Committee noted the following other Information Paper submitted under this agenda item:

- IP 15 rev. 1 *Notice of intention to prepare a Comprehensive Environmental Evaluation for redevelopment of Scott Base* (New Zealand), which noted that New Zealand was considering the redevelopment of Scott Base, no earlier than the 2021/22 season. It noted that New Zealand intended to submit a draft CEE for the project in early 2020, using a sustainability assessment tool in the design and specification process. New Zealand welcomed discussion and input from other Members on such tools, and on the CEE process.

(35) The following paper was also submitted under this agenda item:

- SP 9 *Annual list of Initial Environmental Evaluations (IEE) and Comprehensive Environmental Evaluations (CEE) prepared between 1 April 2017 and 31 March 2018* (ATS).

Item 4: Management Plans

i.) Revised Draft Management Plans which have not been reviewed by the Subsidiary Group on Management Plans

(36) The Committee considered the following papers presenting revised management plans for Antarctic Specially Protected Areas (ASPAs). In each case the proponent(s) summarised the suggested changes to the existing management plan and recommended its approval by the Committee and referral to the ATCM for adoption.

- WP 4 *Revision of the Management Plan for Antarctic Specially Protected Area (ASPA) No. 117 Avian Island, Marguerite Bay, Antarctic Peninsula* (United Kingdom).
- WP 5 *Revision of the Management Plan for Antarctic Specially Protected Area (ASPA) No. 170, Marion Nunataks, Charcot Island, Antarctic Peninsula* (United Kingdom).
- WP 6 *Revision of the Management Plan for Antarctic Specially Protected Area (ASPA) No. 108, Green Island, Berthelot Islands, Antarctic Peninsula* (United Kingdom).
- WP 7 *Revision of the Management Plan for Antarctic Specially Protected Area (ASPA) No. 147, Ablation Valley and Ganymede Heights, Alexander Island* (United Kingdom).

- WP 10 *Revised Management Plan for Antarctic Specially Protected Area (ASPA) No. 172 Lower Taylor Glacier and Blood Falls, McMurdo Dry Valleys, Victoria Land* (United States).

- WP 31 *Revision of the Management Plan for Antarctic Specially Protected Area (ASPA) No. 132, Potter Peninsula* (Argentina).

(37) With respect to WP 4 (ASPA 117), WP 5 (ASPA 170), WP 6 (ASPA 108), and WP 7 (ASPA 147) the United Kingdom noted that only minor changes to the existing management plan were proposed, and included minor updates to supplementary materials in the plans, additional information on Important Bird Areas, provisions for the operation of RPAS, and minor editorial amendments.

(38) With respect to WP 10 (ASPA 172), the United States noted that the changes to the existing management plan included minor textual changes, the change of a helicopter landing site due to rising lake levels, the addition of a prohibition of overflight below 100 metres of the area, and inclusion of additional advice for glacier access.

(39) With respect to WP 31 (ASPA 132), Argentina noted that the changes to the existing management plan included updated information on the natural values of the ASPA, the inclusion of more scientific information regarding ecosystem monitoring, provisions for the operation of RPAS in the boundaries of the ASPA, and waste management.

(40) The Committee approved all of the revised management plans that had not been reviewed by the SGMP.

CEP advice to the ATCM on revised management plans for ASPAs

(41) The Committee agreed to forward the following revised management plans to the ATCM for approval by means of a Measure:

#	Name
ASPA 108	Green Island, Berthelot Islands, Antarctic Peninsula
ASPA 117	Avian Island, Marguerite Bay, Antarctic Peninsula
ASPA 132	Potter Peninsula, King George Island (Isla 25 de Mayo), South Shetland Islands
ASPA 147	Ablation Valley and Ganymede Heights, Alexander Island
ASPA 170	Marion Nunataks, Charcot Island, Antarctic Peninsula
ASPA 172	Lower Taylor Glacier and Blood Falls, McMurdo Dry Valleys, Victoria Land

ii.) Prior assessment of proposed new protected areas

(42)   The Committee considered Working Papers relating to the prior assessment of proposed new protected areas, in accordance with the Guidelines: A prior assessment process for the designation of ASPAs and ASMAs.

(43)   The United Kingdom introduced WP 18 rev. 1 *Prior assessment of a proposed Antarctic Specially Protected Area within the Léonie Islands, Ryder Bay, Antarctic Peninsula*, submitted jointly with the Netherlands. The paper outlined the environmental, scientific, wilderness and aesthetic values of a proposed multi-site ASPA. It noted that the proposed ASPA would afford protection to 10% of the global population of south polar skuas, 1.9% of the global population of Antarctic shags, and rich areas of terrestrial vegetation. It would also protect important long-term and ongoing biological research, as well as provide a control area against which to compare human impacts at Rothera Station. The paper noted that the proposed area also had considerable wilderness and aesthetic values.

(44)   The Committee welcomed the comprehensive information presented in the paper, consistent with the purpose and provisions of the *Guidelines: A prior assessment process for the designation of ASPAs and ASMAs*. The Committee agreed that the values within the proposed ASPA merit special protection, and expressed its support for the development of a draft management plan for the area, led by the United Kingdom and the Netherlands.

(45)   Members raised several matters for further consideration by the proponents, including:

- the potential for disruption of scientific programmes that may arise from designating the area as an ASPA;
- the potential impact of refuges in the area, and their use, on the intended purpose of the area as a control area against which to compare human impacts at Rothera Station; and
- whether the designation of a new ASPA as a control area would result in a review of the status and continued utility of ASPA 129.

(46)   The Netherlands noted that its scientists were enthusiastic about the potential for the proposed ASPA to support research objectives, and the United Kingdom expected that the proposed ASPA would actually reduce risks to scientific activities. The Netherlands and the United Kingdom advised that they had held some discussions about the value of retaining ASPA 129, and would consider the matter further. The United Kingdom also clarified that

the proposed ASPA contained multiple sites, and refuges were not in a site that was being considered for inclusion as a control area.

(47)   The Committee encouraged interested Members and Observers to work with the United Kingdom and the Netherlands during the intersessional period in the development of a management plan for potential submission at CEP XXII, and noted that those discussions could also usefully give further consideration to issues raised during the meeting, as appropriate.

(48)   China introduced WP 30 *Prior assessment of a Proposed Antarctic Specially Protected Area (ASPA) on the Inexpressible Island*. The paper outlined the environmental, scientific and historic values of the proposed ASPA, noting that the area would be designated primarily to protect an Adélie penguin and south polar skua colony identified by BirdLife International as Antarctic Important Bird Area (IBA) 178 from increasing human activities, to protect Historic Site and Monument (HSM) 14 Ice Cave used by the British Antarctic Expedition team in 1912, and for long-term monitoring. The Adélie penguin colony on Inexpressible Island is the only one which has had a continuous occupation for the past ~7000 years based on the present knowledge. The preserved remains (bones, tissues and eggshells) in the frozen environment provide ideal material for evolution and climate or environmental change research. The south polar skua colony represents more than 1% of the global population of the species.

(49)   The Committee welcomed the comprehensive information presented in the paper, consistent with the purpose and provisions of the *Guidelines: A prior assessment process for the designation of ASPAs and ASMAs*. The Committee agreed that due to the combination of scientific, environmental and historic values present, and the increasing human activities, the area merited to be designated as an ASPA.

(50)   Members raised several matters for further consideration by the proponent, including:

- the availability of results of Italian research in the area;
- the value of conducting further investigations on the distribution of the skua population;
- the possible inclusion of the nearby stream and lake within the area boundary;
- incorporation of additional research results obtained on-site during the most recent field season; and

- the consideration of alternatives to designating a visitor area within the proposed ASPA.

(51) Italy expressed its interest in joining China as a co-proponent of the ASPA. Information on Italian scientific activities and peer-review literature had been recently condensed in a document that summarised all the research activities performed so far, which had been made publicly available in a repository facility along with all the papers at *https://cloud.cnr.it/owncloud/index.php/s/teEKRd0tQHNqlBe*.

(52) Other Members expressed interest in contributing to the development of the management plan. IAATO, noting the area's historical significance, also offered to facilitate consultation with its member operators that had extensive experience of the area. The Committee encouraged interested Members and Observers to work with China during the intersessional period to develop a draft management plan for submission at CEP XXII.

(53) The Committee noted that the comprehensive information provided in WP 18 rev. 1 and WP 30, and the resulting productive discussions during the meeting, demonstrated the value of the prior assessment process.

(54) Norway noted that discussions regarding the further development of the protected area system that would take place at the planned workshop (WP 16) and ongoing discussions relating to IBAs in the context of the protected area system could have a bearing on the designation of new protected areas, and noted that it in a broader sense may be useful to consider the relevance of these overarching discussions.

(55) ASOC welcomed WP 18 rev. 1 and WP 30, which presented solid evidence to support the creation of new ASPAs with clear scientific, environmental and wilderness values and that include representative examples of terrestrial ecosystems. ASOC hoped that the undertaking of the prior assessment process, which is a voluntary step, would facilitate the adoption of the proposed ASPAs. ASOC additionally suggested that the proposed Inexpressible Island ASPA could be increased in size to protect a site that was previously relatively pristine and now was experiencing an increase in infrastructure and human activities.

(56) The Committee noted the following Information Paper submitted under this agenda item:

- IP 42 *Update on the proposed Antarctic Specially Protected Area (ASPA) in the Western Sør Rondane Mountains* (Belgium). Following discussions at CEP XX, the paper provided a synthesis of the scientific literature available and a map of the general area as a next step of the prior assessment for the proposed new ASPA in the Sør Rondane Mountains.

iii.) Other matters relating to management plans for protected areas

(57) The United States introduced WP 2 *Review of the Management Plans for Antarctic Specially Protected Areas (ASPAs) No. 137 Northwest White Island, McMurdo Sound and No. 138 Linnaeus Terrace, Asgard Range, Victoria Land.*

(58) The Committee noted the United States' advice that it had conducted a five-yearly review of the management plans for ASPA 137 and ASPA 138 in accordance with the requirements of Article 6.3 of Annex V to the Protocol, and had determined that these management plans did not require revision.

(59) New Zealand introduced WP 15 *Review of Management Plan for ASPA No. 156, Lewis Bay, Mount Erebus, Ross Island.*

(60) The Committee noted New Zealand's advice that it had conducted a five-yearly review of the management plan for ASPA 156, and had determined that the plan did not require revision.

(61) The Committee noted a further Information Paper submitted under this agenda item:

- IP 35 *Review of the Management Plans for Antarctic Specially Protected Areas (ASPAs) 135, 143 and 160* (Australia). This paper presented the results of five-yearly reviews by Australia of the management plans for ASPA 135, ASPA 143 and ASPA 160, which had concluded that no revisions were required.

CEP advice to the ATCM on the five-yearly review of management plans for ASPAs

(62) The Committee agreed to advise the ATCM that five-yearly reviews of the management plans for the following ASPAs had been conducted in accordance with Article 6.3 of Annex V to the Protocol, and that the existing management plans remain in force with the next reviews to be initiated in 2023:

- ASPA 137 North-West White Island, McMurdo Sound
- ASPA 138 Linnaeus Terrace, Asgard Range, Victoria Land
- ASPA 156 Lewis Bay, Mount Erebus, Ross Island

---

(63)   Chile introduced WP 11 *Status of Antarctic Specially Protected Area No. 144, Chile Bay (Discovery Bay), Greenwich Island.* This paper reported on an analysis of the status of ASPA 144 based on the *Checklist to assist in the inspection of Antarctic Specially Protected Areas* adopted in Resolution 4 (2008) and the *Guidelines for implementation of the Framework for Protected Areas* adopted in Resolution 1 (2000). Additionally, Chile presented supporting information in IP 9 *Analysis of the current status of the Antarctic Specially Protected Area No. 144, Chile Bay (Discovery Bay), Greenwich Island.* Chile reported that it had determined that the original designation of the ASPA as a control area for the study of Port Foster, Deception Island, was no longer valid and that due to the low level of activity in the area the values for which the Area was originally designated were no longer threatened. Chile noted that the area had not been subject to significant human activity and recommended that the Committee evaluate the continuing need for protection of the area as an ASPA.

(64)   The Committee thanked Chile for presenting the results of its comprehensive and systematic evaluation of the status of ASPA 144. The Committee noted the conclusions drawn by Chile as a result of that evaluation and acknowledged that the information presented gave good cause to reconsider continuing the status of Chile Bay (Discovery Bay) as an ASPA. The Committee recalled its earlier agreement on the importance of the Antarctic protected area system being dynamic and also of the importance of being rigorous in the consideration of proposals to delist ASPAs. The Committee also recalled that it had previously welcomed an offer by Norway to lead the development of guidance / criteria for delisting ASPAs.

(65)   Norway advised that it was continuing to work on the guidance / criteria, and intended to bring forward a proposal for consideration at CEP XXII. The Committee agreed that it would be appropriate to reconsider the possible delisting of ASPA 144 in light of such guidance.

(66)   Members also noted that it would be appropriate to consider the possible continuing value of the ASPA for other research conducted in nearby area, and possible alternatives to delisting such as revising the objectives for the Area.

(67)   ASOC expressed its view that delisting of ASPAs should not be taken lightly. ASOC further noted that the fact that an area had been documented in the past and protected for a long time was in itself a value that merited consideration of extended protection.

(68) The Committee welcomed Chile's willingness to keep the proposal under consideration, and noted that it would be appropriate for the SGMP's consideration of the management plan to be placed on hold, pending further discussions and decisions on the possible de-designation of the Area.

(69) The Committee noted the following Information Paper submitted under this agenda item:

- IP 8 *Progress in the revision process of the Management Plan for Antarctic Specially Protected Area No. 133, Harmony Point, Nelson Island, South Shetland Islands* (Argentina, Chile). This paper reported on a preliminary evaluation that had determined that the management plan for ASPA 133 required major changes, including an adjustment to the Area boundary. The co-authors noted that the next steps would be: further exchanges with scientific personnel working on projects on-site; field work for the assessment of current environmental values and for the collection of further information on boundaries; and the redrafting of maps and submission of a joint Working Paper once the revised plan was drafted.

Item 5: Site Guidelines

(70) The United Kingdom introduced WP 32 *Review of Site Guidelines for Visitors*, jointly submitted with Argentina, and in conjunction with ASOC and IAATO. The paper described work conducted during the 2017/18 season to review a number of sites either with established Site Guidelines for visitors or currently receiving regular visitation in order to draft new guidelines if deemed appropriate. The co-authors also raised a number of broader issues related to visitor Site Guidelines. The United Kingdom noted that the paper contained several general observations and recommendations arising from the site visits, and drew the Committee's attention to: the importance of regularly reviewing Site Guidelines and the need for more Site Guidelines; the suggestion that precautionary revisions of Site Guidelines could be based on relevant information, and not necessarily require formal on-site reviews; the suggestion to keep a visual record of photographs of sites to aid in the ongoing monitoring of changes; and the potential usefulness of developing a checklist to aid future reviews.

(71) The Committee thanked the co-authors for their work during the previous season to visit several sites in order to inform reviews of existing Site Guidelines and to consider the possible need for new Site Guidelines. Regarding the recommendations presented in WP32, the Committee noted

the importance of regular reviews of existing Site Guidelines including, when appropriate, on the basis of relevant information and without the need for formal on-ground site visits. The Committee also noted that any resulting proposed changes to Site Guidelines would be considered and agreed by the CEP and ATCM in accordance with accepted practice.

(72) The Committee expressed support for further work in relation to other points raised in WP 32, including: the development of a formal checklist to aid the future review of Site Guidelines, noting that such a checklist could also be utilised by researchers active at such sites; and development of an online repository of pictures from sites with Site Guidelines to aid in ongoing monitoring and formal site review.

(73) The Committee welcomed IAATO's willingness to collaborate on these initiatives, and its commitment to continuing to gather and report information on site visits by its operators.

(74) The Russian Federation expressed concerns about regulating the number and size of vessels that could visit certain sites.

(75) In response to a query raised in WP 32, SCAR advised that it was not aware of evidence that a six-hour break, or curfew period, would be beneficial, or otherwise, for wildlife at visited sites, and encouraged further research on this matter.

(76) The Committee agreed to forward the revised Site Guidelines for Half Moon Island, presented in WP 32, to the ATCM for adoption.

(77) The United Kingdom introduced WP 33 *Proposed Amendment for Antarctic Treaty Site Guidelines for Visitors to Pendulum Cove, Telefon Bay and Whalers Bay, Deception Island*, jointly submitted with Argentina, Chile, Norway, Spain and the United States, and in conjunction with ASOC and IAATO. Following a site visit and review by representatives of the United Kingdom, Argentina, IAATO and ASOC, as described in WP 32, the Deception Island Management Group suggested revisions to the Site Guidelines for visitors to the three sites on the interior of the island: Pendulum Cove, Telefon Bay and Whalers Bay. The United Kingdom noted that all three sites required some revision, and highlighted that the co-authors had proposed changes to restrict the maximum number of vessels visiting each site to two per day, restrictions in approaches to various old structures, and alternative routes to avoid fauna.

(78) A concern was raised regarding the proposed reductions in vessel numbers. The co-authors of the paper highlighted some of the background to the proposal, noting that any limitations should be based on numbers of visitors going ashore, it had represented a precautionary approach that took into consideration the potential cumulative impacts of both tourist and national Antarctic programme personnel visits to these highly visited sites, as well as the special circumstances of Deception Island as an active volcano.

(79) Following modifications made during the meeting to the maximum number and size of ships per day (which was altered to three ships per day, two of which carried no more than 500 passengers, and one of which had no more than 200 passengers), the Committee agreed to forward the revised Site Guidelines for Pendulum Cove, Telefon Bay and Whalers Bay, Deception Island to the ATCM for adoption. It was noted that the Deception Island Management Group would keep this issue under consideration.

(80) Argentina introduced WP 34 *Review of Guidelines for Visitor Sites in the Antarctic Peninsula: Revised Guidelines for Paulet Island,* jointly submitted with the United Kingdom, Norway and Sweden, ASOC and IAATO. The co-authors proposed revised Site Guidelines for visitors for Paulet Island, following a site visit and review by representatives of the United Kingdom, Argentina, IAATO and ASOC, as described in WP 32. It reported that the most significant changes stemmed from the increased number and dispersal of the penguins on the island, which had made landing and walking around the island difficult, especially when penguins were fledging.

(81) The Committee agreed to forward the revised Site Guidelines for Paulet Island to the ATCM for adoption.

(82) The United Kingdom introduced WP 35 *Review of Guidelines for Visitor Sites in the Antarctic Peninsula: New and Amended Guidelines*, jointly submitted with Argentina, and in conjunction with ASOC and IAATO. The paper suggested revisions to the existing Site Guidelines for two sites: Brown Bluff and Devil Island. It also proposed new Site Guidelines for three sites: Astrolabe Island, Georges Point, and Portal Point. The United Kingdom noted that the revisions were necessary due to fauna, increases in visitor numbers to an area seldom visited before, and additional restrictions in approaches to snow petrel sites.

(83) The Committee agreed to forward the new Site Guidelines for Astrolabe Island, Georges Point, and Portal Point, and the revised Site Guidelines for Brown Bluff and Devil Island, to the ATCM for adoption.

CEP advice to the ATCM on new and revised Site Guidelines

(84) The Committee agreed to forward the following new and revised Site Guidelines to the ATCM for adoption:

- Astrolabe Island (new)
- Brown Bluff
- Devil Island
- Georges Point, Rongé Island (new)
- Half Moon Island
- Paulet Island
- Pendulum Cove
- Portal Point (new)
- Telefon Bay
- Whalers Bay

(85) ASOC presented IP 61 *Anticipated growth of Antarctic tourism: Effects on existing regulation.* It noted the growing demand for Antarctic tourism, including from newer markets, and that a global increase of polar ship capacity would drive significant tourism growth in coming years. ASOC considered this growth could have an effect on resilience and effectiveness of the Antarctic tourism regulation system in the future. ASOC suggested that Parties pursue timely, proactive and precautionary approaches to address tourism growth, which included the following steps: 1) review the current Antarctic tourism regulation system to ensure adequate resilience and effectiveness in the future, including the adoption and/or review of Site Guidelines; 2) improve impact assessment and monitoring, particularly in respect of cumulative impacts; and 3) expand the network of ASPAs and ASMAs.

(86) The Committee expressed general support for the recommendations in IP 61 and encouraged Members to consider these matters further and bring forward related proposals for consideration at future meetings.

(87) IAATO presented IP 72 *Report on IAATO Operator Use of Antarctic Peninsula Landing Sites and ATCM Visitor Site Guidelines, 2017-18 Season.* This paper presented data collected by IAATO from IAATO Operator Post Visit Report Forms for the 2017-18 season. No non-IAATO visits were included in this analysis. The total number of passengers from ships making landings in the Antarctic Peninsula in 2017-18 (41,517) had surpassed the

previous 2016-17 landing total (of 33,580). This was due in part to vessels being operated with higher passenger capacity, with all vessels benefiting from the current world economic strength and operating at near-full passenger capacity for the whole season. Pre-season and in-season co-ordination between IAATO field staff remained very effective utilising the IAATO Ship Scheduler, which manages visits following the Site Guidelines. Therefore, all operations remained well within individual Site Guideline visitation capacities with all of the most-visited sites covered by site-specific management plans, either through ATCM Visitor Site Guidelines or national programme management.

(88)   The Committee welcomed IAATO's continuing commitment to collect and report information on IAATO operator landing site and Site Guidelines use, and thanked IAATO for the details provided in the paper which were relevant to the Committee's ongoing consideration of matters relating to the environmental management of Antarctic tourism. Several Members noted that the information presented in the paper raised interesting questions, including with regard to the increase in land-based activities and approaches to the management of sites regularly receiving high numbers of visitors.

(89)   The Committee agreed that it would be appropriate to consider actions it could take to understand better and address the environmental implications of increasing numbers of tourists visiting landing sites. The Committee recalled that the *2012 CEP Tourism Study: Tourism and Non-Governmental Activities in the Antarctic, Environmental Aspects and Impacts* had identified recommendations relevant to the discussion. It also noted that SCAR and IAATO were continuing to develop a systematic approach to conservation planning for tourism on the Peninsula, and that Members were encouraged to contribute.

(90)   The Committee noted the following other Information Paper submitted under this agenda item:

- IP 54 *Recovery Status of Moss Communities Near the Trails of Barrientos Island (Aitcho Islands)* (Ecuador, Spain). This paper reported on the current situation on Barrientos Island, where the island's trails were closed for the last six years to foster the recovery of moss communities damaged by trampling. Noting recovery on the coastal trail, and no significant changes to the central trail, the co-authors recommended continued long term follow-up of the recolonisation process.

Item 6: Inspection Reports

(91) Norway introduced WP 26 *Summary of findings and reflections on trends from the Inspections undertaken by Norway under Article VII of the Antarctic Treaty and Article 14 of the Environmental Protocol*. The inspections were carried out from 9-17 February 2018 on seven installations—four scientific research stations (Halley VI, Neumayer III, SANAE IV, and Princess Elisabeth Antarctica), one field station/logistical support base/e-base (SANAP summer station) and two installations that provide support functions to national Antarctic programmes (Novo Airbase and Airfield, and Perseus Runway). Norway noted that the inspection team maintained a focus on an overarching, rather than detailed, level during the inspection and that Inspection Checklist A had been used as guidance in preparing for and conducting the inspections. It highlighted that overall the inspection team was impressed by the high standards and level of environmental commitment at the stations.

(92) Norway reported that as far as the inspection team could discern permits and authorisations were in place for all installations. Norway observed that the framework, provisions and principles of the Protocol had had an overall positive impact on the conduct of national Antarctic programme operations. Although noting differences among stations, the inspection team observed a general desire to implement cleaner, innovative and more efficient technologies. It also noted an ongoing shift towards more complex technological systems that, to a larger degree than before, could be operated remotely, which could in turn have positive implications for the environment. In that respect Norway noted the need for a continued focus on exchanging information and best practices between national programs, operators and personnel at Antarctic stations.

(93) Based on observations, Norway reflected on the current understanding that many of support installations, such as airfield camps are considered non-permanent or semi-permanent. Realizing that such infrastructure often can be removed, as can also research stations, they nevertheless are seemingly long term present and should potentially be treated as such according to the provisions of the Environment Protocol. Norway suggested that Parties continue to consider the use and understanding of the terms non-permanent, semi-permanent and permanent in light of the EIA provisions and requirements of the Environment Protocol.

(94) South Africa thanked Norway for its inspection of SANAE IV and the SANAP summer station, and welcomed the recommendations in the report.

In responding to one of the concerns raised in the report regarding skewing funding efforts towards infrastructure rather than science, South Africa clarified that it had actually expanded its scientific research scope, and had an established peer review process to allocate and review research grants.

(95) Belgium warmly thanked Norway for its inspection report of Princess Elisabeth Antarctic Research Station, and welcomed the comments made by the inspection team relating especially to energy production and consumption. Belgium noted that there were a few aspects to improve and that it would take into account the inspection report's recommendations. It also reported on a new system of permitting adopted by the Federal Parliament in July 2017, a few weeks before the start of the field season, and explained under which conditions a permit should now be requested from the Belgium national authority.

(96) The United Kingdom also thanked Norway for its report, and noted that Halley VI station was happy to host the inspection team. The United Kingdom expressed interest in the general feedback and comments made by Norway, particularly in relation to the use and understanding of the terms non-permanent, semi-permanent and permanent. It also noted that although there were no plans in place to install renewables in Halley VI, it was implementing plans to increase efficiency and achieve the same scientific results with considerably less fuel.

(97) The Russian Federation thanked Norway for the inspection of two of its facilities (Novo Airbase-Airfield and Perseus Runway), and commented on some observations in the inspection report. It indicated that in its opinion there was no need for a CEE in respect of the infrastructure mentioned, since this was only a seasonal, and not a year-round, activity. An alternative approach to the seasonal infrastructure would require a review of the existing IEE/CEE practice. The Russian Federation expressed its readiness to provide further considerations and explanations on the inspection report.

(98) ASOC thanked Norway for providing an inspection report, and noted that it was encouraging that Norway concluded that the Protocol has had an overall positive impact on station operations. However, ASOC also noted that the report mentioned that not all stations had achieved the same level of international coordination and participation with global observation programmes, and that there had been an increase in runways and the number of flights. With respect to the latter, ASOC encouraged the CEP to consider the possible impacts of this increased activity in future discussions on air activities.

(99) Norway thanked inspected Parties for the openness and friendliness with which they were received.

(100) The Committee thanked Norway for the high quality report on the inspections undertaken during the previous season. It was also noted that the inspections constituted a valuable contribution recognising that they imply a logistic and budget effort for the Parties. The Committee welcomed the generally positive findings of the inspection team regarding environmental matters, including: the presence of suitable permits and authorisations, the positive impact of the Environment Protocol on good practices at the stations, and the increase in the use of renewable energy on stations. Regarding the latter point, the Committee noted COMNAP's advice that the use of renewable energy by national Antarctic programmes was increasing, and that COMNAP would be holding a discussion on reducing fossil fuel use at its upcoming annual general meeting. The Committee also noted the suggestion made by the inspection team regarding considering the use of the terms non-permanent, semi-permanent and permanent, and considered that this was an issue the Committee could return to at a future meeting.

(101) The following papers were also submitted under this item:

- BP 1 *Follow-up to the Recommendations of the Inspections at the Eco-Nelson Facility* (Czech Republic).

- BP 23 *Follow-up to the Recommendations of the Inspection at the Johann Gregor Mendel Czech Antarctic Station* (Czech Republic).

Item 7: Reports from Subsidiary Bodies and Intersessional Contact Groups

(102) The convener of the Subsidiary Group on Management Plans (SGMP), Patricia Ortúzar (Argentina) introduced WP 9 *Subsidiary Group on Management Plans Report of activities during the intersessional period 2017-2018* on behalf of the SGMP. In accordance with terms of reference #1 to #3, the Group had been prepared to consider the following five draft Antarctic Specially Protected Area (ASPA) management plans referred by the CEP for intersessional review:

- ASPA 125: Fildes Peninsula, King George Island (25 de Mayo) (Chile).
- ASPA 144: Chile Bay (Discovery Bay), Greenwich Island, South Shetland Islands (Chile).
- ASPA 145: Port Foster, Deception Island, South Shetland Islands (Chile).
- ASPA 146: South Bay, Doumer Island, Palmer Archipelago (Chile).

- ASPA 150: Ardley Island, Maxwell Bay, King George Island (25 de Mayo) (Chile).

(103) The SGMP advised the CEP that the five management plans were still under review by the proponent and the Group would provide advice once the revised versions were available.

(104) In accordance with terms of reference #4 and #5, the Group had not received any new requests for advice from Parties regarding the five-yearly review of management plans, and had agreed to postpone the task of revising the *Guidance for assessing an area for a potential Antarctic Specially Managed Area designation.*

(105) The Committee thanked the SGMP for its advice and encouraged further Members to consider participating in the Group. Uruguay expressed its intention to actively participate in the work of the SGMP. The Committee also welcomed Chile's advice that it was continuing to work on the review of the five ASPA management plans mentioned in the SGMP report, and that it hoped to have them ready for review later in the year. Chile also referred to WP 11 and IP 9 which outlined its work to review the status of ASPA 144.

(106) The Committee adopted the following SGMP work plan for 2018/19:

Terms of Reference	Suggested tasks
ToR 1 to 3	Review draft management plans referred by CEP for intersessional review and provide advice to proponents
ToR 4 and 5	Work with relevant Parties to ensure progress on review of management plans overdue for five-yearly review
	Consider further improvements to the *Guidance for assessing an area for a potential Antarctic Specially Managed Area designation*
	Review and update SGMP work plan
Working Papers	Prepare report for CEP XXII against SGMP ToR 1 to 3

(107) Norway and the United Kingdom jointly introduced WP 20 *Report of the intersessional contact group established to develop guidance material for conservation approaches for the management of Antarctic heritage objects.* The paper outlined the work of the open-ended intersessional contact group (ICG) established at CEP XIX (2016), and which continued at CEP XX (2017), to develop guidance for conservation approaches for the management of Antarctic heritage objects.

(108) Norway and the United Kingdom proposed that the Committee: consider and adopt the attached *Guidelines for the Assessment and Management of Heritage in Antarctica* which had been developed by the ICG; adopt

a revised version of the *Guide to the Presentation of Working Papers containing Proposals for ASPAs, ASMAs or HSMs*; and consider the need for future discussion of overarching issues related to heritage management in Antarctica that were raised during the ICG.

(109) The Committee thanked Norway and the United Kingdom for leading the ICG, and acknowledged the contributions of other Members and Observers that participated. The Committee noted that the ICG had involved rich and challenging discussions on complex but important issues for the CEP and for the broader community. There was broad recognition of the value of the proposed guidelines, both for those making an initial assessment of a heritage site or object and for the CEP in evaluating submissions and proposals for new HSMs. Noting that 2020 marked the 200th anniversary of the first sighting of Antarctica, Members also acknowledged that HSMs offered an important means through which to educate visitors and the general public about Antarctic history and science.

(110) ASOC considered that the draft guidelines offered useful ways to streamline the process of designating historic sites in the context of other obligations in the Protocol, and noted positively that the issue of environmental protection had run through this discussion. ASOC considered that the use of EIA under Article 8(3) of the Protocol applied to a number of instances when an object was transitioning from its original use or status to that of a historic or heritage artefact.

(111) Following modifications suggested during the meeting, including changes in definitions and references to legal issues related to ex situ conservation, the Committee endorsed the *Guidelines for the assessment and management of Heritage in Antarctica*. The Committee also agreed to recommend that the ATCM revise the *Guide to the Presentation of Working Papers containing Proposals for ASPAs, ASMAs or HSMs* to update *Template B: Cover Sheet for a Working Paper on a Historic Site or Monument*, as presented in WP 20.

(112) The Committee recalled its decision at CEP XVIII that future proposals for designation of new HSMs should be put on hold until further guidelines on the assessment and management of heritage were in place, and its related decision at CEP XIX to defer consideration of two HSM proposals. It agreed that if the proponents wished to bring forward those proposals, or that if there were new proposals, it would be appropriate that they be considered and presented in light of the new guidelines and the revised Template B.

(113) The Committee agreed that the ICG had identified several overarching issues that warranted further consideration. In particular, it agreed there

would be value in giving further consideration to: the format of the HSM list; legal issues associated with ownership and potential removal for *ex situ* conservation, noting that this may require guidance from the ATCM; involvement of heritage expertise when assessing options for heritage management; and the possible need for EIA documentation as part of new HSM proposals. The CEP encouraged interested Members to work on these issues and to bring forward further papers for the Committee's consideration.

CEP advice to the ATCM on Guidelines for the assessment and management of Heritage in Antarctica

(114) The Committee endorsed the *Guidelines for the assessment and management of Heritage in Antarctica* and agreed to forward to the ATCM for adoption a draft Resolution encouraging the use of the guidelines.

(115) The Committee also endorsed a revision to the *Guide to the presentation of Working Papers containing proposals for Antarctic Specially Protected Areas, Antarctic Specially Managed Areas or Historic Sites and Monuments,* to reflect the *Guidelines for the assessment and management of Heritage in Antarctica*, which provide guidance with regard to required information for the purpose of HSM listings, and agreed to forward to the ATCM for approval a draft Resolution on updating the Guide.

(116) The Committee recalled its advice to ATCM XXXVIII that future proposals for new designations of HSM should be put on hold until further guidance had been established regarding assessment and management of Antarctic heritage. The Committee agreed to advise the ATCM that, with the adoption of the *Guidelines for the assessment and management of Heritage in Antarctica,* proposals for new designations of HSM could again proceed as appropriate.

(117) Germany introduced WP 29 *Report of the CEP Intersessional Contact Group to develop Guidelines on the Environmental Aspects of the use of Un-manned Aerial Vehicles (UAVs) / Remotely Piloted Aircraft Systems (RPAS) in Antarctica.* In accordance with the ICG terms of reference agreed at CEP XX (2017), the paper presented the report of the ICG convened by Germany, including an updated literature review, a summary of national operator experience in use of RPAS, draft *Environmental Guidelines for Operation of Remotely Piloted Aircraft Systems (RPAS) in Antarctica*, and a draft Resolution for consideration by the CEP.

(118) Germany informed the Committee that at the conclusion of the ICG's work there were several items still open for discussion in relation to the draft

guidelines, including: whether to specify wildlife separation distances in the guidelines; whether to retain a reference list in the guidelines; the extent to which guidance on operational matters should be incorporated in the guidelines; and whether the guidelines should apply to all RPAS activities or be restricted only to professional uses.

(119) The Committee thanked Germany for leading the ICG and commended all participants for contributing to this valuable and complex discussion. Following modifications made during the meeting, including to remove references to separation distances from wildlife, the CEP endorsed the *Environmental guidelines for the operation of Remotely Piloted Aircraft Systems (RPAS) in Antarctica.*

(120) The Committee encouraged support for further research into the environmental impacts and benefits of RPAS, especially with respect to impacts on wildlife. It noted the importance of reviewing and revising the guidelines, as appropriate, to reflect the current state of scientific knowledge of the environmental impacts and benefits of RPAS. The Committee agreed that it would be useful to have a central source of related information and welcomed the offer by COMNAP and SCAR to compile peer-reviewed literature and provide a summary that could be used to inform content to be included in the Antarctic Environments Portal. The Committee noted that the literature review presented in WP 29 would also be very useful in this regard.

(121) The Committee noted that the question of the circumstances under which recreational uses of RPAS should or should not be allowed had not been resolved during the ICG, and that it would be appropriate to keep under consideration the outcomes of any relevant RPAS-related discussion in the ATCM.

CEP advice to the ATCM on Environmental guidelines for the operation of Remotely Piloted Aircraft Systems (RPAS) in Antarctica

(122) The Committee endorsed the *Environmental guidelines for the operation of Remotely Piloted Aircraft Systems (RPAS) in Antarctica* and agreed to forward to the ATCM for approval a draft Resolution encouraging the use and further development of the guidelines.

(123) The Committee noted the following Information Papers submitted under this agenda item:

- IP 36 *Intersessional Contact Group on Review of the Antarctic Clean-up Manual: Progress report* (Australia) reported on the progress made by the ICG during the last year. Noting the limited time available and reduced agenda of CEP XXI, the ICG would finalise its work through the 2018-19 intersessional period and provide its report and any recommendations to CEP XXII. All CEP Members and Observers were invited to participate.

- IP 43 *COMNAP Antarctic Remotely Piloted Aircraft Systems (RPAS) Operator's Handbook* (COMNAP). This paper presented the current edition of the handbook, prepared by the COMNAP RPA Working Group, that included guidance on environmental aspects of RPAS deployment, taking into consideration ATCM XI - WP 20 *State of Knowledge of Wildlife Responses to Remotely Piloted Aircraft Systems (RPAS)* (SCAR), the views of the CEP Members that participated in the initial rounds of the CEP RPAS ICG, and first-hand experiences of the national Antarctic programmes in the Antarctic. The paper noted that COMNAP continues to recognise the risks and benefits (including cost-effectiveness and fuel savings) of RPA operations, and that there are many examples of the benefits of these technologies as science support instruments, monitoring, data-collection and operations and logistics tools. The handbook remained open and available through the COMNAP website.

- IP 46 *Report from the Subsidiary Group on Climate Change Response (SGCCR)* (Norway). This paper reported on the work of the SGCCR during the intersessional period. The SGCCR had initiated discussions on operating mechanisms for the group. One of the SGCCR's first steps would be to develop a more user-friendly format for the Climate Change Response Work Program (CCRWP).

Item 8: Five-Year Work Plan

(124) SCAR introduced WP 1 *SCAR's Environmental Code of Conduct for Terrestrial Scientific Field Research in Antarctica*. SCAR recalled the Committee's discussion of the Code of Conduct at CEP XX (2017), and reported on further consultations made during the intersessional period, including those with COMNAP, and the resulting revisions.

(125) The Committee recognised the broad and extensive consultation undertaken in the review and revision of the non-mandatory Code of Conduct, and agreed to encourage the dissemination and use of the Code of Conduct when planning and undertaking terrestrial scientific research in Antarctica.

CEP advice to the ATCM on SCAR's Environmental Code of Conduct for Terrestrial Scientific Field Research in Antarctica

(126) The Committee endorsed *SCAR's Environmental Code of Conduct for Terrestrial Scientific Field Research in Antarctica*, and agreed to forward to the ATCM for approval a draft Resolution on encouraging its dissemination and use.

(127) Australia introduced WP 16 *Proposal for a joint SCAR/CEP workshop on further developing the Antarctic protected area system* jointly prepared with Argentina, Belgium, Chile, China, the Czech Republic, France, Germany, Japan, New Zealand, Norway, the Russian Federation, SCAR, the United Kingdom, and the United States. To address actions in the Five-year Work Plan and the Climate Change Response Work Programme (CCRWP), the co-authors proposed that the CEP support the convening of a joint SCAR/CEP workshop on further developing the Antarctic protected area system. The paper presented a proposed workshop outline. The proponents recommended that the Committee agree to this proposal, adopt terms of reference for the workshop, and support the establishment of a joint SCAR/CEP steering committee to consult with CEP Members and workshop participants to finalise and communicate the workshop arrangements.

(128) The Committee strongly supported the proposal to convene a joint SCAR/CEP workshop on further developing the Antarctic protected area system, consistent with actions identified in the CEP Five-year Work Plan and the CCRWP, and supported the following workshop terms of reference as outlined in WP 16:

- Review the current status of the Antarctic protected area system.
- Identify information and resources relevant to designating ASPAs within a systematic environmental-geographic framework.
- Identify actions that could be taken to support the further development of the Antarctic protected area system.
- Prepare a report for consideration by the CEP.

(129) The Committee warmly welcomed the offer by the Czech Republic to host the workshop in Prague on the Thursday and Friday, in the end of June 2019, prior to the commencement of CEP XXII.

(130) The Committee agreed that it would be appropriate to establish a steering committee comprising representatives from the CEP, SCAR and the host country to consult with CEP Members and workshop participants to finalise

and communicate the workshop arrangements, and agreed that SCAR, the Czech Republic, Australia and the United Kingdom would serve on the steering committee. The Committee agreed that the steering committee could consult with CEP Members and relevant SCAR contacts on practical details, including to identify an appropriate recommended maximum number of workshop participants based on the venue, once identified. The Committee agreed that participation in the workshop would be open to representatives of CEP Members and Observers, and representatives and experts from relevant SCAR bodies and invited external experts.

(131) The Committee noted that the steering committee could also give further consideration to related issues raised by Members during the meeting regarding specific matters that could be discussed during the workshop, when further developing the detailed plans and agenda for the workshop in consultation with CEP Members and Observers and relevant contacts within SCAR. Such issues included: the possible designation of Important Bird Areas (IBAs) as ASPAs; taking tourism growth into consideration in the expansion of the protected area system; processes for review and delisting of areas; and the relevance of considering risk in assessing the potential for new ASPAs.

(132) The Committee looked forward to further consultation between the steering committee and CEP Members and Observers, and to considering the outcomes of the workshop at CEP XXII.

(133) The CEP Chair introduced WP 17 *Supporting the work of the Committee for Environmental Protection (CEP): A paper by the CEP Chair*, which followed on from discussions at CEP XX, and sought to facilitate further discussion about ways to ensure the CEP could remain well placed to support Parties' efforts to comprehensively protect the Antarctic environment. The CEP Chair invited Members to: review the attached list of CEP science needs and options for its presentation, communication and review; and consider options presented for obtaining and managing CEP funding.

(134) The Committee thanked the Chair for preparing the paper. It noted the value of having a consolidated list of science knowledge and information needs identified by the Committee, including as a useful communications tool for its engagement with the ATCM and other stakeholders. The Committee agreed to incorporate the science needs presented in Attachment A to WP 17 into the CEP Five-year Work Plan. It noted that the science needs would then be available via the ATS public website, and agreed that it would also be beneficial to communicate the CEP science needs directly to relevant

groups, and to consider alternative formats that may be more accessible to the relevant target audience. For those science needs that were relevant to matters identified in the CCRWP, the Committee noted that the SGCCR could play an important communication role.

(135) The Committee agreed to bring the CEP science needs to the attention of the ATCM in accordance with Article 12(k) of the Environment Protocol, including to inform ongoing discussions under the ATCM Multi-Year Strategic Work Plan on strategic science priorities. It encouraged Members, SCAR and other organisations involved in research and monitoring in the Antarctic region to draw on the CEP science needs to help promote and support science to better understand and address the environmental challenges facing Antarctica. The Committee welcomed SCAR's advice that the list of CEP science needs would be helpful for SCAR in its consideration of new scientific research programmes. It also noted SCAR's interest to work with Members to incorporate the CEP's science, knowledge and information needs into its new research programmes. The Committee agreed that it was important to regularly review and revise the CEP science needs, as appropriate, during annual CEP meetings.

(136) The Committee recognised that modest funding could assist it to undertake priority work to develop advice and recommendations to the ATCM. The Committee noted that it did not anticipate that there would be a large number of requests for funding, and recognised the previous and ongoing generous support of Members and Observers to assist the work of the CEP. The Committee expressed support for the possible process for considering proposals for CEP funding, as outlined in Attachment C to WP 17, noting that such a process would assist to ensure that any proposals were structured and targeted towards supporting agreed priorities. Members expressed the view that appropriate sources of CEP funding might include any surplus from Parties' annual contributions to the Secretariat of the Antarctic Treaty or voluntary contributions by Parties.

(137) China also noted that using funding for online forums or internet meetings was preferable to intersessional workshops or meetings to make it easier for all interested parties to contribute and improve the efficiency of communication, and that the possible uses for funds needed more discussion.

(138) The Committee agreed to seek advice from the ATCM on possible opportunities for obtaining funding.

CEP advice to the ATCM on supporting the work of the CEP

(139) In accordance with Article 12 (k) of the Environment Protocol, and noting the ATCM Multi-Year Strategic Work Plan priority relating to strategic science priorities, the Committee agreed to advise the ATCM that it had incorporated a list of CEP science needs into the CEP Five-year Work Plan, and that it had agreed to regularly review and revise these science needs as appropriate.

(140) The Committee also recognised that modest funding could assist it to undertake priority work to develop high quality and timely advice and recommendations in line with its functions under Article 12 of the Environment Protocol, and that it had agreed to seek advice from the ATCM on possible opportunities for obtaining such funding. In this regard, the Committee had noted that WP 17 presented a possible process for consideration of funding proposals that could assist to ensure that any funding proposals were structured and targeted to agreed priorities.

(141) The Committee noted the following papers submitted under this agenda item:

- IP 28 *Anthropogenic Noise in the Southern Ocean: an Update* (SCAR). This paper reported progress in the 2017-18 intersessional period on the SCAR review of anthropogenic noise in the Southern Ocean for the CEP. A comprehensive literature review had been completed, an expert panel convened and consulted, and input from a variety of sources considered. These inputs had been combined in a draft Background Paper that would continue to be revised and refined until final submission to ATCM XLII - CEP XXII in 2019.

- IP 50 *Joint monitoring activities during 2017/18 summer season to manage non-native flies in King George Island, South Shetland Islands* (Uruguay, Republic of Korea, Poland, Russian Federation). This paper reported on coordinated actions by countries operating on King George Island to monitor and manage the presence of the non-native fly *Trichocera maculipennis* on the island.

(142) The Committee revised and updated its Five-year Work Plan (Appendix 1). The major changes comprised updates to reflect actions agreed during the Meeting, including those relating to: incorporation of the CEP science knowledge and information needs; the outcomes of discussions on matters related to Site Guidelines; the joint SCAR/CEP workshop on further developing the Antarctic protected area system; and management of Antarctic heritage.

(143) Noting that, due to the abbreviated format of the meeting, some items identified in the Five-year Work Plan for consideration at CEP XXI had been deferred, the Committee welcomed the following updates:

- Bulgaria informed the Committee that, during the 2017-18 intersessional work of the ATCM ICG on Education and Outreach, various activities were carried out relevant to the work of the CEP. These included a webinar organized by the Association of Polar Early Career Scientists and the European Polar Board on the Antarctic Treaty and Environmental Protection. The webinar was presented by Dr Yves Frenot, who gave a presentation on the Antarctic Treaty and Environment Protocol. Other activities highlighted in the ATCM Forum included Polar Weeks and Antarctica Day 2017, in which IAATO shared its new app named "Polar Guide: Antarctica". Bulgaria also reported that the ATCM ICG on Education and Outreach would continue its work in the next intersessional period.

- The Netherlands informed the Committee that it planned to convene an informal workshop to undertake a stocktake of tourism priorities, in collaboration with the United Kingdom and IAATO.

Item 9: Cooperation with Other Organisations

(144) The Committee welcomed the following Information Papers submitted by Observers participating in the meeting in accordance with Rule 4(b) of the CEP Rules of Procedure:

- IP 11 *Annual Report for 2017/18 of the Council of Managers of National Antarctic Programs (COMNAP)* (COMNAP). This paper noted that 2018 was the 30th anniversary of COMNAP, and reported that Kazuyuki Shiraishi of Japan's National Institute of Polar Research completed his three-year term as COMNAP Chair and Kelly Falkner of the US Antarctic Program was elected to a three-year term as Chair. It noted that its Remotely Piloted Aircraft (RPA) Working Group continued to share first-hand knowledge of Antarctic air activity and to develop the COMNAP Antarctic RPAS Operator's Handbook based on peer-reviewed scientific knowledge. The paper further noted that the 2018 COMNAP annual General Meeting and Symposium would include an environmental session on identifying sources of plastics in the Antarctic environment, fossil fuel use/reduction and further understanding of cumulative impacts.

- IP 33 *Update on activities of the Southern Ocean Observing System (SOOS)* (SCAR). This paper summarised key activities of SOOS *(www.soos.aq),* highlighted future efforts and identified challenges facing SOOS in the coming year. It noted that SOOS is a joint initiative of SCAR and the Scientific Committee on Oceanic Research (SCOR) aimed at facilitating the collection and delivery of observations on dynamics and change of the Southern Ocean through cost-effective observing and data delivery systems.

- IP 66 *Report by the SC-CAMLR Observer to CEP* (CCAMLR). CCAMLR noted that the Scientific Committee had made significant progress with a number of work programmes previously reported as of interest to the CEP. In particular, in 2017 it had recommended to the Commission a Climate Change Response Work Program, and that the loss of a 5800 km^2 section of floating ice from the Larsen C Ice Shelf should be recognised by designation of a 10-year Special Area for scientific study in the area. It had also approved a Research and Monitoring Program for the Ross Sea MPA.

(145) On behalf of the Committee, the Chair thanked COMNAP, SCAR and SC-CAMLR for the collaboration and contributions to the work of the CEP, and congratulated SCAR on its 60th anniversary and COMNAP on its 30th anniversary. COMNAP advised the Committee that it had recently welcomed the national Antarctic programmes of Switzerland and Turkey to Observer status membership.

(146) WMO presented IP 47 *WMO Annual Report 2017-2018* and IP 48 *The Southern Hemisphere Special Observing Period of the Year of Polar Prediction.* WMO reported that its activities related to Antarctica during the last year included the Global Cryosphere Watch, the Year of Polar Prediction (YOPP), and progress on the development of the concept of an Antarctic Polar Regional Climate Centre. WMO noted that it would be inviting a CEP representative to a scoping workshop on an Antarctic Polar Regional Climate Centre (PRCC) Network, provisionally planned for May 2019, to ensure that the needs of the CEP are taken into account. With respect to IP 48, WMO provided an update on activities carried out in the context of the YOPP, including a special Observing Period planned for November 2018 to February 2019. It encouraged Members to get involved in the YOPP and to read more about the initiative at: *http://www.polarprediction.net/yopp-activities/getting-involved-with-yopp/.* With reference to IP 44, WMO noted that it would jointly launch with SCAR a WMO-SCAR Fellowship Program for early career scientists.

Nomination of CEP Representatives to other organisations

(147) The Committee nominated:

- Ms Patricia Ortúzar (Argentina) to represent the CEP at the 30th COMNAP Annual General Meeting, to be held in Garmisch, Germany, from 11 to 13 June 2018, and also welcomed the kind offer by Dr Antonio Quesada Del Corral (Spain) to assist as appropriate;

- Ms Birgit Njåstad (Norway) to represent the CEP at the 35th SCAR Delegates Meeting, to be held in Davos, Switzerland, from 24 to 26 June 2018; and

- Dr Polly Penhale (United States) to represent the CEP at the 37th meeting of SC-CAMLR, to be held in Hobart, Australia, from 22 to 26 October 2018.

Item 10: General Matters

(148) The Russian Federation introduced WP 3 *Consideration of Current Climate Changes in the Antarctic Treaty System*. Recalling that Parties submitted documents on climate change to both the ATCM and the CEP, the Russian Federation proposed that, in order to avoid duplication of discussions, papers submitted to the ATCM should address the role of Antarctica in global climate changes, while papers to the CEP should refer to the influence of global climate changes on the Antarctic environment and on matters relating to local anthropogenic influence on the environment of the region.

(149) SCAR drew the Committee's attention to the conclusions of the IPCC Fifth Assessment Report, and specifically to the conclusion that warming in the climate system is unequivocal and that the human influence on the climate system is clear. SCAR also noted the rapid growth of scientific knowledge about the role of Antarctica in the climate system, the extent to which the Antarctic system is changing and impacts on Antarctic ecology. SCAR further reported that it would continue to contribute advice about those matters on an annual basis, both to the CEP, and, in keeping with Article 10.2 of the Protocol, to the ATCM.

(150) WMO supported the conclusion of WP 3 that the brevity and sparse distribution of observational records pose significant challenges to understanding climatic trends in the Antarctic region. However, it noted that many of the instrumental records do go back more than 100 years, with significant data from the IGY (1957/58) and the advent of satellite

data from the 1970s. WMO explained that by combining information from instrumental, satellite, palaeoclimate and reanalysis data, along with climate model simulations, serious scientific conclusions could be drawn. WMO drew the Committee's attention to the significant strengthening of the westerly winds associated with changes in the Southern Annular Mode and a marked warming since the mid-20th century on the Antarctic Peninsula. It highlighted that regional warming had an impact on the terrestrial biota and had played a part in the retreat of 90% of the glaciers around the Peninsula. It further noted that these scientific conclusions had been published in numerous papers in highly rated journals and that as scientists continue to analyse the data WMO, like SCAR, would continue to highlight important updates both to the CEP and the ATCM, as appropriate.

(151) In responding, the Russian Federation noted that while sharing of the views of WMO and SCAR it emphasised that the task of the paper was to optimize operations related to paper submissions and avoid overloading the agenda.

(152) The Committee thanked the Russian Federation for providing the paper and recognised that matters related to climate change implications for the environment were clearly relevant to the work of the CEP, including the ongoing work of the Subsidiary Group on Climate Change Response. The Committee agreed with the sentiment expressed by the Russian Federation of seeking to avoid duplication of discussions by the ATCM and CEP by seeking to ensure that papers are directed to the appropriate body. However, it was noted that it was challenging in some instances to identify a clear distinction, and that some matters may be relevant to both bodies.

(153) The Committee welcomed the commitment from SCAR and WMO to continue to bring forward relevant scientific advice to inform the Committee's discussions.

(154) New Zealand introduced WP 12 *Harmonisation of Marine Protection Initiatives across the Antarctic Treaty System (ATS)*, prepared jointly with Belgium, Chile, France, Germany, Netherlands and the United States. The paper recommended that the CEP establish an ICG to support harmonisation of marine protection initiatives across the Antarctic Treaty System. The ICG would be tasked with identifying options, within its mandate, to contribute to the Ross Sea Region Marine Protected Area (RSRMPA) as well as capturing related broader issues raised.

(155) Noting the ATCM's request to the CEP in Resolution 5 (2017) and the action in the CEP Five-year Work Plan, many Members strongly supported

the proposal to establish an ICG on harmonisation of marine protection initiatives across the Antarctic Treaty System.

(156) Some Members raised generic issues, including the independent procedure and role of the ATCM from CCAMLR, the nature of MPAs as a tool to achieve CCAMLR objectives and principles, and the differences between conservation and protection. With respect to Resolution 5 (2017), some Members suggested that the proposed ICG should only be established after a Research and Monitoring Plan for the Ross Sea Region MPA is adopted by CCAMLR according to its Conservation Measures.

(157) The Representative from SC-CAMLR informed the Committee that the Research and Monitoring Plan for the RSRMPA, having been developed at the Ross Sea region MPA Research and Monitoring Plan Workshop in Rome (2017), had been adopted by SC-CAMLR, but noted it had yet to be adopted by CCAMLR. The Representative from SC-CAMLR also informed the Committee that a CCAMLR Workshop on Spatial Management was going to occur in July 2018 in Cambridge. The workshop would consider the scope and potential mechanisms for future cooperation and collaboration with other scientific programmes (e.g. SCAR, SOOS and ICED), in terms of the provision of data relating to the development of spatial management and MPA research and monitoring.

(158) ASOC thanked the co-sponsors of WP 12 for a useful and timely paper and expressed strong support for efforts to harmonise the work of CCAMLR on MPAs with the work of the ATCM and CEP. ASOC noted that IP 58 *ASOC update on Marine Protected Areas in the Southern Ocean 2017-2018* provided an update on discussions on MPAs that had taken place at the CCAMLR XXXVI meeting in October 2017. In that paper ASOC recommended, *inter alia,* that the ATCM and CEP work to harmonise ASPAs and ASMAs with CCAMLR MPAs, starting with the Ross Sea. ASOC noted that there were several proposals for CCAMLR MPAs at various stages in the design and discussion processes, all of which are located in the Antarctic Treaty Area. ASOC expressed its hope that the proposed ICG would be the first step towards creating a process in which the ATCM, CEP and CCAMLR and its advisory bodies could work together to create effective protection for the Antarctic environment.

(159) The Committee recalled:

- Resolution 5 (2017), which invited "the Committee on Environmental Protection to consider any appropriate actions within the Antarctic Treaty Consultative Meeting's competence to contribute to the achievement of the specific objectives set forth in CCAMLR Conservation Measure 91-05, particularly in the designation and implementation of Antarctic Specially Protected Areas and Antarctic Specially Managed Areas in the Ross Sea region and the management of relevant human activities"; and

- the action in the CEP Five-year Work Plan "to consider connectivity between land and ocean, and complementary measures that could be undertaken by Parties with respect to MPAs".

(160) New Zealand offered to lead informal intersessional work on these matters over the next intersessional period and report back at CEP XXII, and encouraged interested Members to participate.

(161) China introduced WP 14 *Report of the Informal Discussion for the intersessional period of 2017/18 on the draft Code of Conduct for the Exploration and Research in Dome A Area in Antarctica.* The paper presented a report on informal intersessional discussions led by China with interested Members on developing a draft Code of Conduct for the Exploration and Research in Dome A in Antarctica. China thanked the four Members who took part in the informal intersessional discussion regarding the Code of Conduct. In noting that it was seeking to establish two more telescopes at Kunlun Station to study extra-terrestrial activities, China emphasised that such scientific endeavours needed protection from disturbance by other activities. Comparisons were drawn between the prospective telescopes at Kunlun and the United States Green Bank Telescope, which has a large exclusion area. China emphasised that it welcomed and promoted international scientific collaboration within the Dome A and Kunlun Station areas, and advised that it planned to make further changes to the draft Code of Conduct based on suggestions to be provided by Members. China encouraged interested Members and Observers to contribute to the draft and share their thoughts on how to improve the Code of Conduct.

(162) The United Kingdom introduced WP 21 *Notification of pre-1958 historic remains: Wreck of Sir Ernest Shackleton's vessel Endurance.* While the location of the *Endurance* was unknown, the United Kingdom reported that it was aware of an upcoming non-governmental expedition to locate the wreck and it wished to confirm the protection status of the vessel in the event that the wreck was found. The United Kingdom sought the Committee's agreement that, in the event that it was located, protection of the vessel would commence in accordance with Resolution 5 (2001). The United Kingdom also informed the Committee of its intention to seek formal Historic Site and Monument

status for the wreck of the vessel, and noted that it would be a unique historical site, as it would be the first one to be completely marine in nature.

(163) Norway highlighted the historical relevance of Shackleton's expedition and noted the importance of developing an appropriate protection mechanism. It recalled that the designation of Roald Amundsen's tent, which had not been located, as an HSM could be considered a precedent for this case.

(164) In response to a question raised, the United Kingdom explained that the plan was for the expedition to locate the wreck and take photographs, but under no circumstance to touch the wreck or remove any artefacts. It stressed that when issuing the permit the United Kingdom's competent authority would make it very clear that no authorisation would be granted to interfere with the wreck in any way.

(165) The Committee thanked the United Kingdom for providing notice of the possible discovery of the site of the wreck of Sir Ernest Shackleton's vessel *Endurance*, consistent with provisions of Resolution 5 (2001). The Committee agreed that should the exact location of the wreck be identified, both the wreck and all its associated artefacts would be afforded interim protection under the terms of Resolution 5 (2001). The Committee noted the United Kingdom's intention to submit a proposal to a future meeting to list the vessel as a HSM.

(166) ASOC presented IP 49 *Emperor Penguin Population Variability in a Region Subject to Climate Warming*, jointly prepared with the United Kingdom. This paper presented preliminary findings of a collaborative study between the British Antarctic Survey and ASOC member WWF. The study attempted to estimate the population size of the 16 known emperor penguin colonies situated between 0 to 90°W (covering the Antarctic Peninsula and the Weddell Sea) using high resolution satellite imagery taken between 2009-2016. The initial results demonstrated that colonies in this sector ranged from about 650 to over 15,000 pairs, with an average colony size of less than 5,000 pairs. Results also demonstrated that all colonies were highly variable from year to year, and that there were no common inter-annual patterns of change across all sites, suggesting that a longer dataset at a circum-Antarctic scale would be beneficial to determine more accurate population trends. ASOC and the United Kingdom suggested that these results could be used to inform precautionary protection of emperor penguins, including those places where refugia from climate change were most likely to exist, for example, in the high-latitude Weddell Sea.

(167) ASOC presented IP 60 *Enacting the Climate Change Work Response Programme under a Changing Antarctic Environment*. ASOC focussed on five

core recommendations: investing in robust monitoring of the Antarctic region, investing in ecological monitoring, developing precautionary or rapid-response management plans, establishing protected areas as climate reference areas, and implementing specific, measurable, achievable, realistic, and time-bound (SMART) monitoring and evaluation in response plans. ASOC had linked the recommendations to specific items that could be included in the CCRWP and had provided an annotated CCRWP for reference. ASOC stressed that climate change was impacting Antarctica and that the CEP and ATCM needed to move away from simply reviewing information on climate change towards making management decisions such as establishing new protected areas and making commitments to fill gaps in monitoring.

(168) The Committee welcomed IP 49 and IP 60 and noted the relevance of these papers to its work. In particular, the Committee observed that IP 60 presented information that would be useful for the SGCCR's work to support implementation of the CCRWP. China thanked ASOC for the Information Paper and suggested that the information used for the SGCCR be validated by scientific data. The SGCCR convener highlighted that the SGCCR was open to all interested Members and Observers.

(169) New Zealand observed that the study presented in IP 49 would be useful in updating the climate change and emperor penguin Information Summary in the Antarctic Environments Portal.

(170) Argentina observed that there are other important criteria to specially protect determined areas or values, including the consideration of the pressure of human activities.

(171) In response to a question, ASOC clarified that climate reference areas represented areas set aside in which human activities were limited with the aim of allowing scientists to distinguish between the effects of climate change and human activities. It noted the importance of these reference areas in regions that were rapidly changing like the Antarctic Peninsula.

(172) Colombia informed the Committee that, in January 2018, the President of the Republic of Colombia approved the ratification of the Environment Protocol. It noted that the ratification was undergoing Constitutional Control, and that it anticipated completing the ratification process in the next year. Colombia thanked the six countries who supported Colombia in the environmental aspects of its recent expedition and reaffirmed that it would continue to collaborate with the CEP and its intersessional groups.

(173) The Committee thanked Colombia for reporting that it was in the process of ratifying the Environment Protocol and looked forward to welcoming Colombia as a CEP Member.

(174) The Committee noted the following Information Papers submitted under this agenda item:

- IP 3 *Antarctic Environments Portal: Progress Report* (New Zealand, SCAR). This paper reported on the development of the Antarctic Environments Portal including an attached update to the Portal's Content Management Plan. The proponents encouraged Members to provide feedback on the Content Management Plan and to nominate a representative to fill a vacancy on the Portal Editorial Group.

- IP 5 *Environmental Monitoring of the Reconstruction Work of the Brazilian Antarctic Station (2017/2018)* (Brazil). This paper provided an update on the environmental monitoring activities carried out by Brazil during the reconstruction of the Comandante Ferraz Antarctic Station over the last summer season.

- IP 10 *New Data on Seawater Temperature in South Bay, Doumer Island* (Chile). This paper provided the results of the first annual, continuous, high-resolution temperature record for ASPA 146, South Bay, Doumer Island.

- IP 12 *Preliminary Survey for the International Exploration Programme of Subglacial Lakes in Southern Victoria Land, Antarctica* (Republic of Korea). The paper outlined the Republic of Korea's preparations for the future exploration of subglacial lakes upstream of David Glacier in Southern Victoria Land, East Antarctica. It also noted that baseline data for the preparation of a CEE would be obtained until the 2019/20 season at the latest.

- IP 17 *Towards Application of Atmospheric Deposition Modeling for Quantitative Assessment of Cumulative Impacts on Soils* (Belarus). This paper drew attention to the application of atmospheric deposition modeling within a quantitative assessment of the cumulative impacts on soils within the framework of the CEE. In particular, this assessment could be applied during construction and operation of facilities in the Antarctic using this modeling as an important part of cumulative impact assessment. The paper reported on Belarus' particulate deposition modelling of stationary sources emissions from the Belarusian Antarctic Station on Mount Vechernyaya, and was presented as a demonstration of the application of this concept.

- IP 22 *Supporting the Regional-Scale Analysis of Antarctica: A Tool to Enable Broader-Scale Environmental Management* (New Zealand). This paper provided an update on New Zealand's work to develop a tool to support the assessment of environmental impacts of Antarctic activities. New Zealand encouraged Members to participate in the development of the tool and to attend a workshop to showcase it at the POLAR2018 conference.

- IP 24 *Accession of Turkey to the Protocol on Environmental Protection to the Antarctic Treaty* (Turkey). This paper reported on Turkey's accession to the Environment Protocol and the next steps towards its ratification.

- IP 27 *Implementation of Nature Protection Measures During The Xth Belarusian Antarctic Expedition 2017-2018* (Belarus). The paper reported on the continued removal of historical waste from Vechernyaya Mountain on Enderby Land, East Antarctica by the Belarusian Antarctic Expedition in close cooperation with the Russian Antarctic Expedition. The paper also noted Belarus' plans to start the procedure of ratifying Annex VI to the Environment Protocol in 2019.

- IP 30 *Hull Damage of the Russian M/V Ivan Papanin in Quilty Bay, Larsemann Hills, East Antarctica* (India, Russian Federation). This paper reported on an accident near Bharati Station that damaged the hull of the *M/V Ivan Papanin*. It noted that 38 people were evacuated from the ship (excluding 28 crew members) as well as crucial cargo and helicopters, with the assistance of the Russian Programme. The South African Antarctic programme also offered their assistance during the incident. Although damage to the hull was severe, there were no injuries to crew/expedition members and no oil spillage. After temporary repairs, the ship left Prydz Bay on 7 March and safely reached Cape Town on 21 March 2018.

- IP 31 *Non-native Species Response Protocol: An Update* (United Kingdom, Argentina, Spain). This paper reported on informal discussions initiated to improve the Non-native Species Response Protocol and encouraged Members to participate informally in the ongoing development of the Response Protocol during the intersessional period.

- IP 34 *Fatal Accident During Convoy Operation at Indian Barrier, Maitri Station, East Antarctica* (India). This paper reported that a student participating in the XXXVII Indian Scientific Expedition to Antarctica (ISEA) had passed away following a vehicle accident on 26 March 2018.

- IP 45 *The Initial Environmental Evaluation for the Construction of a New Garage for the Inland Traverse Vehicles in Zhongshan Station, Larsemann Hills, East Antarctica* (China). It noted that the IEE was conducted by Tongji University in accordance with Annex I of the Environment Protocol and the Guidelines for EIA in Resolution 1 (2016), and that construction started during the 2017/18 season and would be finished in the next season.

- IP 52 *On Permit for Implementing Activity of the Russian Antarctic Expedition in 2018-2022* (Russian Federation). This paper reported on the internal procedures conducted by the Russian Federation to renew the permit granted to the Arctic and Antarctic Research Institute (AARI) to conduct operations of the Russian Antarctic Expedition.

- IP 59 *The Polar Code and Marine Mammal Avoidance Planning in the International Maritime Organization* (ASOC). This paper drew attention to requirements in the Polar Code for voyage planning in relation to marine mammal avoidance. ASOC proposed that the CEP and ATCM consider the implementation of the Polar Code provisions on voyage planning. It requested Parties consider how to make progress on the implementation of the provisions of the Polar Code and how to make relevant data on marine mammal densities and seasonal migration routes available to mariners.

- IP 64 *Progress on the Development of a Preliminary Proposal for the Establishment of a Marine Protected Area (MPA) West of the Antarctic Peninsula and South of the Scotia Arc* (Argentina, Chile). The paper reported on the latest developments in the designation of a MPA in CCAMLR's Domain 1. The co-authors encouraged more Members to become part of the designation process and follow debates regarding the development of the Domain 1 MPA.

- IP 67 *Committee for Environmental Protection (CEP): Summary of Activities During the 2017/18 Intersessional Period* (Australia). This paper presented a summary by the CEP Chair of intersessional activities since CEP XX.

(175) The following papers were also submitted under this agenda item:

- BP 11 *Visit to Chilean Antarctic Station Prof. Julio Escudero by Turkey* (Turkey).

- BP 34 *Brazil/Australia Remediation Workshop* (Australia, Brazil).

Item 11: Election of Officers

(176) The Committee elected Patricia Ortúzar from Argentina for a second two-year term as Vice-Chair. The Committee thanked Patricia for her many valued contributions as Vice-Chair, and congratulated her on her re-appointment to the role.

(177) The Committee elected Birgit Njåstad from Norway as Chair for a two-year term and congratulated her on her appointment to the role.

(178) Noting Birgit Njåstad's election as CEP Chair would result in a vacancy for the convenor of the SGCCR, the Committee agreed to appoint CEP Vice-Chair, Kevin Hughes from the United Kingdom as SGCCR convenor. The Committee thanked Birgit Njåstad for her work in leading the SGCCR in its first year.

(179) The Committee warmly thanked and congratulated Ewan McIvor from Australia for his excellent work and significant contributions throughout his four-year term as Chair.

Item 12: Preparation for the Next Meeting

(180) The Committee adopted the Preliminary Agenda for CEP XXII (Appendix 2).

Item 13: Adoption of the Report

(181) The Committee adopted its Report.

Item 14: Closing of the Meeting

(182) The Chair closed the Meeting on Tuesday 15th May 2018.

Appendix 1

CEP Five-Year Work Plan 2018

Issue / Environmental Pressure: Introduction of non-native species	
Priority: 1	
Actions:	
1. Continue developing practical guidelines & resources for all Antarctic operators. 2. Implement related actions identified in the Climate Change Response Work Programme. 3. Consider the spatially explicit, activity-differentiated risk assessments to mitigate the risks posed by terrestrial non-native species. 4. Develop a surveillance strategy for areas at high risk of non-native species establishment. 5. Give additional attention to the risks posed by intra-Antarctic transfer of propagules.	
Intersessional period 2018/19	• Initiate work to develop a non-native species response strategy, including appropriate responses to diseases of wildlife • To help the Committee in assessing the effectiveness of the Manual, request a report from COMNAP on the implementation of quarantine and biosecurity measures by its members • United Kingdom to lead discussion with interested Members and Observers, on the further development of a non-mandatory non-native species response protocol
CEP XXII 2019	• Discuss the intersessional work concerning the development of a response strategy for inclusion in the Non-native Species Manual, and the implementation of quarantine and biosecurity measures by COMNAP members. Review IMO report on biofouling guidelines • Consider report on intersessional discussion on non-native species response protocol and its inclusion in the Non-native Species Manual. • SCAR to present information on existing mechanism to assist with the identification of non-native species
Intersessional period 2019/20	• Ask SCAR to compile a list of available biodiversity information sources and databases to help Parties establish which native species are present at Antarctic sites and thereby assist with identifying the scale and scope of current and future introductions • Develop generally applicable monitoring guidelines. More detailed or site-specific monitoring may be required for particular locations • Request a report from Parties and Observers on the application of biosecurity guidelines by their members
CEP XXIII 2020	• Discuss the intersessional work concerning the development of monitoring guidelines for inclusion in the NNS Manual. • Consider the reports from Parties and Observers on the application of biosecurity guidelines by their members
Intersessional period 2020/21	• Initiate work to assess the risk of marine non native species introductions
CEP XXIV 2021	• Discuss the intersessional work concerning the risks of marine non-native species

Intersessional period 2021/22	• Develop specific guidelines to reduce non-native species release with wastewater discharge • Review the progress and contents of the CEP Non-native Species Manual
CEP XXV 2022	• CEP to consider if intersessional work is required to review/update the Non-native Species Manual
Intersessional period 2022/23	• As appropriate, intersessional work to review the Non-native Species Manual
CEP XXVI 2023	• CEP to consider report of ICG, if established, and consider adoption of revised Non-native Species Manual by the ATCM through a resolution

Science knowledge and information needs:
- Identify terrestrial and marine regions and habitats at risk of introduction
- Identify native species at risk of relocation and vectors and pathways for intra-continental transfer
- Synthesise knowledge of Antarctic biodiversity, biogeography and bioregionalisation and undertake baseline studies to establish which native species are present
- Identify pathways for the introduction of marine species (including risks associated with wastewater discharge)
- Assess risks and pathways for introduction of microorganisms that might impact on existing microbial communities
- Monitor for non-native species in the terrestrial and marine environments (including microbial activity near sewage treatment plant discharges)
- Identify techniques to rapidly respond to non-native species introductions
- Identify pathways for introduction of non-native species without any direct human intervention

Issue / Environmental Pressure: Tourism and NGO activities	
Priority: 1	

Actions:
1. Provide advice to ATCM as requested.
2. Advance recommendations from ship-borne tourism ATME.

Intersessional period 2018/19	• Further develop methodology for site sensitivity assessment and to consider trigger levels (recommendations 3 and 7 of the CEP Tourism Study)
CEP XXII 2019	• Discuss the recommendations from the CEP Tourism Study, and other relevant recommendations, and determine priority actions and next steps to be put forward
Intersessional period 2019/20	
CEP XXIII 2020	
Intersessional period 2020/21	
CEP XXIV 2021	
Intersessional period 2021/22	
CEP XXV 2022	
Intersessional period 2022/23	
CEP XXVI 2023	

Science knowledge and information needs:
- Consistent and dedicated monitoring of tourism impacts
- Monitor visitor sites covered by Site Guidelines

Issue / Environmental Pressure: Climate Change Implications for the Environment	
Priority: 1	
Actions:	
1. Consider implications of climate change for management of Antarctic environment. 2. Implement the Climate Change Response Work Programme.	
Intersessional period 2018/19	• Subsidiary group conducts work in accordance with agreed work plan
CEP XXII 2019	• Standing agenda item • Consider advice on how WMO activities map to CCRWP • Consider subsidiary group report • SCAR provides update to the Antarctic Climate Change and the Environment (ACCE) report, with input as appropriate from WMO, the Integrating Climate and Ecosystem Dynamics in the Southern Ocean (ICED) programme and SOOS
Intersessional period 2019/20	• Subsidiary group conducts work in accordance with agreed work plan
CEP XXIII 2020	• Standing agenda item • Consider subsidiary group report • SCAR provides update to ACCE report, with input as appropriate from WMO, ICED and SOOS • Consider review of subsidiary group • Review implementation of actions arising from 2016 joint CEP/SC-CAMLR workshop • Plan for five-yearly joint SC-CAMLR/CEP workshop during 2021/22 intersessional period
Intersessional period 2020/21	
CEP XXIV 2021	• Finalise plans for joint SC-CAMLR/CEP workshop during 2021/22 intersessional period
Intersessional period 2021/22	• Regular five-yearly joint SC-CAMLR CEP workshop
CEP XXV 2022	
Intersessional period 2022/23	
CEP XXVI 2023	

Science knowledge and information needs:
- Improve understanding of current and future change to the terrestrial (including aquatic) biotic and abiotic environment due to climate change
- Long-term monitoring of change to the terrestrial (including aquatic) biotic and abiotic environment due to climate change
- Continue to develop biogeographic tools to provide a sound basis for informing Antarctic area protection and management at regional and continental scales in light of climate change, including identifying the need to set aside reference areas for future research and identifying areas resilient to climate change
- Identify and prioritise Antarctic biogeographic regions most vulnerable to climate change
- Understand and predict near-shore marine changes and impacts of the change
- Long-term monitoring of change to the near-shore marine biotic and abiotic environment due to climate change
- Assessment on impact of ocean acidification to marine biota and ecosystems
- Understand population status, trends, vulnerability and distribution of key Antarctic species
- Understand habitat status, trends, vulnerability and distribution
- Southern Ocean observations and modelling to understand climate change
- Identify areas that may be resilient to climate change
- Monitor emperor penguin colonies, including using remote sensing and complementary techniques, to identify trends in populations and potential climate change *refugia*

Issue / Environmental Pressure: Processing new and revised protected / managed area management plans	
Priority: 1	
Actions:	
1. Refine the process for reviewing new and revised management plans. 2. Update existing guidelines. 3. Develop guidelines to ASMAs preparation.	
Intersessional period 2018/19	• SGMP conducts work as per agreed work plan • Norway and interested Members prepare paper on guidance for delisting ASPAs
CEP XXII 2019	• Consider SGMP report • Consider paper by Norway and interested Members on guidance for delisting ASPAs
Intersessional period 2019/20	• SGMP conducts work as per agreed work plan
CEP XXIII 2020	• Consider SGMP report
Intersessional period 2020/21	• SGMP conducts work as per agreed work plan
CEP XXIV 2021	• Consider SGMP report
Intersessional period 2021/22	• SGMP conducts work as per agreed work plan
CEP XXV 2022	• Consider SGMP report
Intersessional period 2022/23	• SGMP conducts work as per agreed work plan
CEP XXVI 2023	• Consider SGMP report
Science knowledge and information needs: • Monitoring to assess the status of values at ASPA 107 Emperor Island • Use remote sensing techniques to monitor changes in vegetation within ASPAs • Long-term monitoring of biological values in ASPAs	

Issue / Environmental Pressure: Operation of the CEP and Strategic Planning	
Priority: 1	
Actions:	
1. Keep the five-year work plan up to date based on changing circumstances and ATCM requirements. 2. Identify opportunities for improving the effectiveness of the CEP. 3. Consider long-term objectives for Antarctica (50-100 years time). 4. Consider opportunities for enhancing the working relationship between the CEP and the ATCM.	
Intersessional period 2018/19	
CEP XXII 2019	
Intersessional period 2019/20	
CEP XXIII 2020	
Intersessional period 2020/21	
CEP XXIV 2021	
Intersessional period 2021/22	
CEP XXV 2022	
Intersessional period 2022/23	
CEP XXVI 2023	

Issue / Environmental Pressure: Repair or Remediation of Environmental Damage	
Priority: 2	
Actions:	
1. Respond to further request from the ATCM related to repair and remediation, as appropriate. 2. Monitor progress on the establishment of Antarctic-wide inventory of sites of past activity. 3. Consider guidelines for repair and remediation. 4. Members develop practical guidelines and supporting resources for inclusion in the Clean-up Manual. 5. Continue developing bioremediation and repair practices for inclusion in the Clean-up Manual.	
Intersessional period 2018/19	• Continue ICG to review the Clean-up Manual
CEP XXII 2019	• Consider ICG report on review of the Clean-up Manual
Intersessional period 2019/20	
CEP XXIII 2020	
Intersessional period 2020/21	
CEP XXIV 2021	
Intersessional period 2021/22	
CEP XXV 2022	
Intersessional period 2022/23	
CEP XXVI 2023	
Science knowledge and information needs:	
• Research to inform the establishment of appropriate environmental quality targets for the repair or remediation of environmental damage in Antarctica • Techniques to prevent mobilisation of contaminants such as melt water diversion and containment barriers • Techniques for *in situ* and *ex situ* remediation of sites contaminated by fuel spills or other hazardous substances	

Issue / Environmental Pressure: Monitoring and state of the environment reporting	
Priority: 2	
Actions:	
1. Identify key environmental indicators and tools. 2. Establish a process for reporting to the ATCM. 3. SCAR to support information to COMNAP and CEP.	
Intersessional period 2018/19	
CEP XXII 2019	• Consider *SCAR's Code of Conduct for the Use of Animals for Scientific Purposes in Antarctica*
Intersessional period 2019/20	
CEP XXIII 2020	
Intersessional period 2020/21	
CEP XXIV 2021	• Consider monitoring report by UK on ASPA 107
Intersessional period 2021/22	
CEP XXV 2022	
Intersessional period 2022/23	
CEP XXVI 2023	

<table>
<tr><td>

Science knowledge and information needs:
- Long-term monitoring of change to the terrestrial (including aquatic) biotic and abiotic environment due to climate change
- Long-term monitoring of change to the near-shore marine biotic and abiotic environment due to climate change
- Monitor bird populations to inform future management actions
- Use remote sensing techniques to monitor changes in vegetation within ASPAs and more widely
- Monitor emperor penguin colonies, using remote sensing and complementary techniques, to identify potential climate change *refugia*
- Long-term monitoring of biological values in ASPAs
- Long-term monitoring to verify or detect environmental impacts associated with human activities
- Long-term monitoring and sustained observations of environmental change
- Consistent and dedicated monitoring of tourism impacts
- Systematic and regular monitoring of visitor sites covered by Site Guidelines
- Long-term monitoring of biological indicators at sites visited by tourists

</td></tr>
</table>

Issue / Environmental Pressure: Marine spatial protection and management

Priority: 2

Actions:
1. Cooperation between the CEP and SC-CAMLR on common interest issues.
2. Cooperate with CCAMLR on Southern Ocean bioregionalisation and other common interests and agreed principles.
3. Identify and apply processes for spatial marine protection.
4. Consider connectivity between land and ocean, and complementary actions that could be taken by Parties with respect to MPAs.

Intersessional period 2018/19	• Informal discussions led by New Zealand on matters relating to Resolution 5 (2017)
CEP XXII 2019	• Consider outcomes from informal discussions
Intersessional period 2019/20	
CEP XXIII 2020	
Intersessional period 2020/21	
CEP XXIV 2021	
Intersessional period 2021/22	
CEP XXV 2022	
Intersessional period 2022/23	
CEP XXVI 2023	

Issue / Environmental Pressure: Site specific guidelines for tourist-visited sites

Priority: 2

Actions:
1. Periodically review the list of sites subject to Site Guidelines and consider whether development of guidelines should be need for additional sites.
2. Regular review of all existing Site Guidelines to ensure that they are accurate and up to date, this includes precautionary updates where appropriate.
3. Provide advice to ATCM as required.
4. Review the format of the Site Guidelines.

Intersessional period 2018/19	• Development of a Site Guideline review checklist • Development of a repository of pictures to aid in the regular review of Site Guidelines

CEP XXII 2019	• Standing agenda item; Parties to report on their reviews of Site Guidelines • Consider a checklist to aid in the conducting of on the ground Site Guideline reviews
Intersessional period 2019/20	
CEP XXIII 2020	• Standing agenda item; Parties to report on their reviews of Site Guidelines
Intersessional period 2020/21	
CEP XXIV 2021	• Standing agenda item; Parties to report on their reviews of Site Guidelines
Intersessional period 2021/22	
CEP XXV 2022	
Intersessional period 2022/23	
CEP XXVI 2023	

Science knowledge and information needs:
- Long-term monitoring to assess the status and recovery of vegetation at Barrientos Island
- Systematic and regular monitoring of visitor sites covered by Site Guidelines

Issue / Environmental Pressure: Overview of the protected areas system

Priority: 2

Actions:
1. Apply the Environmental Domains Analysis (EDA) and Antarctic Conservation Biogeographic Regions (ACBR) to enhance the protected areas system.
2. Maintain and develop Protected Area database.
3. Assess the extent to which Antarctic IBAs are or should be represented within the series of ASPAs.

Intersessional period 2018/19	• Plan for joint SCAR/CEP workshop on further developing the Antarctic protected area system to be held immediately prior to CEP XXII • United Kingdom to lead discussion with interested Members and Observers, on Antarctic Specially Protected Areas and Important Bird Areas
CEP XXII 2019	• Consider outcomes from joint SCAR/CEP workshop on further developing the Antarctic protected area system • Provide a report to the ATCM on the status of the Antarctic Protected Areas network • Consider report of intersessional work on Antarctic Specially Protected Areas and Important Bird Areas
Intersessional period 2019/20	
CEP XXIII 2020	
Intersessional period 2020/21	
CEP XXIV 2021	
Intersessional period 2021/22	
CEP XXV 2022	
Intersessional period 2022/23	
CEP XXVI 2023	

<table>
<tr><td colspan="2">Science knowledge and information needs:</td></tr>
<tr><td>•</td><td>Continue to develop biogeographic tools to provide a sound basis for informing Antarctic area protection and management at regional and continental scales in light of climate change, including identifying the need to set aside reference areas for future research and identifying areas resilient to climate change</td></tr>
<tr><td>•</td><td>Use remote sensing techniques to monitor changes in vegetation within ASPAs and more widely, to inform the further development of the Antarctic protected areas system</td></tr>
</table>

Issue / Environmental Pressure: Outreach and education	
Priority: 2	
Actions:	
1. Review current examples and identify opportunities for greater education and outreach.	
2. Encourage Members to exchange information regarding their experiences in this area.	
3. Establish a strategy and guidelines for exchanging information between Members on Education and Outreach for long term perspective.	
Intersessional period 2018/19	
CEP XXII 2019	• Bulgaria to draw to the Committee's attention any outcomes from the ICG on Education and Outreach of direct relevance to the work of the CEP
Intersessional period 2019/20	
CEP XXIII 2020	
Intersessional period 2020/21	
CEP XXIV 2021	
Intersessional period 2021/22	
CEP XXV 2022	
Intersessional period 2022/23	
CEP XXVI 2023	

Issue / Environmental Pressure: Implementing and improving the EIA provisions of Annex I	
Priority: 2	
Actions:	
1. Refine the process for considering CEEs and advising the ATCM accordingly.	
2. Develop guidelines for assessing cumulative impacts.	
3. Review EIA guidelines and consider wider policy and other issues.	
4. Consider application of strategic environmental assessment in Antarctica.	
Intersessional period 2018/19	• Establish ICG to review draft CEEs as required • Members and Observers work to progress and coordinate information that will assist development of guidance on identifying and assessing cumulative impacts • Consider potential changes required to EIA database to improve its utility
CEP XXII 2019	• Discuss changes to the EIA database with a view to giving proposals to the Secretariat • Consideration of ICG reports on draft CEE, as required
Intersessional period 2019/20	• Establish ICG to review draft CEEs as required • Members and Observers work to progress and coordinate information that will assist development of guidance on identifying and assessing cumulative impacts
CEP XXIII 2020	• Consideration of ICG reports on draft CEE, as required

Intersessional period 2020/21	• Establish ICG to review draft CEEs as required • Members and Observers work to progress and coordinate information that will assist development of guidance on identifying and assessing cumulative impacts
CEP XXIV 2021	• Ask SCAR to provide guidance on how to do an environmental baseline condition survey, and consider their advice in due course • Consideration of ICG reports on draft CEE, as required
Intersessional period 2021/22	• Establish ICG to review draft CEEs as required • Members and Observers work to progress and coordinate information that will assist development of guidance on identifying and assessing cumulative impacts
CEP XXV 2022	• Encourage parties to provide feedback on the utility of the revised set of *Guidelines for Environmental Impact Assessment in Antarctica* in the preparation of EIAs • Consideration of the options for preparing guidance on identifying and assessing cumulative impacts • Consideration of ICG reports on draft CEE, as required
Intersessional period 2022/23	• Establish ICG to review draft CEEs as required
CEP XXVI 2023	• Consideration of ICG reports on draft CEE, as required

Issue / Environmental Pressure: Designation and management of Historic Sites and Monuments
Priority: 2
Actions: 1. Maintain the list and consider new proposals as they arise. 2. Consider strategic issues as necessary, including issues relating to designation of HSM versus clean-up provisions of the Protocol. 3. Review the presentation of the HSM list with the aim to improve information availability.

Intersessional period 2018/19	• Argentina and the United States to lead work to examine the format of the list of Historic Sites and Monuments
CEP XXII 2019	• Review a proposed new format for the list of Historic Sites and Monuments
Intersessional period 2019/20	• Work to consider how the CEP can better bring conservation management plans into its wider tools to protect Antarctic heritage
CEP XXIII 2020	• Review proposals relating to how conservation management plans can contribute to the management of HSMs
Intersessional period 2020/21	• Consider how environmental impact assessments can form a part of Historic Site and Monument assessment
CEP XXIV 2021	• Review proposals relating to EIAs and the HSM listing process
Intersessional period 2021/22	
CEP XXV 2022	
Intersessional period 2022/23	
CEP XXVI 2023	

Issue / Environmental Pressure: Biodiversity knowledge	
Priority: 3	
Actions: 1. Maintain awareness of threats to existing biodiversity. 2. CEP to consider further scientific advice on wildlife disturbance.	
Intersessional period 2018/19	
CEP XXII 2019	• Discussion of SCAR update on underwater noise
Intersessional period 2019/20	
CEP XXIII 2020	
Intersessional period 2020/21	
CEP XXIV 2021	
Intersessional period 2021/22	
CEP XXV 2022	
Intersessional period 2022/23	
CEP XXVI 2023	

Science knowledge and information needs:
- Research on the environmental impacts of remotely piloted aircraft systems (RPAS), particularly on wildlife responses including:
    - a range of species including flying seabirds and seals;
    - both behavioural and physiological responses;
    - demographic effects, including breeding numbers and breeding success;
    - ambient environmental conditions, for example, wind and noise;
    - the effects of RPAS of different sizes and specifications;
    - the contribution of RPAS noise to wildlife disturbance;
    - comparisons with control sites and human disturbance; and
    - habituation effects.
- Collection and submission of further spatially explicit biodiversity data
- Research on the impacts of underwater noise on Antarctic marine mammals
- Synthesis of available knowledge on the biogeography, bioregionalisation and endemism within Antarctica
- Site-specific, timing-specific and species-specific studies to understand the impacts arising from interactions between human activities and wildlife and support evidence-based guidelines to avoid disturbance
- Inventory of Mt Erebus ice caves and microbial communities
- Regular population counts and research to understand the status and trends in the southern giant petrel population

Issue / Environmental Pressure: Protection of outstanding geological values	
Priority: 3	
Actions: 1. Consider further mechanisms for protection of outstanding geological values.	
Intersessional period 2018/19	
CEP XXII 2019	• Consider advice from SCAR
Intersessional period 2019/20	
CEP XXIII 2020	
Intersessional period 2020/21	
CEP XXIV 2021	
Intersessional period 2021/22	
CEP XXV 2022	
Intersessional period 2022/23	
CEP XXVI 2023	

Appendix 2

Preliminary Agenda for CEP XXII (2019)

1. Opening of the Meeting
2. Adoption of the Agenda
3. Strategic Discussions on the Future Work of the CEP
4. Operation of the CEP
5. Cooperation with other Organisations
6. Repair and Remediation of Environment Damage
7. Climate Change Implications for the Environment
    a. Strategic Approach
    b. Implementation and Review of the Climate Change Response Work Programme
8. Environmental Impact Assessment (EIA)
    a. Draft Comprehensive Environmental Evaluations
    b. Other EIA Matters
9. Area Protection and Management Plans
    a. Management Plans
    b. Historic Sites and Monuments
    c. Site Guidelines
    d. Marine Spatial Protection and Management
    e. Other Annex V Matters
10. Conservation of Antarctic Flora and Fauna
    a. Quarantine and Non-native Species
    b. Specially Protected Species
    c. Other Annex II Matters
11. Environmental Monitoring and Reporting
12. Inspection Reports
13. General Matters
14. Election of Officers
15. Preparation for the Next Meeting
16. Adoption of the Report
17. Closing of the Meeting

3. Appendices

Preliminary Agenda for ATCM XLII, Working Groups and Allocation of Items

Plenary

1. Opening of the Meeting

2. Election of Officers and Creation of Working Groups

3. Adoption of the Agenda, Allocation of Items to Working Groups and Consideration of the Multi-year Strategic Work Plan

4. Operation of the Antarctic Treaty System: Reports by Parties, Observers and Experts

5. Report of the Committee for Environmental Protection

Working Group 1: *(Policy, Legal, Institutional)*

6. Operation of the Antarctic Treaty System: General matters

7. Operation of the Antarctic Treaty System: Matters related to the Secretariat

8. Liability

9. Biological Prospecting in Antarctica

10. Exchange of Information

11. Education Issues

12. Multi-year Strategic Work Plan

Working Group 2: *(Science, Operations, Tourism)*

13. Safety and Operations in Antarctica

14. Inspections under the Antarctic Treaty and Environment Protocol

15. Science issues, future science challenges, scientific cooperation and facilitation

16. Implications of Climate Change for Management of the Antarctic Treaty Area

17. Tourism and Non-governmental Activities in the Antarctic Treaty Area, including Competent Authorities Issues

Plenary

18. Preparation of the 43rd Meeting

19. Any other Business

20. Adoption of the Final Report

21. Close of the Meeting

Appendix 2

Host Country Communique

The 41st Antarctic Treaty Consultative Meeting (ATCM XLI) was held in Buenos Aires, Argentina, from May 16th to 18th, 2018. The meeting was chaired by Ambassador María Teresa Kralikas, from the Ministry of Foreign Affairs and Worship of Argentina. The 21st Meeting of the Committee for Environmental Protection (CEP) was held from May 13th to 15th, 2018 and was chaired by Mr Ewan McIvor (Australia). The meetings, which took place at the Palacio San Martín, were organized by the Ministry of Foreign Affairs and Worship of Argentina and very efficiently assisted by the Antarctic Treaty Secretariat.

Participants from 53 Antarctic Treaty Parties, observers and experts from international organisations were invited to attend the annual Meeting. Ambassador Jorge Faurie, Head of the Ministry of Foreign Affairs of Argentina officially opened the ATCM 41 on May 16th, 2018 and offered a welcoming reception at the Palacio San Martín, where he was accompanied by other government authorities.

Due to unexpected changes in the regular schedule as originally foreseen, on this occasion the ATCM 41 and CEP 21 meetings worked under a reduced programme, which did not prevent them from addressing the most relevant issues on their agendas. Discussions at the ATCM focused on: operation of the Antarctic Treaty System, biological prospecting in Antarctica, inspections under the Antarctic Treaty, and tourism trends and environmental impacts in the Antarctic Treaty area, as well as the updating of the multi-year strategic work plan. The CEP discussed the environmental impact of human activities, including construction of new facilities, management of tourism and operation of unmanned vehicles; the management of protected areas and preservation of Antarctic heritage, and the environmental aspects of inspection reports.

Ms. Birgit Njåstad from Norway was elected as Chair of the CEP for the 2018-2020 term. Parties extended their congratulations to Ms Njåstad and appreciation for the excellent performance of Mr McIvor over the past four years. Ms Patricia Ortúzar from Argentina was re-elected as Vice Chair of the CEP.

Parties congratulated the Scientific Committee of Antarctic Research (SCAR) on its 60th anniversary, and the Council of Managers of Antarctic National Programs (COMNAP) on its 30th anniversary, both key organizations of the Antarctic Treaty System.

Parties expressed their gratitude to Argentina for having organized ATCM 41 and CEP 21 under extraordinary circumstances and with such short notice and their appreciation for the excellent facilities provided for the meeting.

The next ATCM will be hosted by Czech Republic in July 2019.

PART II
Measures, Decisions and Resolutions

1. Measures

Antarctic Specially Protected Area No 108
(Green Island, Berthelot Islands, Antarctic Peninsula): Revised Management Plan

The Representatives,

Recalling Articles 3, 5 and 6 of Annex V to the Protocol on Environmental Protection to the Antarctic Treaty, providing for the designation of Antarctic Specially Protected Areas ("ASPA") and approval of Management Plans for those Areas;

Recalling

- Recommendation IV-9 (1966), which designated Green Island, Berthelot Islands, Antarctic Peninsula as Specially Protected Area ("SPA") No. 9;

- Recommendation XVI-6 (1991), which annexed a Management Plan for the Area;

- Decision 1 (2002), which renamed and renumbered SPA 9 as ASPA 108;

- Measures 1 (2002) and 1 (2013), which adopted revised Management Plans for ASPA 108;

Recalling that Recommendation IV-9 (1966) was designated as no longer current by Decision 1 (2011) and that Recommendation XVI-6 (1991) did not become effective and was withdrawn by Decision 3 (2017);

Noting that the Committee for Environmental Protection has endorsed a revised Management Plan for ASPA 108;

Desiring to replace the existing Management Plan for ASPA 108 with the revised Management Plan;

Recommend to their Governments the following Measure for approval in accordance with paragraph 1 of Article 6 of Annex V to the Protocol on Environmental Protection to the Antarctic Treaty:

That:

1. the revised Management Plan for Antarctic Specially Protected Area No. 108 (Green Island, Berthelot Islands, Antarctic Peninsula), which is annexed to this Measure, be approved; and

2. the Management Plan for the Antarctic Specially Protected Area No. 108 annexed to Measure 1 (2013) be revoked.

Antarctic Specially Protected Area No 117
(Avian Island, Marguerite Bay, Antarctic Peninsula): Revised Management Plan

The Representatives,

Recalling Articles 3, 5 and 6 of Annex V to the Protocol on Environmental Protection to the Antarctic Treaty, providing for the designation of Antarctic Specially Protected Areas ("ASPA") and approval of Management Plans for those Areas;

Recalling

- Recommendation XV-6 (1989), which designated Avian Island, North-West Marguerite Bay as Site of Special Scientific Interest ("SSSI") No. 30 and annexed a Management Plan for the site;

- Recommendation XVI-4 (1991), which redesignated SSSI 30 as Specially Protected Area ("SPA") No. 21 and annexed a revised Management Plan for the Area;

- Decision 1 (2002), which renamed and renumbered SPA 21 as ASPA 117;

- Measures 1 (2002) and 2 (2013), which adopted revised Management Plans for ASPA 117;

Recalling that Recommendations XV-6 (1989) and XVI-4 (1991) did not become effective and were designated as no longer current by Decision 1 (2011);

Noting that the Committee for Environmental Protection has endorsed a revised Management Plan for ASPA 117;

Desiring to replace the existing Management Plan for ASPA 117 with the revised Management Plan;

Recommend to their Governments the following Measure for approval in accordance with paragraph 1 of Article 6 of Annex V to the Protocol on Environmental Protection to the Antarctic Treaty:

That:

1. the revised Management Plan for Antarctic Specially Protected Area No. 117 (Avian Island, Marguerite Bay, Antarctic Peninsula), which is annexed to this Measure, be approved; and

2. the Management Plan for Antarctic Specially Protected Area No. 117 annexed to Measure 2 (2013) be revoked.

Antarctic Specially Protected Area No 132
(Potter Peninsula, King George Island [Isla 25 de Mayo], South Shetland Islands): Revised Management Plan

The Representatives,

Recalling Articles 3, 5 and 6 of Annex V to the Protocol on Environmental Protection to the Antarctic Treaty, providing for the designation of Antarctic Specially Protected Areas ("ASPA") and approval of Management Plans for those Areas;

Recalling

- Recommendation XIII-8 (1985), which designated Potter Peninsula, King George Island (Isla 25 de Mayo), South Shetland Islands as Site of Special Scientific Interest ("SSSI") No. 13 and annexed a Management Plan for the site;

- Measure 3 (1997), which annexed a revised Management Plan for SSSI 13;

- Decision 1 (2002), which renamed and renumbered SSSI 13 as ASPA 132;

- Measures 2 (2005) and 4 (2013), which adopted revised Management Plans for ASPA 132;

Recalling that Measure 3 (1997) has not become effective yet;

Noting that the Committee for Environmental Protection has endorsed a revised Management Plan for ASPA 132;

Desiring to replace the existing Management Plan for ASPA 132 with the revised Management Plan;

Recommend to their Governments the following Measure for approval in accordance with paragraph 1 of Article 6 of Annex V to the Protocol on Environmental Protection to the Antarctic Treaty:

That:

1. the revised Management Plan for Antarctic Specially Protected Area No. 132 (Potter Peninsula, King George Island [Isla 25 de Mayo], South Shetland Islands), which is annexed to this Measure, be approved; and

2. the Management Plan for the Antarctic Specially Protected Area No. 132 annexed to Measure 4 (2013) be revoked.

Antarctic Specially Protected Area No 147
(Ablation Valley and Ganymede Heights, Alexander Island): Revised Management Plan

The Representatives,

Recalling Articles 3, 5 and 6 of Annex V to the Protocol on Environmental Protection to the Antarctic Treaty, providing for the designation of Antarctic Specially Protected Areas ("ASPA") and approval of Management Plans for those Areas;

Recalling

- Recommendation XV-6 (1989), which designated Ablation Valley and Ganymede Heights, Alexander Island as Site of Special Scientific Interest ("SSSI") No. 29 and annexed a Management Plan for the site;

- Resolution 3 (1996), which extended the expiry date for SSSI 29;

- Measure 2 (2000), which extended the expiry date for the Management Plan for SSSI 29;

- Decision 1 (2002), which renamed and renumbered SSSI 29 as ASPA 147;

- Measures 1 (2002) and 10 (2013), which adopted revised Management Plans for ASPA 147;

Recalling that Recommendation XV-6 (1989) and Resolution 3 (1996) were designated as no longer current by Decision 1 (2011);

Recalling that Measure 2 (2000) did not become effective and was withdrawn by Measure 5 (2009);

Noting that the Committee for Environmental Protection has endorsed a revised Management Plan for ASPA 147;

Desiring to replace the existing Management Plan for ASPA 147 with the revised Management Plan;

Recommend to their Governments the following Measure for approval in accordance with paragraph 1 of Article 6 of Annex V to the Protocol on Environmental Protection to the Antarctic Treaty:

That:

1. the revised Management Plan for Antarctic Specially Protected Area No. 147 (Ablation Valley and Ganymede Heights, Alexander Island), which is annexed to this Measure, be approved; and

2. the Management Plan for Antarctic Specially Protected Area No. 147 annexed to Measure 10 (2013) be revoked.

Antarctic Specially Protected Area No 170
(Marion Nunataks, Charcot Island, Antarctic Peninsula): Revised Management Plan

The Representatives,

Recalling Articles 3, 5 and 6 of Annex V to the Protocol on Environmental Protection to the Antarctic Treaty, providing for the designation of Antarctic Specially Protected Areas ("ASPA") and approval of Management Plans for those Areas;

Recalling

- Measure 4 (2008) which designated Marion Nunataks, Charcot Island, Antarctic Peninsula as ASPA 170 and adopted a Management Plan for the Area;

- Measure 16 (2013), which adopted a revised Management Plan for ASPA 170;

Noting that the Committee for Environmental Protection has endorsed a revised Management Plan for ASPA 170;

Desiring to replace the existing Management Plan for ASPA 170 with the revised Management Plan;

Recommend to their Governments the following Measure for approval in accordance with paragraph 1 of Article 6 of Annex V to the Protocol on Environmental Protection to the Antarctic Treaty:

That:

1. the revised Management Plan for Antarctic Specially Protected Area No. 170 (Marion Nunataks, Charcot Island, Antarctic Peninsula), which is annexed to this Measure, be approved; and

2. the Management Plan for Antarctic Specially Protected Area No. 170 annexed to Measure 16 (2013) be revoked.

Antarctic Specially Protected Area No 172
(Lower Taylor Glacier and Blood Falls, McMurdo Dry Valleys, Victoria Land): Revised Management Plan

The Representatives,

Recalling Articles 3, 5 and 6 of Annex V to the Protocol on Environmental Protection to the Antarctic Treaty, providing for the designation of Antarctic Specially Protected Areas ("ASPA") and approval of Management Plans for those Areas;

Recalling Measure 9 (2012) which designated Lower Taylor Glacier and Blood Falls, McMurdo Dry Valleys, Victoria Land as ASPA 172 and adopted a Management Plan for the Area;

Noting that the Committee for Environmental Protection has endorsed a revised Management Plan for ASPA 172;

Desiring to replace the existing Management Plan for ASPA 172 with the revised Management Plan;

Recommend to their Governments the following Measure for approval in accordance with paragraph 1 of Article 6 of Annex V to the Protocol on Environmental Protection to the Antarctic Treaty:

That:

1. the revised Management Plan for Antarctic Specially Protected Area No. 172 (Lower Taylor Glacier and Blood Falls, McMurdo Dry Valleys, Victoria Land), which is annexed to this Measure, be approved; and

2. the Management Plan for Antarctic Specially Protected Area No. 172 annexed to Measure 9 (2012) be revoked.

2. Decisions

Secretariat Report, Programme and Budget

The Representatives,

Recalling Measure 1 (2003) on the establishment of the Secretariat of the Antarctic Treaty;

Recalling Decision 2 (2012) on the establishment of the open-ended Intersessional Contact Group on Financial Issues to be convened by the host country of the next Antarctic Treaty Consultative Meeting ("ATCM");

Bearing in mind the Financial Regulations for the Secretariat annexed to Decision 4 (2003);

Decide:

1. to approve the audited Financial Report for 2016/17, annexed to this Decision (Annex 1);

2. to take note of the Secretariat Report 2017/18, which includes the Provisional Financial Report for 2017/18, annexed to this Decision (Annex 2);

3. to take note of the Five Year Forward Budget Profile 2019/20-2023/24 and approve the Secretariat Programme 2018/19, including the Budget for 2018/19, annexed to this Decision (Annex 3); and

4. to invite the host country for the next Antarctic Treaty Consultative Meeting to request that the Executive Secretary open the ATCM forum for the open-ended Intersessional Contact Group on Financial Issues, and provide assistance to it.

Audited Financial Report for 2016/17

AUDITOR'S REPORT

To: The Secretary of the Antarctic Treaty Secretariat

Maipú 757, 4° piso

CUIT (Taxpayer ID) 30-70892567-1

Subject: ATCM XLI - CEP XXI, Antarctic Treaty Consultative Meeting, 2018

Buenos Aires, Argentina

1. Report on Financial Statements

We have audited the attached Financial Statements of the Antarctic Treaty Secretariat, which include the following Statement of Income and Expenditure, Statement of Financial Position, Statement of Changes in Shareholders' Equity, Cash Flow Statement and Explanatory Notes for the financial year commencing 1st April 2016 and ending 31st March 2017.

2. Management Responsibility for Financial Statements

The Antarctic Treaty Secretariat, established under Argentine Law No. 25,888 dated 14th May 2004, is responsible for the preparation and fair presentation of the attached financial statements in accordance to accounting principles based on cash transactions, pursuant to International Accounting Standards and specific standards for Antarctic Treaty Consultative Meetings. Such responsibility includes: design, implementation and maintenance of internal controls on the preparation and presentation of the Financial Statements, such that they are free of misstatements due to error or fraud, selection and implementation of appropriate accounting policies and preparation of accounting estimates which are reasonable under the circumstances.

3. Auditor's Responsibility

Our responsibility is to express an opinion on these Financial Statements based on our audit.

The audit was conducted in accordance with International Auditing Standards and the Annex to Decision 3 (2012) of the XXXI Antarctic Treaty Consultative Meeting, which describes the tasks to be carried out by the external audit.

These standards require compliance with ethical requirements, and planning and execution of the audit so as to provide reasonable assurance that the Financial Statements are free of material misstatements.

An audit includes the execution of procedures in order to obtain evidence on the amounts and exposure reflected in the Financial Statements. Relevant procedures are selected based on the auditor's judgement, including the assessment of the risks of significant errors in the financial statements.

On conducting such assessment of risks, the auditor considers the internal control relevant to the preparation and reasonable presentation of the Financial Statements by the organisation, in order to design suitable procedures that are appropriate to the circumstances.

An audit also includes an evaluation of appropriateness, of the accounting principles used, an opinion on whether the accounting estimates made by management are reasonable, as well as an assessment of the general presentation of the Financial Statements.

We believe that the evidence obtained provides a sufficient and appropriate basis for our audit opinion.

4. Opinion

In our opinion, the attached Financial Statements of the Antarctic Treaty Secretariat for the financial year ending on 31st March 2017 have been prepared, in all material respects, in accordance with International Accounting Standards, specific standards for Antarctic Treaty Consultative Meetings and accounting principles based on cash transactions.

5. Other Matters

Disclosures on Note 1 to the attached financial statements, establishing that they have been prepared by the Antarctic Treaty Secretariat pursuant to the provisions established in the Financial Regulations, annexed to Decision 4 (2003), which differ in terms of specific valuation and presentation, from accounting standards applicable and in force for the City of Buenos Aires, Argentine Republic.

6. Additional Information Required by Law

Pursuant to the analysis described in point 3, we report that the abovementioned Financial Statements arise from accounting records that are not transcribed into books in accordance with Argentine standards in force.

We also report that, according to bookkeeping as at 31st March 2017, the liabilities accrued in favour of the Argentine Single Social Security System in Argentine pesos and pursuant to calculations made by the Secretariat amounted to ARS 174,375.28 (USD 11,177.90), none of which was due and payable in Argentine pesos as at that date.

It is worth noting that labour relationships are governed by the Staff Regulations of the Antarctic Treaty Secretariat.

City of Buenos Aires, 12th April 2018

[signature]
Héctor Horacio Canaveri
Certified Accountant (U.M.)

1. Statement of Income and Expenses for all funds for the period 1ˢᵗ April 2016 to 31ˢᵗ March 2017, comparatively with the prior year.

INCOME	31/03/2016	Budget 31/03/2017	31/03/2017
Contributions (Note 10)	1,378,099	1,378,097	1,378,097
Other income (Note 2)	13,956	2,000	59,182
Total Income	1,392,055	1,380,097	1,437,279

EXPENSES

	31/03/2016	31/03/2017	31/03/2017
Salaries and wages	692,454	716,869	699,021
T&I Services	304,821	326,326	302,260
Travel and accommodation	92,238	99,000	70,972
Information Technology	39,259	53,000	38,569
Printing, editing and copying payment	23,963	25,194	16,650
General Services	53,818	45,549	77,443
Communications	20,827	21,204	17,890
Office Expenses	25,772	23,690	18,138
Management	7,101	21,955	9,307
Representation expenses	4,154	4,000	4,473
Financing	2,251	11,893	7,881
Total Expenses	1,266,656	1,348,680	1,262,603

FUND ALLOCATION

	31/03/2016	31/03/2017	31/03/2017
Staff Termination Fund	32,988	31,417	31,419
Staff Replacement Fund	-	-	-
Working Capital Fund	-	-	-
Contingency fund	-	-	-
Total Fund allocation	32,988	31,417	31,419
Total Expenses & allocation	1,299,644	1,380,097	1,294,022
Surplus for the period	92,412	-	143,257

This statement should be read together with Notes 1 to 10 attached.

2. Statement of Financial Position as at 31ˢᵗ March 2017, comparatively with the prior year

ASSETS	31/03/2016	31/03/2017
Current assets		
Cash and cash equivalents (Note 3)	1,227,598	1,462,262
Contributions owed (Note 9 and 10)	136,347	40,649
Other debtors (Note 4)	44,805	32,800
Other current assets (Note 5)	65,550	115,523
Total current assets	1,474,300	1,651,235
Non-current assets		
Fixed assets (Note 1.3 and 6)	100,459	89,397
Total non-current assets	100,459	89,397
Total Assets	1,574,760	1,740,632
LIABILITIES		
Current liabilities		
Accounts payable (Note 7)	17,163	25,358
Contributions received in advance (Notes 10)	347,173	376,722
Special voluntary fund for specific purposes (Note 1.9)	14,546	22,889
Remuneration and payable contributions (Note 8)	73,345	29,511
Total current liabilities	452,227	454,480
Non-current liabilities		
Staff Termination Fund (Note 1.4)	240,181	271,600
Staff Replacement Fund (Note 1.5)	50,000	50,000
Contingency fund (Note 1.6)	30,000	30,000
Fixed Asset Replacement Fund (Note 1.7)	34,163	23,101
Total non-current liabilities	354,344	374,701
Total Liabilities	806,571	829,181
NET ASSETS	768,189	911,451

This statement should be read together with Notes 1 to 10 attached.

3. Statement of changes in Net Assets as at 31ˢᵗ March 2016 and 2017

Represented by	Net Assets 31/03/2016	Income	Expenses and Allocation	Other Income	Net Assets 31/03/2017
General Fund	538,237	1,378,097	-1,294,022	59,187	681,499
Working Capital Fund (Note 1.8)	229,952		-		229,952
Net Assets	768,189				911,451

This statement should be read together with Notes 1 to 10 attached.

4. Cash Flow Statement for the period 1ˢᵗ April 2016 as at 31ˢᵗ March 2017, comparatively with the prior year

Variation in cash & cash equivalents		**31/03/2017**	**31/03/2016**
Cash & cash equivalent at beginning of the year	1,227,598		
Cash & cash equivalent at year end	1,462,262		
Net increase in cash and cash equivalents		234,664	170,428
Causes of variations in cash & cash equivalents			
Operating activities			
Contributions received	1,086,686		
Payment of salaries and wages	746,795		
Payment of translation services	-302,260		
Payment of travel, accommodation, etc.	-71,148		
Payment of printing, editing and copying	-16,650		
Payment of general services	-30,855		
Other payments to providers	-57,077		
Net cash & cash equivalents from operating activities		-138,099	-157,497
Investment activities			
Purchase of fixed assets	-35,921		
Net cash & cash equivalents from investment activities		-35,921	-38,362
Financing activities			
Contributions received in advance	376,722		
Collection pt. 5.6 of Staff Regulations	182,980		
Payment pt. 5.6 of Staff Regulations	-162,698		
Net lease prepayment	29,966		
Net AFIP reimbursement	-15,951		
Miscellaneous revenues	5,516		
Net cash & cash equivalents from financing activities		416,535	367,995
Foreign currency activities			
Net loss	-7,852		
Net cash & cash equivalents from foreign currency activities		-7,852	-1,260
Net increase in cash and cash equivalents		234,664	170,428

This statement should be read together with Notes 1 to 10 attached.

Notes to the Financial Statements
as at 31ˢᵗ March 2016 and 2017

1. Basis for Preparation of Financial Statements

These financial statements are presented in US dollars, following the guidelines established in Financial Regulations, annexed to Decision 4 (2003). These financial statements have been prepared in accordance with International Financial Reporting Standards (IFRS), as issued by the International Accounting Standards Board (IASB).

1.1. Historical Cost

The accounts are prepared in accordance with the historical cost rule, except where otherwise indicated.

1.2. Office

The Secretariat Offices are provided by the Ministry of Foreign Affairs, International Trade and Cult of the Argentine Republic. Premises are free of rent and common expenses.

1.3. Fixed Assets

All items are valued at historical cost, less accumulated depreciation. Depreciation is calculated on a straight-line basis at annual rates estimated to write off the assets over their expected useful lives. The aggregate residual value of fixed assets does not exceed their use value.

1.4. Executive Staff Termination Fund

Pursuant to Section 10.4 of the Staff Regulations, this fund shall be sufficiently funded to compensate executive staff members at a rate of one month base pay for each year of service.

1.5. Staff Replacement Fund

This fund is used to cover Secretariat executive staff travel expenses to and from the Secretariat.

1.6. Contingency Fund

Pursuant to Decision 4 (2009), this Fund was created to cover the translation expenses arising from the unexpected increase in the volume of documentation filed with the ATCM for translation purposes.

1.7. Fixed Assets Replacement Fund

Pursuant to IAS, assets with a useful life beyond the current financial year shall be reflected as an asset in the Statement of Financial Position. Up to March 2010, the balancing entry was an adjustment to the General Fund. As from April 2010, the balancing entry shall be reflected as a liability under such heading.

1.8. Working Capital Fund

Pursuant to Financial Regulations 6.2 (a), the fund shall stand at one-sixth (1/6) of the budget for the current financial year.

1.9. Special Voluntary Fund for Specific Purposes

Pt (82) of the XXXV ATCM Final Report, to receive voluntary contributions by the parties. The voluntary fund refers to money to pay lease rents and common expenses for the fiscal year.

1.10. Chilean Special Contribution

The Government of Chile and the Secretariat have agreed to employ the services of international rapporteurs for ATCM XXXIX, such costs shall be borne by the Government of Chile, paid by means of a voluntary contribution.

Notes to the Financial Statements
as at 31st March 2016 and 2017

			31/03/2016	31/03/2017
2	**Other income**			
		Earned interest	13,810	4,786
		Chilean special contribution (Note 1.1(	-	54,000
		Discounts obtained	146	396
		Total	13,956	59,182
3	**Cash and cash equivalents**			
		Cash US Dollars	965	2,125
		Cash Argentine Pesos	63	153
		BNA special US Dollar account	611,910	1,442,553
		BNA Argentine Peso account	34,327	17,431
		Investments	580,334	-
		Total	1,227,598	1,462,262
4	**Other debtors**			
		Staff Regulations pt. 5.6	44,807	32,800
5	**Other current assets**			
		Advance payments	8,848	44,293
		VAT receivable	51,995	66,234
		Other recoverable expenses	4,706	4,995
		Total	65,550	115,523
6	**Fixed assets**			
		Books & subscriptions	10,406	14,085
		Office equipment	37,234	40,826
		Furniture	49,818	50,971
		IT equipment and software	135,452	141,788
		Total original cost	232,910	247,670
		Accumulated depreciation	-132,451	-158,272
		Total	100,459	89,397
7	**Accounts payable**			
		Trade	5,022	9,815
		Accrued expenses	11,991	11,267
		Other	150	4,275
		Total	17,163	25,358
8	**Remuneration and payable contributions**			
		Remuneration	38,774	9,001
		Contributions	34,579	20,510
		Total	73,353	29,511

9 Contributions not received

At the end of each year, there are unsettled contributions. This implies that the
General Fund is increased by an amount equal to unsettled contributions. Pursuant to
Financial Regulation 6 (3), "... notify Consultative Parties about any cash surplus
in the General Fund", $40,649 should be deducted for the year ended 31 March 2017.
Such deduction amounted to $ 136,347 in the previous fiscal year.

Notes to the Financial Statements
as at 31st March 2016 and 2017

10 Contributions owed, committed, paid and received in advance.

Contributions Parties	Owed 31/03/2016	Committed	Cancelled $	Owed 31/03/2017	Prepaid 31/03/2017
Argentina		60,347	60,347	-	-
Australia	25	60,347	60,347	25	60,347
Belgium	50	40,021	40,021	50	-
Brazil	40,236	40,021	79,930	327	-
Bulgaria		33,923	33,923	-	-
Czech Republic		40,021	40,021	-	-
Chile		46,119	46,119	-	-
China	25	46,119	46,119	25	-
Ecuador		33,923	33,923	-	-
Finland		40,021	40,021	-	40,001
France		60,347	60,335	12	-
Germany	12	52,217	52,216	13	-
India	75	46,119	46,119	75	-
Italy	25	52,217	52,242	-	-
Japan		60,347	60,347	-	-
Korea		40,021	40,021	-	-
Netherlands		46,119	46,119	-	-
New Zealand	-20	60,347	60,342	-15	60,322
Norway	60	60,347	60,407	-	60,347
Peru	1,162	33,923	35,085	-	19,116
Poland		40,021	39,996	25	-
Russia		46,119	46,119	-	-
South Africa		46,119	46,119	-	-
Spain		46,119	46,119	-	-
Sweden		46,119	46,119	-	-
Ukraine	94,606	40,021	134,627	-	15,895
UK		60,347	60,347	-	60,347
USA	25	60,347	60,347	25	60,347
Uruguay	66	40,021	-	40,087	-
Total	136,347	1,378,097	1,473,797	40,649	376,722

Dr. Manfred Reinke
Executive Secretary

Roberto A. Fennell
Finance Officer

Provisional Financial Report for 2017/18

**Estimate of Income and Expenditure for all Funds
for the Period 1 April 2017 to 31 March 2018**

APPROPRIATION LINES		Audited Statement 2016/17		Budget 2017/18		Prov Statement 2017/18
INCOME						
CONTRIBUTIONS pledged	$	-1,378,097	$	-1,378,097	$	-1,378,097
*) Other Income	$	-59,182	$	-53,000	$	-53,000
Total Income	$	-1,437,279	$	-1,431,097	$	-1,431,097
EXPENDITURE						
SALARIES						
Executive	$	336,376	$	326,636	$	326,637
General Staff	$	327,459	$	362,892	$	358,968
ATCM Support Staff	$	18,810	$	21,160	$	20,743
Trainee	$	2,738	$	9,600	$	800
Overtime	$	13,638	$	16,000	$	15,151
	$	699,021	$	736,288	$	722,299
TRANSLATION AND INTERPRETATION						
Translation and Interpretation	$	302,260	$	316,388	$	291,085
TRAVEL						
Travel	$	70,972	$	103,000	$	107,381
INFORMATION TECHNOLOGY						
Hardware	$	5,028	$	10,000	$	10,455
Software	$	2,116	$	6,000	$	2,896
Development	$	23,128	$	22,000	$	22,834
Hardware and Software Maintenance	$	1,850	$	2,250	$	2,706
Support	$	6,447	$	7,500	$	7,208
	$	38,569	$	47,750	$	46,099
PRINTING, EDITING & COPYING						
Final report	$	14,276	$	20,000	$	16,525
Compilation	$	2,374	$	2,500	$	662
Site guidelines	$	0	$	3,205	$	1,288
	$	16,650	$	25,705	$	18,475
GENERAL SERVICES						
Legal advice	$	1,123	$	3,000	$	1,322
External audit	$	9,207	$	11,139	$	9,236
*) Rapporteur Services	$	44,247	$	0	$	0
Cleaning, maintenance & security	$	10,209	$	11,000	$	8,300
Training	$	3,950	$	8,000	$	6,774
Banking	$	6,203	$	9,983	$	8,022
Rental of equipment	$	2,503	$	3,042	$	2,503
	$	77,442	$	46,164	$	36,157
COMMUNICATION						
Telephone	$	5,010	$	7,210	$	5,563
Internet	$	3,176	$	2,500	$	2,353
Web hosting	$	7,680	$	8,500	$	7,650
Postage	$	2,024	$	2,785	$	2,247
	$	17,890	$	20,995	$	17,813

	Audited Statement 2016/17	Budget 2017/18	Prov Statement 2017/18
OFFICE			
Stationery & supplies	$ 3,480	$ 4,789	$ 6,243
Books & subscriptions	$ 1,507	$ 3,342	$ 1,570
Insurance	$ 3,644	$ 4,326	$ 3,034
Furniture	$ 97	$ 1,255	$ 0
Office equipment	$ 3,907	$ 4,455	$ 1,679
Office improvement	$ 5,503	$ 2,785	$ 0
	$ 18,138	**$ 20,952**	**$ 12,526**
ADMINISTRATIVE			
Office Supplies	$ 3,063	$ 5,013	$ 2,653
Local transport	$ 426	$ 890	$ 791
Miscellaneous	$ 2,824	$ 4,455	$ 2,603
Utilities (Energy)	$ 2,994	$ 7,262	$ 4,729
	$ 9,307	**$ 17,620**	**$ 10,776**
REPRESENTATION			
Representation	$ 4,473	$ 4,000	$ 3,929
FINANCING			
Exchange loss	$ 7,881	$ 12,249	$ 14,222
SUBTOTAL Expenditures	**$ 1,262,605**	**$ 1,351,111**	**$ 1,280,762**
ALLOCATION TO FUNDS			
Translation Contingency Fund	$ 0	$ 0	$ 0
**) Staff Replacement Fund	$ 0	$ 50,000	$ 29,500
Staff Termination Fund	$ 31,417	$ 29,986	$ 29,986
Working Capital Fund	$ 0	$ 0	$ 0
	$ 31,417	**$ 79,986**	**$ 59,486**
TOTAL Expenditures	**$ 1,294,021**	**$ 1,431,097**	**$ 1,340,248**
FUND EXPENDITURES			
***) General Fund	$ 0	$ 50,000	$ 50,000
Working Capital Fund	$ 0	$ 0	$ 0
Translation Contingency Fund	$ 0	$ 0	$ 0
*****) Staff Termination Fund	$ 0	$ 127,438	$ 127,438
******) Staff Replacement Fund	$ 0	$ 50,000	$ 29,500
	$ 0	**$ 227,438**	**$ 206,938**
·······) **Unpaid Contributions**	**$ 49,165**	**$ 0**	**$ 79,121**
BALANCE	**$ 94,093**	**$ 0**	**$ 11,728**
SUMMARY OF FUNDS			
Translation Contingency Fund	$ 30,000	$ 30,000	$ 30,000
Staff Replacement Fund	$ 50,000	$ 50,000	$ 50,000
Staff Termination Fund	$ 271,599	$ 174,065	$ 174,065
*******) Working Capital Fund	$ 229,952	$ 229,952	$ 229,952

* Audited Statement 2016/17: Chile reimbursed the costs for Rapporteur Services in the form of a special contribution and intrests of investements
Budget 17/18 and Prov Statement 2017/18: amount carried over from General Fund (see ***) and intrests of investment

** Budget 2017/18 and Prov Statement 2017/18: The Staff Replacement Fund is filled up from the General Fund (see ***and *****) to its nominal level of 50,000 USD

*** Budget 2017/18 and Prov Statement 2017/18: The Staff Replacement Fund is filled up from the General Fund (see ** and *****) to its nominal level of 50,000 USD

**** Budget 2017/18 and Prov Statement 2017/18: Staff termination compensation (Staff Regulation 10.4 and Final Report ATCM XXXIII para 100) for the Executive Secretary in 2017 and the Assistant Executive Secretary in 2018

***** Budget 2017/18 and Prov Statement 2017/18: Expected expenditures for executive staff replacement from the Staff Replacement Fund (see ** and ***)

****** Unpaid contributions as of 31 March 2018

******* Maximum Required Amount

| Working Capital Fund (Fin. Reg. 6.2) | $ 229,683 | $ 229,683 | $ 229,683 |

Secretariat Programme for 2018/19

Introduction

This work programme outlines the activities proposed for the Secretariat in the Financial Year 2018/19 (1 April 2018 to 31 March 2019). The main areas of activity of the Secretariat are treated in the first four parts, followed by a section on management and a forecast of the programme for the Financial Year 2019/20.

The Budget for the Financial Year 2018/19, the Forecast Budget for the Financial Year 2019/20, and the accompanying contribution and salary scales are included in the appendices.

The programme and the accompanying budget figures for 2018/19 are based on the Forecast Budget for the Financial Year 2018/19 (Decision 5 [2017], Annex 3).

The programme focuses on the regular activities, such as the preparation of the ATCM XLI and ATCM XLII, the publication of Final Reports, and the various specific tasks assigned to the Secretariat under Measure 1 (2003).

Contents:

1. ATCM/CEP support
2. Information Technology
3. Documentation and Public Information
4. Management
5. Forecast Programme for the Financial Year 2019/20 and the Financial Year 2020/21
   - Appendix 1: Provisional Report for the Financial Year 2017/18, Budget for the Financial Year 2018/19, Forecast Budget for the Financial Year 2019/20
   - Appendix 2: Contribution Scale for the Financial Year 2019/20
   - Appendix 3: Salary Scale
   - Appendix 4: ATS – COMNAP Data Management Cooperation Report
   - Appendix 5: Proposed procedure and dates for selection of the new Assistant Executive Secretary

1. ATCM/CEP Support

ATCM XLI

Given the extraordinary characteristics of the ATCM XLI and CEP XXI meetings, the Secretariat will actively cooperate with the authorities of the Argentine government in the organisation of these events by providing logistic and financial support. The details of the expenses to be incurred for this purpose are provided in the provisional budget 2018/19 included in this document.

The Secretariat will also support the ATCM XLI by gathering and collating the documents for the meeting and publishing them in a restricted section of the Secretariat website, and providing in a USB flash drive distributed to all delegates an application that allows offline browsing of all documents and automatic synchronisation with the online database for the latest updates. The Delegates section will provide online registration for delegates and a downloadable, up-to-date list of delegates.

The Secretariat will support the functioning of the ATCM through the production of Secretariat Papers, a Manual for Delegates, and summaries of papers for the ATCM and the CEP.

The Secretariat will organise the services for translation and interpretation. It is responsible for pre- and post-sessional translation and for the translation services during the ATCM. It maintains contact with the provider of interpretation services, ONCALL.

The Secretariat will organise the note-taking services and is responsible for the compilation and editing of the Reports of the CEP and ATCM for adoption during the final plenary meetings. For this Meeting, the Secretariat has also contracted and covered the expenses related to the work of a Chief rapporteur and four rapporteurs.

ATCM XLII

The Host Country Secretariat of the Czech Republic and the Secretariat of the Antarctic Treaty will jointly prepare the ATCM XLII, which will take place in Prague in the first half of July 2019.

Coordination and contact

Aside from maintaining constant contact via email, telephone and other means with the Parties and international institutions of the Antarctic Treaty System, attendance at meetings is an important tool to maintain coordination and communication.

The travelling to be undertaken is as follows:

- COMNAP Annual General Meeting (AGM) XXX, Garmisch-Partenkirchen, Germany, 11-13 June 2018. Attendance to the meeting will provide an opportunity to further strengthen the connections and interaction with COMNAP.
- SCAR: The Executive Secretary received the invitation to attend as observer the XXXV SCAR Delegates Meeting, to be held in Davos, Switzerland on 25 and 26 June 2018.
- CCAMLR-XXXVII, Hobart, Australia, 22 October to 2 November 2018. The CCAMLR meeting, which takes place roughly halfway between succeeding ATCMs, provides an opportunity for the Secretariat to brief the ATCM

Representatives, many of whom attend the CCAMLR meeting, on developments in the Secretariat's work. Liaison with the CCAMLR Secretariat is also important for the Antarctic Treaty Secretariat, as many of its regulations are modelled after those of the CCAMLR Secretariat.

- Coordination Meetings with the Czech Republic as Host Country of ATCM XLII in Prague, tentatively in March or April 2019.

Support of intersessional activities

During recent years both the CEP and the ATCM have produced an important amount of intersessional work, mainly through Intersessional Contact Groups (ICGs). The Secretariat will provide technical support for the online establishment of the ICGs agreed at the ATCM XLI and CEP XXI and will produce specific documents if required by the ATCM or the CEP.

The Secretariat will update its website with the measures adopted by the ATCM and with the information produced by the CEP and the ATCM.

The Secretariat has received from the Permanent Court of Arbitration (PCA) an updated list of arbitrators designated by State Parties to the Protocol on Environmental Protection to the Antarctic Treaty according to Article 2 of the Schedule to the Protocol. The PCA's Secretary General has committed to keep the Antarctic Treaty Secretariat informed of changes to this list. The secretariat will update the records accordingly and make it available to the Parties.

Printing

The Secretariat will translate, publish and distribute the ATCM XLI Final Report and its Annexes in the four Treaty languages pursuant to the Procedures for the Submission, Translation and Distribution of Documents for the ATCM and the CEP. The text of the Final Report will be published on the website of the Secretariat and will be printed in book form. The full text of the Final Report will be available in book form (two volumes) through online retailers and also in electronic book form.

2. Information Technology

Information Exchange and the Electronic Information Exchange System

As informed in SP 4 *Secretariat Report 2017/18*, the ATCM XL asked the Secretariat to cooperate with COMNAP in ways to reduce duplication and increase compatibility across their databases (Decision 7 [2017] Annex: ATCM Multi-Year Strategic Work Plan, page 1, #1). Both Secretariats have worked together during the intersessional period and a proposed roadmap of joint developments and collaboration has been included as Appendix 4 below.

The Secretariat will continue to assist Parties in posting their information exchange materials, as well as processing information uploaded using the File Upload functionality.

Development of the Secretariat website

Based on the proposals to be presented to ATCM XLI the Secretariat will continue to develop a complete redesign of the institutional website, with the aim of introducing, at the next ATCM in Prague 2019, a renovated graphic interface featuring improved navigation and increased visibility of the most relevant sections and information of the Secretariat's website.

Mapping tools

The experience acquired in incorporating geographic information related to Inspections of Antarctic stations (see SP 8) will be leveraged to explore the possibility of using the same GIS (Geographic Information System) tool for a variety of georeferenced content already existing in other Secretariat databases. Geographical data layers related to Antarctic Protected Areas, Land- and Ship-Based Expeditions, and Visitor Sites, among others, will be gradually incorporated.

3. Documentation and Public Information

Documents of the ATCM

The Secretariat will continue its efforts to complete its archive of the Final Reports and other records of the ATCM and other meetings of the Antarctic Treaty System in the four Treaty languages. Assistance from Parties in searching for their files will be essential in order to achieve a complete archive at the Secretariat. The project will continue in the Financial Year 2018/19. A complete and detailed list of missing papers in our database is available to all delegations interested in collaborating.

Glossary

The Secretariat will continue to develop the Secretariat's glossary of terms and expressions of the ATCM to generate a nomenclature in the four Treaty languages. The aim of this vocabulary database is to manage, publish and share these ATCM ontologies, which are data systems that define the relationships between the concepts, abbreviations and acronyms used in the Antarctic Treaty System. The glossary will evolve mainly based on the contributions of terms from Parties interested in contributing to the system.

Antarctic Treaty database

The database of Recommendations, Measures, Decisions and Resolutions of the ATCM is at present complete in English and nearly complete in Spanish and French, although the Secretariat still lacks various Final Report copies in those languages. In Russian, further Final Reports are lacking. The Secretariat is willing at all times to incorporate any Final Reports or discussion documents from Consultative and Special Meetings that are still missing in our database.

Image Bank

The Secretariat will continue to incorporate to the image bank photographic material currently available in its archive. Likewise, we would like to invite Parties to provide the Secretariat with original photographic material to be published in the image bank under a Creative Commons license. We would especially appreciate receiving pictures corresponding to the first Antarctic Treaty Meetings.

Public Information

The Secretariat and its website will continue to function as a clearinghouse for information on the Parties' activities and relevant developments in Antarctica.

4. Management

Personnel

On 1 April 2018 the Secretariat staff consisted of the following personnel:

Executive staff

Name	Position	Since	Rank	Step	Term
Albert Lluberas	Executive Secretary (ES)	01-09-2017	E1	1	31-08-2021
José María Acero	Assistant Executive Secretary (AES)	01-01-2005	E3	14	15-07-2019

General staff

Name	Position	Since	Rank	Step
José Luis Agraz	Information Officer	1-11-2004	G1	6
Diego Wydler	Information Technology Officer	01-02-2006	G1	6
Roberto Alan Fennell	Finance Officer (part time)	01-12-2008	G2	6
Pablo Wainschenker	Editor	01-02-2006	G2	4
Violeta Antinarelli	Librarian (part time)	01-04-2007	G3	6
Anna Balok	Communications Specialist (part time)	01-10-2010	G4	3
Viviana Collado	Office Manager	15-11-2012	G4	3
Margarita Tolaba	Cleaning Professional	01-07-2015	G7	3

On 31 December 2018 the contract term of the AES, José Maria Acero, will end. Mr Acero has demonstrated a high commitment and efficiency in his tasks during the last years, and it is the intention of the ES to extend Mr Acero's contract for a period of six and a half months, until the middle of 2019, in coincidence with the date planned for his retirement, 15 July 2019, and allowing his participation at the Antarctic Treaty Consultative Meeting

XLII. The new AES would begin his/her tasks immediately after the ATCM XLII, which, according to what was informed by the Czech Republic, will take place in Prague during the first half of July 2019. In accordance with Regulation 6 of the Staff Regulations, the Executive Secretary has consulted with the Consultative Parties and has found full support for this proposal. The Executive Secretary will take a decision after further consultation during the ATCM XLI.

Appendix 5 contains the proposed procedure and dates for selection of the new AES.

Following a request of ATCM XL, the Secretariat is presenting a separate paper (SP 7) on Human Resource Policy for the Antarctic Treaty Secretariat staff.

The Secretariat will invite international trainees from Parties for internships with the Secretariat. It has extended an invitation to the Czech Republic as host of the ATCM XLII to send one member of its organisational team for an internship in Buenos Aires.

Financial Matters

The Budget for the Financial Year 2018/19 and the Forecast Budget for the Financial Year 2019/20 are shown in Appendix 1.

Salaries

The cost of living continued to rise in Argentina in the year 2017. The inflation rate (Índice de Precios al Consumidor) for 2017 published by INDEC (Instituto Nacional de Estadística y Censos de la República Argentina) was 25%. Taking into account the devaluation of the Argentine Peso against the US$ of 20.4%, the rise of public salaries in Argentine Pesos of 24.9%, and some effects from the devaluation of the Argentine Peso in 2015 and 2016, the Executive Secretary proposes to maintain a zero percent increase to the salaries of the General Staff. The salary of the Cleaning Professional (G7) will be adjusted by 7.9% to coincide with the salaries of the same field in Argentina. There will be no increase for the Executive Staff.

Regulation 5.10 of the Staff Regulations requires the compensation of General Staff members when they are required to work more than 40 hours per week. Overtime is requested during the ATCM meetings.

With the termination of his contract the outgoing Assistant Executive Secretary will be entitled to receive the payment for staff termination under Regulation 10.4 of the ATCM Staff Regulations. At ATCM XXXIII (Punta del Este) 2010, "the ATCM agreed that Regulation 10.4 applied to all departures from service of executive staff, subject to the specific caveats set out in Regulation 10" (Final Report ATCM XXXIII, para. 100).

Funds

Working Capital Fund

According to Financial Regulation 6.2 (a), the Working Capital Fund must be maintained at 1/6 of the Secretariat's budget of 229,952 US$ in the upcoming years. The contributions of the Parties form the basis of the calculation of the level of the Working Capital Fund.

Staff Termination Fund

The Staff Termination Fund will be credited with 26,372 US$ in accordance with Staff Regulation 10.4 (scc Appcndix 1).

Staff Replacement Fund

Relocation costs for the incoming AES are calculated at 25,000 US$. They will be covered by the "Staff Replacement Fund" (see Appendix 1, appropriation line "Fund Expenditures").

25,000 US$ will be credited to the Staff Replacement Fund (see Appendix 1 appropriation line "Allocation to Funds") to maintain it at 50,000 US$ (Decision 1 [2006], Annex 3, Appendix 1: Budget 2006/7 and Forecast budget 2007/8 and allocation of resources).

General Fund

On 31 Mar 2018, the cash surplus of the General Fund amounted to 90,849 US$. Outstanding contributions amounted to 79,281. US$. 29,500 US$ were transferred from the Surplus General Fund to "Income" to maintain the requested level of the Staff Replacement Fund.

Further Details of the Draft Budget for the Financial Year 2018/19

As was informed to the Consultative Parties, for the ATCM XLI the Secretariat will be responsible for some expenses normally covered by the Host Country. These include IT and audiovisual support, rapporteurs, catering and other logistic support expenses. For these a new appropriation line, "ATCM 2018", has been added.

The rest of the allocation to the appropriation lines follows the proposal from last year. Some smaller adjustments have been implemented according to the foreseen expenses in the Financial Year 2018/2019.

Appendix 1 shows the Budget for the Financial Year 2018/2019. The salary scale is provided in Appendix 3.

Contributions for the Financial Year 2019/20

The contributions for the Financial Year 2019/2020 will not rise.

Appendix 2 shows the contributions of the Parties for the Financial Year 2019/2020.

5. Forecast Programme for the Financial Year 2019/20 and the Financial Year 2020/21

It is expected that most of the ongoing activities of the Secretariat will be continued in the Financial Year 2019/2020 and the Financial Year 2020/2021, and therefore, unless the programme undergoes major changes, no change in staff positions is foreseen for the following years.

Appendix 1

Provisional Statement FY 2017/18, Forecast FY 2018/19, Budget FY 2018/19 and Forecast FY 2019/20

APPROPRIATION LINES	Prov Statement 2017/18 *)		Forecast 2018/19		Budget 2018/19		Forecast 2019/20	
INCOME								
CONTRIBUTIONS pledged	$	-1,378,097	$	-1,378,097	$	-1,378,097	$	-1,378,097
**) from General Fund	$	-50,000	$	-25,000	$	-129,038	$	-25,000
Interest Investments	$	-3,000	$	-3,000	$	-3,000	$	-3,000
Total Income	$	**-1,431,097**	$	**-1,406,097**	$	**-1,510,135**	$	**-1,406,097**
EXPENDITURES								
SALARIES								
Executive	$	326,637	$	313,333	$	321,841	$	302,657
General Staff	$	358,968	$	372,992	$	373,143	$	383,877
ATCM Support Staff	$	20,743	$	21,160	$	9,932	$	21,160
Trainee	$	800	$	9,600	$	9,600	$	9,600
Overtime	$	15,151	$	16,000	$	11,000	$	16,000
	$	**722,299**	$	**733,085**	$	**725,516**	$	**733,294**
TRANSLATION AND INTERPRETATION								
Translation and Interpretation	$	291,085	$	334,967	$	175,000	$	330,773
TRAVEL								
Travel	$	107,381	$	91,000	$	61,300	$	95,000
INFORMATION TECHNOLOGY								
Hardware	$	10,455	$	10,000	$	10,000	$	10,050
Software	$	2,896	$	3,000	$	3,000	$	3,015
Development	$	22,834	$	22,500	$	31,500	$	22,613
Hardware and Software Maintenance	$	2,706	$	2,250	$	2,250	$	2,261
Support	$	7,208	$	7,750	$	9,000	$	9,045
	$	**46,099**	$	**45,500**	$	**55,750**	$	**46,984**
PRINTING, EDITING & COPYING								
Final report	$	16,525	$	20,100	$	19,000	$	19,095
Compilation	$	662	$	2,512	$	2,500	$	2,512
Site guidelines	$	1,288	$	3,221	$	2,500	$	2,512
	$	**18,475**	$	**25,833**	$	**24,000**	$	**24,119**
GENERAL SERVICES								
Legal advice	$	1,322	$	3,060	$	2,500	$	2,660
External audit	$	9,236	$	11,362	$	13,000	$	13,260
Cleaning, maintenance & security	$	8,300	$	11,220	$	11,000	$	11,220
Training	$	6,774	$	8,160	$	5,000	$	5,100
Banking	$	8,022	$	10,183	$	7,000	$	7,140
Rental of equipment	$	2,503	$	3,102	$	2,503	$	2,553
	$	**36,157**	$	**47,087**	$	**41,003**	$	**41,823**
COMMUNICATION								
Telephone	$	5,563	$	7,354	$	7,500	$	7,650
Internet	$	2,353	$	2,550	$	3,200	$	3,264
Web hosting	$	7,650	$	8,670	$	9,600	$	9,792
Postage	$	2,247	$	2,841	$	2,700	$	2,754
	$	**17,813**	$	**21,415**	$	**23,000**	$	**23,460**

	Prov Statement 2017/18		Forecast 2018/19		Budget 2018/19		Forecast 2019/20	
OFFICE								
Stationery & supplies	$	6,243	$	4,885	$	4,885	$	4,983
Books & subscriptions	$	1,570	$	3,409	$	3,409	$	3,477
Insurance	$	3,034	$	4,413	$	4,413	$	4,501
Furniture	$	0	$	1,280	$	1,280	$	1,306
Office equipment	$	1,679	$	4,544	$	4,544	$	4,635
Office improvement	$	0	$	2,841	$	2,841	$	2,898
	$	**12,526**	**$**	**21,372**	**$**	**21,372**	**$**	**21,799**
ADMINISTRATIVE								
Office Supplies	$	2,653	$	5,113	$	5,113	$	5,215
Local transport	$	791	$	908	$	908	$	926
Miscellaneous	$	2,603	$	4,544	$	4,544	$	4,635
Utilities (Energy)	$	4,729	$	7,407	$	7,407	$	7,555
	$	**10,776**	**$**	**17,972**	**$**	**17,972**	**$**	**18,331**
REPRESENTATION								
Representation	$	3,929	$	4,000	$	4,000	$	4,000
FINANCING								
Exchange loss	$	14,222	$	12,494	$	12,494	$	12,744
ATCM								
IT and Audiovisual					$	235,000		
Rapporteurs					$	40,700		
Catering					$	26,000		
Miscellaneous					$	20,000		
***)					**$**	**321,700**		

	Prov Statement 2017/18	Forecast 2018/19	Budget 2018/19	Forecast 2019/20
SUBTOTAL APPROPRIATIONS	**$ 1,280,762**	**$ 1,354,725**	**$ 1,483,107**	**$ 1,352,328**

	Prov Statement 2017/18		Forecast 2018/19		Budget 2018/19		Forecast 2019/20	
ALLOCATION TO FUNDS								
Translation Contingency Fund	$	0	$	0	$	0	$	0
Staff Replacement Fund	$	29,500	$	25,000	$	0	$	25,000
Staff Termination Fund	$	29,986	$	26,372	$	27,028	$	28,769
Working Capital Fund	$	0	$	0	$	0	$	0
	$	**59,486**	**$**	**51,372**	**$**	**27,028**	**$**	**53,769**

	Prov Statement 2017/18	Forecast 2018/19	Budget 2018/19	Forecast 2019/20
TOTAL APPROPRIATIONS	**$ 1,340,248**	**$ 1,406,097**	**$ 1,510,135**	**$ 1,406,098**

		Prov Statement 2017/18		Forecast 2018/19		Budget 2018/19		Forecast 2019/20	
FUND EXPENDITURES									
**)	General Fund	$	50,000	$	25,000	$	129,038	$	25,000
	Working Capital Fund	$	0	$	0	$	0	$	0
	Translation Contingency Fund	$	0	$	0	$	0	$	0
***)	Staff Termination Fund	$	127,438	$	175,282	$	0	$	185,099
****)	Staff Replacement Fund	$	29,500	$	25,000	$	0	$	25,000
		$	**206,938**	**$**	**225,282**	**$**	**129,038**	**$**	**235,099**

		Prov Statement 2017/18	Forecast 2018/19	Budget 2018/19	Forecast 2019/20
*****)	**Unpaid Contributions**	**$ 79,281**	**$ 0**	**$ 0**	**$ 0**
	BALANCE	**$ 11,568**	**$ 0**	**$ 0**	**$ 0**

		Prov Statement 2017/18		Forecast 2018/19		Budget 2018/19		Forecast 2019/20	
SUMMARY OF FUNDS									
	Translation Contingency Fund	$	30,000	$	30,000	$	30,000	$	30,000
	Staff Replacement Fund	$	50,000	$	50,000	$	50,000	$	50,000
	Staff Termination Fund	$	174,065	$	25,156	$	201,093	$	44,765
*******)	Working Capital Fund	$	229,952	$	229,952	$	229,952	$	229,952
	General Fund (Fin.Reg. 6.3)	$	633,464	$	687,585	$	583,547	$	558,547

* Provisional Statement
as of 31 Mar 2018

** The Staff Replacement Fund is filled up
from the Gerneral Fund to its nominal level
of 50,000 USD. Extraordinary cost for
ATCM are born by the General Fund.

*** Staff termination compensation (Staff
Regulation 10.4 and Final Report ATCM
XXXIII para 100) for the Executive
Secretary in 2017 and the Assistant
Executive Secretary in 2018

**** Removal costs (Staff Regulations 9.6 (b)
and 10.6 (b)) for the Executive Secretaries
in 2017 and the Assistant Executive
Secretary in 2018 compensated from Staff
Replacement Fund

***** Unpaid contributions
as of 31 March 2018

****** Maximum Required Amount
Working Capital Fund (Fin. Reg. 6.2) $ 229,683 $ 229,683 $ 229,683 $ 229,683

Appendix 2

Contribution Scale FY 2019/20

2019/20	Cat.	Mult.	Variable	Fixed	Total
Argentina	A	3.6	$ 36,587	$ 23,760	$ 60,347
Australia	A	3.6	$ 36,587	$ 23,760	$ 60,347
Belgium	D	1.6	$ 16,261	$ 23,760	$ 40,021
Brazil	D	1.6	$ 16,261	$ 23,760	$ 40,021
Bulgaria	E	1	$ 10,163	$ 23,760	$ 33,923
Chile	C	2.2	$ 22,359	$ 23,760	$ 46,119
China	C	2.2	$ 22,359	$ 23,760	$ 46,119
Czech Republic	D	1.6	$ 16,261	$ 23,760	$ 40,021
Ecuador	E	1	$ 10,163	$ 23,760	$ 33,923
Finland	D	1.6	$ 16,261	$ 23,760	$ 40,021
France	A	3.6	$ 36,587	$ 23,760	$ 60,347
Germany	B	2.8	$ 28,456	$ 23,760	$ 52,216
India	C	2.2	$ 22,359	$ 23,760	$ 46,119
Italy	B	2.8	$ 28,456	$ 23,760	$ 52,216
Japan	A	3.6	$ 36,587	$ 23,760	$ 60,347
Republic of Korea	D	1.6	$ 16,261	$ 23,760	$ 40,021
Netherlands	C	2.2	$ 22,359	$ 23,760	$ 46,119
New Zealand	A	3.6	$ 36,587	$ 23,760	$ 60,347
Norway	A	3.6	$ 36,587	$ 23,760	$ 60,347
Peru	E	1	$ 10,163	$ 23,760	$ 33,923
Poland	D	1.6	$ 16,261	$ 23,760	$ 40,021
Russian Federation	C	2.2	$ 22,359	$ 23,760	$ 46,119
South Africa	C	2.2	$ 22,359	$ 23,760	$ 46,119
Spain	C	2.2	$ 22,359	$ 23,760	$ 46,119
Sweden	C	2.2	$ 22,359	$ 23,760	$ 46,119
Ukraine	D	1.6	$ 16,261	$ 23,760	$ 40,021
United Kingdom	A	3.6	$ 36,587	$ 23,760	$ 60,347
United States	A	3.6	$ 36,587	$ 23,760	$ 60,347
Uruguay	D	1.6	$ 16,261	$ 23,760	$ 40,021

Budget   **$1,378,097**

Salary Scale FY 2018/19

Schedule A

SALARY SCALE FOR THE EXECUTIVE STAFF

(United States Dollar)

2018/19 Level		I	II	III	IV	V	VI	VII	VIII	IX	X	XI	XII	XIII	XIV	XV
E1	A	$135,302	$137,819	$140,337	$142,855	$145,373	$147,890	$150,407	$152,926							
E1	B	$169,127	$172,274	$175,421	$178,569	$181,716	$184,863	$188,009	$191,158							
E2	A	$113,932	$116,075	$118,218	$120,359	$122,501	$124,642	$126,783	$128,926	$131,069	$133,211	$135,352	$135,595	$137,709		
E2	B	$142,415	$145,093	$147,772	$150,449	$153,126	$155,802	$158,479	$161,158	$163,837	$166,513	$169,190	$169,494	$172,136		
E3	A	$95,007	$97,073	$99,140	$101,207	$103,275	$105,341	$107,408	$109,476	$111,542	$113,608	$115,675	$116,915	$118,154	$120,193	$122,231
E3	B	$118,758	$121,341	$123,925	$126,509	$129,094	$131,676	$134,260	$136,845	$139,427	$142,010	$144,594	$146,143	$147,693	$150,242	$152,788
E4	A	$78,779	$80,693	$82,609	$84,518	$86,435	$88,347	$90,257	$92,174	$94,089	$96,000	$97,915	$98,448	$100,336	$102,223	$104,110
E4	B	$98,474	$100,866	$103,262	$105,648	$108,044	$110,434	$112,822	$115,217	$117,611	$119,999	$122,393	$123,060	$125,413	$127,778	$130,137
E5	A	$65,315	$67,029	$68,739	$70,452	$72,162	$73,873	$75,586	$77,293	$79,007	$80,719	$82,427	$82,981			
E5	B	$81,644	$83,786	$85,924	$88,065	$90,203	$92,342	$94,482	$96,617	$98,759	$100,899	$103,034	$103,726			
E6	A	$51,706	$53,351	$54,994	$56,641	$58,284	$59,928	$61,575	$63,219	$64,862	$65,862	$66,508				
E6	B	$64,632	$66,689	$68,742	$70,801	$72,855	$74,910	$76,969	$79,024	$81,078	$82,328	$83,135				

STEPS

Note: Row B is the base salary (shown in Row A) with an additional 25% for salary on-costs (retirement fund and insurance premiums, installation and repatriation grants, education allowances etc.) and is the total salary entitlement for executive staff in accordance with regulation 5.

Schedule B

SALARY SCALE FOR THE GENERAL STAFF

(United States Dollar)

Level		I	II	III	IV	V	VI	VII	VIII	IX	X	XI	XII	XIII	XIV	XV
G1		$64,788	$67,810	$70,834	$73,856	$77,006	$80,291									
G2		$53,990	$56,508	$59,028	$61,546	$64,172	$66,909									
G3		$44,990	$47,089	$49,189	$51,288	$53,477	$55,760									
G4		$37,493	$39,242	$40,991	$42,741	$44,564	$46,466									
G5		$30,972	$32,419	$33,863	$35,310	$36,818	$38,391									
G6		$25,388	$26,571	$27,756	$28,941	$30,177	$31,465									
G7		$13,724	$14,317	$14,911	$15,505	$16,124	$16,770									

STEPS

Appendix 4

ATS - COMNAP Data Management Cooperation Report

Both secretariats started work immediately after ATCM XL, exchanging ideas on possible topics on which cooperation could be useful for the Parties. The Treaty Electronic Information Exchange System (EIES) and Inspections Database, along with the use of compatible mapping tools, were selected as first candidates for collaboration. In September 2017 COMNAP hosted a meeting in Christchurch, NZ with the participation of the Antarctic Treaty Secretariat's IT Officer, COMNAP's Executive Secretary, and experts from various organisations. In this Data Management meeting the practical issues of cooperation on those topics were discussed, and a set of actions to increase the compatibility of the respective organisations' information systems were defined. The following is a summary of these topics:

Electronic Information Exchange System (EIES)

The main challenge concerning the EIES, as reflected in SP 10 - ATCM XL (p. 4), was to allow the Antarctic Treaty Secretariat to receive updates of the public subset of data from the COMNAP database for various EIES Operational Information - National Expeditions sections when those sections were updated by a representative from the National Antarctic Programs in the COMNAP system.

To this end, the following process was envisioned:

1. The process would start when a COMNAP Member representative adds or modifies data in the COMNAP system.

2. Once that information is verified by the COMNAP Secretariat staff, and if it is included in the public subset of data, it would be transferred to the ATS System using web-service technology.

3. The Web Service at the EIES would insert the information into the EIES in a pending state and send an alert to the Treaty Party's EIES Operator, informing that new information has been received from COMNAP.

4. The Party's EIES Operator would then be able to accept the information as it was received, modify it (by changing or complementing it), or reject it completely.

To make the two information systems compatible, the Meeting would need to adopt, as part of the Information Exchange requirements, the classification which was provided by COMNAP in IP 12 - ATCM XL (as advice to the ATCM in response to the requirement in ATCM XXXIX Final Report Appendix IV p. 190): namely, adding the status and seasonality data fields for facilities, and slightly modifying the list of types of facilities.

Inspections Database

To provide a list of non-inspected facilities (one of the new features described in SP 8 Inspections Database developments and Mapping Tools) the AT Secretariat will use the COMNAP Facilities list.

Additionally, the updating process described above for the EIES could also be used to keep the Inspections Database Facilities list updated.

It was also defined that the ATS, being the authoritative source for information on Inspections under the Treaty and the Environment Protocol, could share that information with COMNAP for inclusion in their databases as required.

Mapping Tools

Since both organisations would use the same GIS tool (ESRI ArcGis cloud), geographical information layers produced by each organisation could be shared, thus reducing the need for duplication in this field as well. Examples of those layers from the ATS side are Protected Areas locations and Expeditions Itineraries informed through the EIES.

Appendix 5

Procedure for the selection of the new Assistant Executive Secretary

Regulation 6.2 of the Staff Regulations for the Secretariat establishes that: "In accordance with Article 3 of Measure 1 (2003) the Executive Secretary shall appoint, direct, and supervise other staff members. The paramount consideration in the appointment, transfer or promotion of staff members shall be the need to secure the highest standards of efficiency, competence and integrity. Subject to this, due consideration should be given to recruiting Executive staff on as wide a basis as possible from among the nationals of Consultative Parties."

On 15 July 2019, the Secretariat must replace the current Assistant Executive Secretary, José María Acero of Argentina. In order to allow for sufficient time for the selection process, the following procedure is proposed for the consideration of the Parties:

Vacancy announcement: On 1 September 2018, the Executive Secretary will send a Circular to the Antarctic Treaty Consultative Parties announcing the call for applications for the position of the Assistant Executive Secretary, for Parties to disseminate the information to their nationals[1] in the manner in which they consider appropriate. The call for applications will also be also sent to SCAR, COMNAP and CCAMLR Secretariats and published on the Secretariat website.

The format for the call for applications is proposed as follows:

Call for applications for the position of Assistant Executive Secretary of the Secretariat of the Antarctic Treaty

1. Description of the position: Assistant Executive Secretary (AES).

The Secretariat of the Antarctic Treaty has had its headquarters in the city of Buenos Aires, Argentina since 1 September 2004. Information about the Secretariat can be found at *www.ats.aq*.

The Assistant Executive Secretary occupies one of the two executive-level positions of the Secretariat, along with the Executive Secretary.

2. Responsibilities and tasks: The main functions of the AES are: to assist the Executive Secretary in his functions and to act in charge of the Secretariat during periods of absence of the Executive Secretary.

---

[1] Taking into account the provisions of Regulation 2.8 of the *Staff Regulations for the Secretariat* and, in order that the person replacing Mr Acero be able to carry out procedures on behalf of the Secretariat involving public and private agencies of the Argentine Republic, if the replacement were not of Argentine nationality, it would be necessary that once selected, the Party to which he/she belongs grant him/her a diplomatic passport. In this way, he/she will be able to process, before the Ministry of Foreign Affairs of Argentina, the credentials that enable him/her to function as executive officer of the Secretariat of the Antarctic Treaty.

To assist the ES in his functions the AES should be capable of managing the Secretariat staff and applying internal rules and procedures. The AES should understand the Secretariat information systems and be able to communicate fluently and efficiently in English and desirably also in Spanish.

The AES should also take an active role in the organisation of annual meetings and be able to act as secretary to Antarctic Treaty Consultative Meeting (ATCM) working groups if required. Additionally, the AES serves as the contact point in the Secretariat for matters related to functions of the Committee for Environmental Protection (CEP).

To act in charge of the Secretariat in periods of absence of the ES, the AES should be able to understand and accommodate quickly to financial, banking and administrative rules and customs of Argentina. The AES is also routinely tasked with negotiating contracts with providers and interacting with auditors, advisors and the Argentinean government.

For these functions, the following are required:

   a. Familiarity with the activities of the Antarctic Treaty Consultative Meeting (ATCM) and the Committee for Environmental Protection (CEP).
   b. Experience in attending and/or organising international meetings, preferably related to Antarctic matters.
   c. Demonstrated experience in personnel management.
   d. Basic knowledge of IT and information systems.
   e. Basic finance/accounting knowledge.
   f. Hold a university degree, academic degree, or equivalent qualification.
   g. Fluency in one of the four official languages of the Antarctic Treaty. Given that the Secretariat is located in Buenos Aires, knowledge of the Spanish language is desirable.
   h. Be a national of an Antarctic Treaty Consultative Party.

4. *Duration of the position*: Four years, renewable by decision of the Executive Secretary in consultation with the Antarctic Treaty Consultative Meeting.

5. *Work schedule*: This is a full-time position. Information on the work schedule is provided in the *Staff Regulations for the Secretariat of the Antarctic Treaty*. Updated details of salaries and allowances are available from the Antarctic Treaty Secretariat upon request.

6. *Requirements and deadline for applications:* Applications must be sent by email to *aes.applications@ats.aq* before 30 September 2018. They must include a Cover letter and the attached Application Form providing detailed information on the requirements specified therein, as well as a summarised CV of no more than two pages in length.

7. *Selection criteria:* From the set of applications received, the Executive Secretary will produce a ranking of candidates based on the fulfillment of the items included in the application form and draw a list of the top five candidates with whom he will hold interviews, either personally or through electronic means, on a date agreed between the parties involved. For the sake of transparency both the applications and the rankings will be available on request to all Consultative Parties. Subsequently, the Executive Secretary will inform the Consultative Parties on the results of the interviews and choose the person who will occupy the position. This decision will be communicated before 15 December 2018.

8. Availability: The person chosen for the position must be available to begin work on 16 July 2019 in the city of Buenos Aires, Argentina.

9. Additional information: Please consult the website of the Antarctic Treaty Secretariat, *www.ats.aq* or contact Mr Albert Lluberas by email at *executive.secretary@antarctictreaty.org*. Other relevant information can be found in the *Key Documents of the Antarctic Treaty System.*

Standard application form (to be accompanied by a Cover letter)

Personal information

Name:

Address:

Telephone:

Email:

Nationality:

Date of birth:

Selection Criteria

Please include additional information related to the requirements listed below and attach a curriculum vitae that does not exceed two pages.

1) Familiarity with the activities of the Antarctic Treaty Consultative Meeting (ATCM) and the Committee for Environmental Protection (CEP).

2) Experience in attending and/or organising international meetings, preferably related to Antarctic matters.

3) Demonstrated experience in personnel management.

4) Basic knowledge of IT and information systems.

5) Basic finance/accounting knowledge.

6) University/academic degree or equivalent qualification in a field related to the position.

7) Fluency in one of the four official languages of the Antarctic Treaty. Given that the Secretariat is located in Buenos Aires, knowledge of the Spanish language is desirable.

8) Citizenship of one of the 29 Consultative Parties of the Antarctic Treaty.

Renewal of the Contract of the Secretariat's External Auditor

The Representatives,

Recalling the Financial Regulations for the Secretariat of the Antarctic Treaty ("Financial Regulations for the Secretariat") annexed to Decision 4 (2003), and specifically Regulation 11 (External Audit);

Conscious that the Secretariat of the Antarctic Treaty ("the Secretariat") conducts the majority of its financial transactions in Argentina, and that the detailed rules of book-keeping and accounting are country-specific;

Noting Argentina's proposal to designate the Sindicatura General de la Nación ("SIGEN") as the external auditor of the Secretariat;

Decide:

1. to designate SIGEN as the external auditor of the Secretariat for the Financial Years ending in 2018 to 2021, in accordance with Regulation 11.1 of the Financial Regulations for the Secretariat; and

2. to authorise the Executive Secretary to negotiate a contract with SIGEN to carry out annual external audits for the above-mentioned years in accordance with Regulation 11.3, the Annex to this Decision and the budgetary limits set by the Antarctic Treaty Consultative Meeting ("ATCM").

Tasks to be carried out by the external auditor

To provide external audit reports covering the financial years ending in 2018, 2019, 2020 and 2021 in accordance with Regulation 11.3 of the Financial Regulations annexed to Decision 4 (2003).

The audit report shall address:

- Implementation of regulations adopted by the Antarctic Treaty Consultative Meeting ("ATCM");
- Internal controls - Regulations and Procedures;
- Internal oversight of administrative processes, payments, custody of funds, and assets;
- Budgeting;
- Comparative budget reports;
- Expenditure efficiency analysis;
- Budget execution oversight;
- Analysis of the establishment of new area units;
- Control and reporting of contributions;
- Establishment and oversight of the General Fund, the Working Capital Fund, the Future Meeting Fund, the Staff Replacement Fund, the Staff Termination Fund and any other Funds held by the Secretariat of the Antarctic Treaty ("the Secretariat");
- Income and expense accounts;
- Trust funds;
- Custody of funds - Investments;
- Accounting oversight in accordance with Regulation 10 of Decision 4 (2003);
- Drafting an external auditor report;
- Other matters which may be necessary to ensure sound financial management of the Secretariat.

The provisional financial report for each Financial Year should be submitted by the Executive Secretary to the Sindicatura General de la Nación ("SIGEN") no later than 1 June of the year in which the Financial Year concludes and the final audited report should be submitted by SIGEN to the Executive Secretary no later than 1 September of the year in which the Financial Year concludes.

Multi-Year Strategic Work Plan for the Antarctic Treaty Consultative Meeting

The Representatives,

Reaffirming the values, objectives and principles contained in the Antarctic Treaty and its Protocol on Environmental Protection;

Recalling Decision 3 (2012) on the Multi-Year Strategic Work Plan ("the Plan") and its principles;

Bearing in mind that the Plan is complementary to the agenda of the Antarctic Treaty Consultative Meeting ("ATCM") and that the Parties and other ATCM participants are encouraged to contribute as usual to other matters on the ATCM agenda;

Decide:

1. to adopt the Plan annexed to this Decision; and

2. that the Plan annexed to Decision 7 (2017) is no longer current.

ATCM Multi-year Strategic Work Plan

	Priority	ATCM XL (2017)	Intersessional	ATCM XLI (2018)	Intersessional	ATCM XLII (2019)	Intersessional	ATCM XLIII (2020)
1.	Continue to improve the functioning of the EIES	WG1 to review functioning of the EIES	The ATS to cooperate with COMNAP in ways to reduce duplication and increase compatibility across their databases The ATS to continue to improve the EIES, including the provision of the website interface in the four Treaty languages		The ATS to cooperate with COMNAP in ways to reduce duplication and increase compatibility across their databases The ATS to continue to improve the EIES.	ATCM to keep under review the functioning of the EIES		
2.	Consider coordinated outreach to non-party states whose nationals or assets are active in Antarctica and states that are Antarctic Treaty Parties but not yet to the Protocol	ATCM to identify and reach out to non-party states whose nationals are active in Antarctica				ATCM to identify and reach out to non-party states whose nationals are active in Antarctica		
3.	Contribute to nationally and internationally coordinated education and outreach activities from an Antarctic Treaty perspective	WG1 to consider the report of the ICG on Education and Outreach	ICG on Education and Outreach		ICG on Education and Outreach	WG1 to consider the report of the ICG on Education and Outreach		
4.	Share and discuss strategic science priorities in order to identify and pursue opportunities for collaboration as well as capacity building in science, particularly in relation to climate change	WG2 to collate and compare strategic science priorities with a view to identify cooperation opportunities	Continue informal intersessional discussions on strategic science priorities		Continue informal intersessional discussions on strategic science priorities	Consider outcomes of intersessional discussions on strategic science priorities		
5.	Enhance effective cooperation between Parties (e.g. joint inspections, joint scientific projects and logistic support) and effective participation in meetings (e.g. consideration of effective working methods in meetings)	WG2 to consider the report of the ICG on Joint Inspections	Continue informal consultations on joint inspections	Consider outcomes of informal consultations on joint inspections	Continue informal consultations on joint inspections	Consider outcomes of informal consultations on joint inspections Consider advice from COMNAP on information exchange and search and rescue		

	Priority	ATCM XL (2017)	Intersessional	ATCM XLI (2018)	Intersessional	ATCM XLII (2019)	Intersessional	ATCM XLIII (2020)
6.	Strengthening cooperation between the CEP and the ATCM	ATCM to consider issues raised in CEP report at ATCM XXXIX and XL ATCM to receive advice from CEP that requires follow-up action						
7.	To bring Annex VI in to force and to continue to gather information on repair and remediation of environmental damage and other relevant issues to inform future negotiations on liability	ATCM to evaluate progress made towards Annex VI becoming effective in accordance with Article IX of the Antarctic Treaty, and what action may be necessary and appropriate to encourage Parties to approve Annex VI in a timely manner	The ATS will set up a webpage within the ATS website which will contain the information on national legislation on Annex VI implementation, voluntarily provided by Parties and accessible to Parties Report available at: *https://eies. ats.aq/Ats.IE/ Reports/rptNRLs. aspx?Topic=7*		ATS to be in touch with IGP&I Clubs	ATCM to evaluate progress made towards Annex VI becoming effective in accordance with Article IX of the Antarctic Treaty, and what action may be necessary and appropriate to encourage Parties to approve Annex VI in a timely manner		ATCM to take a decision in 2020 on the establishment of a timeframe for the resumption of negotiations on liability in accordance with Article 16 of the Protocol on Environmental Protection, or sooner if the Parties so decide in light of progress made in approving Measure 1 (2005) – see Decision 5 (2015)
8.	Assess the progress of the CEP on its ongoing work to review best practices and to improve existing tools and develop further tools for environmental protection, including environmental impact assessment procedures	WG1 to consider advice of the CEP and discuss the policy considerations of the review of Environmental Impact Assessment (EIA) Guidelines				WG1 to further discuss the issues raised in part 8b of the CEP XX Report		WG1 to consider advice of the CEP and discuss the policy considerations of the review of Environmental Impact Assessment (EIA)
8 bis	Collection and use of biological material in Antarctica			ATCM to discuss the collection and use of biological material in Antarctica	Informal exchange of information through ATCM forum Request SCAR to present at ATCM XLII an update to its Report contained in WP 2 *Biological Prospecting in the Antarctic* presented at ATCM XXXIII	WG 1 to discuss the collection and use of biological material in Antarctica		
9.	Address the recommendations of the Antarctic Treaty Meeting of Experts on Implications of Climate Change for Antarctic Management and Governance (CEP-ICG)	WG2 to consider recommendations 4-6 WG2 to consider outcomes of the SC-CCAMLR and CEP workshop	Interested Parties to prepare for discussions on outstanding recommendations from the ATME on Climate Change Implications (2010)		Interested Parties to prepare for discussions on outstanding recommendations from the ATME on Climate Change Implications (2010)	Agree how to deal with any outstanding recommendations from the ATME on Climate Change Implications (2010)		Follow up on any decisions regarding handling of any outstanding recommendations from the ATME on Climate Change Implications (2010)

	Priority	ATCM XL (2017)	Intersessional	ATCM XLI (2018)	Intersessional	ATCM XLII (2019)	Intersessional	ATCM XLIII (2020)
10.	Discuss implementation of the Climate Changes Response Work Programme (CCRWP)	WG2 to consider annual update from CEP on implementation of CCRWP				WG2 to consider annual update from CEP on implementation of CCRWP		WG2 to consider annual update from CEP on implementation of CCRWP
11.	Modernisation of Antarctic stations in context of climate change	WG2 to discuss exchange of information and COMNAP advice				WG2 to discuss exchange of information and COMNAP advice		
12.	Review and discuss issues related to increased aviation activity in Antarctica, and assess the need for additional action		Secretariat to write to ICAO to request any information pertinent to aviation in Antarctica and to invite them to attend ATCM XLI Ask COMNAP and IAATO to provide an overview of aviation activity, and to present at the next ATCM XLI to inform discussion		Secretariat to write to ICAO to request any information pertinent to aviation in Antarctica and to invite them to attend ATCM XLII Ask COMNAP and IAATO to provide an overview of aviation activity, and to present at the next ATCM XLII to inform discussion	ATCM XLII WG2 to have a dedicated discussion on aviation activity, including non-government air traffic and UAVs/ RPAs, in Antarctica ATCM XLII WG2 to consider any views presented on air safety issues by ICAO	The meeting to seek advice addressing risks and other issues identified during discussions at ATCM XLII	
12 bis	To take note of the International Code for Ships Operating in Polar Waters; and to continue to strengthen cooperation among Antarctic marine operators; and to take into account developments in the IMO		Secretariat to write to the IMO to set out the ATCM's priority interest in maritime safety and invite them to present an update, and engage in ATCM XLI			WG 2 to consider developments at IMO, and discuss further maritime safety issues		Exchange views on national experiences in authorising vessel activity in Antarctica, following entry into force of the Polar Code
13.	Hydrographic surveying in Antarctica		IHO, in consultation with ATS and host, prepare to deliver a seminar on the status and the impact of hydrography in Antarctic waters at ATCM XLI		IHO, in consultation with ATS and host, prepare to deliver a seminar on the status and the impact of hydrography in Antarctic waters at ATCM XLII	ATCM to have a dedicated seminar on hydrography in Antarctica, with a presentation of IHO		
14.	Review and assess the need for additional actions regarding area management and permanent infrastructure related to tourism, as well as issues related to land based and adventure tourism, and address the recommendations of the CEP Tourism Study	Consider a report from the Secretariat concerning progress against recommendation 1 of 2012 CEP Tourism Study		Discuss the options for developing a standardised monitoring methodology for site management. Discuss proposals in respect of the need for additional actions regarding area management. Review progress against recommendations from CEP Tourism Study	Follow up on any conclusions regarding the CEP Tourism Study CEP to continue its work on the long-term impacts of tourism on the environment	Further consideration of environmental issues relating to tourism based on any new advice from the CEP SCAR and IAATO to provide an interim report on progress of the systematic conservation plan for the Antarctic Peninsula		Consideration of possibly increased search and rescue burdens on national Antarctic programmes due to increased tourism activity in Antarctica

	Priority	ATCM XL (2017)	Intersessional	ATCM XLI (2018)	Intersessional	ATCM XLII (2019)	Intersessional	ATCM XLIII (2020)
15.	Develop a strategic approach to environmentally managed tourism and non-governmental activities in Antarctica	WG2 to consider Secretariat update Develop a strategic vision for tourism and non-governmental activities in Antarctica	Continue discussions to prepare for ATCM XLI	Discuss specific actions to enhance implementation of the 2009 General Principles of Antarctic Tourism	Examine the suitability and rules around forms of tourism that present a threat to the environment and to high standards of health and safety Invite parties to review domestic implementation and permitting processes and work to complete domestic implementation requirements for outstanding Measures Preparation of a report from an informal workshop	Further discussions relating to issues arising from the growth of tourism, including any implications of the potential growth in non-IAATO registered operators		
16.	Visitor site monitoring				Secretariat to explore the possibility of extending the mapping tool to sites covered by existing site guidelines	To analyse CEP progress on recommendations 3 and 7 of the CEP Tourism Study Secretariat to report back to ATCM XLII		

Note: The ATCM Working Groups mentioned above are not permanent but are established by consensus at the end of each Antarctic Treaty Consultative Meeting.

3. Resolutions

Site Guidelines for visitors

The Representatives,

Recalling Resolutions 5 (2005), 2 (2006), 1 (2007), 2 (2008), 4 (2009), 1 (2010), 4 (2011), 4 (2012), 3 (2013), 4 (2014) and 2 (2016) which adopted and updated lists of sites subject to Site Guidelines for visitors ("Site Guidelines");

Believing that Site Guidelines enhance the provisions set out in the Guidance for those organising and conducting tourism and non-governmental activities in the Antarctic annexed to Recommendation XVIII-1 (1994);

Confirming that the term "visitors" does not include scientists conducting research within such sites, or individuals engaged in official governmental activities;

Noting that Site Guidelines have been developed based on the current levels and types of visits at each specific site, and aware that Site Guidelines would require review if there were any significant changes to the levels or types of visits to a site;

Believing that the Site Guidelines for each site must be reviewed and revised promptly in response to changes in the levels and types of visits, or in response to any demonstrable or likely environmental impacts;

Desiring to keep the list of sites subject to Site Guidelines and the Site Guidelines up to date;

Recommend to their Governments that:

1. Astrolabe Island; Georges Point, Rongé Island; and Portal Point be added to the list of sites subject to Site Guidelines annexed to this Resolution, and that the Site Guidelines for those sites, as adopted by the Antarctic Treaty Consultative Meeting, be added to the Site Guidelines;

2. the Secretariat of the Antarctic Treaty ("the Secretariat") update its website accordingly;

3. their Governments urge all potential visitors to ensure that they are fully conversant with and adhere to the relevant Site Guidelines; and

4. the Secretariat post the text of Resolution 2 (2016) on its website in such a way that makes clear that it is no longer current.

List of sites subject to Site Guidelines

Site Guidelines	First Adopted	Latest Version
1. Penguin Island (Lat. 62° 06' S, Long. 57° 54' W)	2005	2005
2. Barrientos Island - Aitcho Islands (Lat. 62° 24' S, Long. 59° 47' W)	2005	2013
3. Cuverville Island (Lat. 64° 41' S, Long. 62° 38' W)	2005	2013
4. Jougla Point (Lat. 64° 49' S, Long. 63° 30' W)	2005	2013
5. Goudier Island, Port Lockroy (Lat. 64° 49' S, Long. 63° 29' W)	2006	2006
6. Hannah Point (Lat. 62° 39' S, Long. 60° 37' W)	2006	2013
7. Neko Harbour (Lat. 64° 50' S, Long. 62° 33' W)	2006	2013
8. Paulet Island (Lat. 63° 35' S, Long. 55° 47' W)	2006	2018
9. Petermann Island (Lat. 65° 10' S, Long. 64° 10' W)	2006	2013
10. Pleneau Island (Lat. 65° 06' S, Long. 64° 04' W)	2006	2013
11. Turret Point (Lat. 62° 05' S, Long. 57° 55' W)	2006	2006
12. Yankee Harbour (Lat. 62° 32' S, Long. 59° 47' W)	2006	2013
13. Brown Bluff, Tabarin Peninsula (Lat. 63° 32' S, Long. 56° 55' W)	2007	2018
14. Snow Hill (Lat. 64° 22' S, Long. 56° 59' W)	2007	2007
15. Shingle Cove, Coronation Island (Lat. 60° 39' S, Long. 45° 34' W)	2008	2008
16. Devil Island, Vega Island (Lat. 63° 48' S, Long. 57° 16.7' W)	2008	2018
17. Whalers Bay, Deception Island, South Shetland Islands (Lat. 62° 59' S, Long. 60° 34' W)	2008	2018
18. Half Moon Island, South Shetland Islands (Lat. 60° 36' S, Long. 59° 55' W)	2008	2018
19. Baily Head, Deception Island, South Shetland Islands (Lat. 62° 58' S, Long. 60° 30' W)	2009	2013
20. Telefon Bay, Deception Island, South Shetland Islands (Lat. 62° 55' S, Long. 60° 40' W)	2009	2018
21. Cape Royds, Ross Island (Lat. 77° 33' 10.7" S, Long. 166° 10' 6.5" E)	2009	2009
22. Wordie House, Winter Island, Argentine Islands (Lat. 65° 15' S, Long. 64° 16' W)	2009	2009
23. Stonington Island, Marguerite Bay, Antarctic Peninsula (Lat. 68° 11' S, Long. 67° 00' W)	2009	2009
24. Horseshoe Island, Antarctic Peninsula (Lat. 67° 49' S, Long. 67° 18' W)	2009	2014
25. Detaille Island, Antarctic Peninsula (Lat. 66° 52' S, Long. 66° 48' W)	2009	2009
26. Torgersen Island, Arthur Harbour, Southwest Anvers Island (Lat. 64° 46' S, Long. 64° 04' W)	2010	2013
27. Danco Island, Errera Channel, Antarctic Peninsula (Lat. 64° 43' S, Long. 62° 36' W)	2010	2013
28. Seabee Hook, Cape Hallett, Northern Victoria Land, Ross Sea, Visitor Site A and Visitor Site B (Lat. 72° 19' S, Long. 170° 13' E)	2010	2010
29. Damoy Point, Wiencke Island, Antarctic Peninsula (Lat. 64° 49' S, Long. 63° 31' W)	2010	2013

Site Guidelines	First Adopted	Latest Version
30. Taylor Valley Visitor Zone, Southern Victoria Land (Lat. 77° 37.59' S, Long. 163° 03.42' E)	2011	2011
31. North-east beach of Ardley Island (Lat. 62° 13' S; Long. 58° 54' W)	2011	2011
32. Mawson's Huts and Cape Denison, East Antarctica (Lat. 67° 01' S; Long. 142 ° 40' E)	2011	2014
33. D'Hainaut Island, Mikkelsen Harbour, Trinity Island (Lat. 63° 54' S, Long. 60° 47' W)	2012	2012
34. Port Charcot, Booth Island (Lat. 65° 04'S, Long. 64° 02'W)	2012	2012
35. Pendulum Cove, Deception Island, South Shetland Islands (Lat. 62°56'S, Long. 60°36' W)	2012	2018
36. Orne Harbour, Southern arm of Orne Harbour, Gerlache Strait (Lat. 64° 38'S, Long. 62° 33'W)	2013	2013
37. Orne Islands, Gerlache Strait (Lat. 64° 40'S, Long. 62° 40'W)	2013	2013
38. Point Wild, Elephant Island (Lat. 61° 6'S, Long. 54°52'W)	2016	2016
39. Yalour Islands, Wilhelm Archipelago (Lat. 65° 14'S, 64°10'W)	2016	2016
40. Astrolabe Island (Lat. 63° 28'S, Long. 58° 77'W)	2018	2018
41. Georges Point, Rongé Island (Lat. 64° 67'S, Long. 62° 67'W)	2018	2018
42. Portal Point (Lat. 64° 30'S, Long. 61° 46'W)	2018	2018

Guidelines for the assessment and management of Heritage in Antarctica

The Representatives,

Recalling the requirement in Annex III to the Protocol on Environmental Protection to the Antarctic Treaty ("the Protocol") to clean up past and present waste disposal sites on land and abandoned work sites of Antarctic activities;

Recalling furthermore that Article 8 of Annex V to the Protocol provides for sites or monuments of recognised historic value to be listed as Historic Sites and Monuments ("HSM"), which shall not be damaged, removed or destroyed;

Recalling also Measure 3 (2003), which revised and updated the *List of Historic Sites and Monuments* ("the List"), and subsequent Measures which have added further HSM to the List;

Recalling further Resolution 3 (2009), which recommended that the *Guidelines for the designation and protection of Historic Sites and Monuments* be used by Parties as guidance on questions related to the designation, protection and preservation of historic sites, monuments, artefacts and other historic remains in Antarctica;

Desiring to ensure that the process for designating HSM advances identification and protection of the recognised historic values of Antarctica;

Noting the importance of consistency in the listing of HSM, the need to appropriately balance environmental protection and heritage conservation considerations in the management of HSM and the value of taking into account the growing expertise in the management of Antarctic heritage values;

Recommend that their Governments that the non-mandatory *Guidelines for the assessment and management of Heritage in Antarctica* annexed to this Resolution be used by Parties as additional guidance on questions related to the assessment and management of sites/objects with heritage values in Antarctica.

Guidelines for the assessment and management of Heritage in Antarctica

1. Introduction

The aim of this document is to provide Parties with some guidance and support in the process of assessing and determining whether a site/object should be managed as heritage, including whether it merits Historic Site and Monument (HSM) listing, both in the context of Annex V and Annex III to the Protocol on Environmental Protection to the Antarctic Treaty (Environment Protocol). Furthermore, it aims to provide guidance as how the heritage site/object can best be managed once a conclusion has been reached. The guidance is non-mandatory, but provides points to consider when a Party or Parties begin to consider HSM listing or other methods of protection for a particular object or site.

The guidance seeks to assist the Committee for Environmental Protection (CEP) and Parties in reaching the following overarching vision:

To recognise, manage, conserve and promote Antarctic heritage for the benefit of current and future generations.

These guidelines take into account that it is essential that the needs of protecting the Antarctic environment, as set out in the Environment Protocol, are appropriately balanced with the desire to protect important heritage sites and objects.

Article 8 of Annex V to the Environment Protocol provides that any sites or monuments of recognised historic value can be proposed for listing as a Historic Site and Monument (HSM), which shall not be damaged, removed or destroyed.

Resolution 3 (2009) contains *Guidelines for the designation and protection of Historic Sites and Monuments*, and provides guidance to Parties on questions related to the designation, protection and preservation of historic sites, monuments, artefacts and other historic remains in Antarctica. These guidelines provide further guidance as to the implementation of Resolution 3 (2009).

The CEP must consider all HSM proposals, which ultimately must be agreed by the Antarctic Treaty Consultative Parties at an Antarctic Treaty Consultative Meeting (ATCM). No further measures are required or specified in the Environment Protocol or through measures adopted by the Antarctic Treaty Parties. The current document does however provide guidance as to potential and relevant management efforts for a heritage site or object, whether listed as HSM or maintained as a general site or object of historic interest.

This document should be regarded as guidance only, to aid in ensuring that all relevant aspects have been considered appropriately and sufficiently in the process leading up to the decision whether to propose an object or site as an HSM or not. Sites, including any objects they contain, considered for HSM listing will have different qualities, past, current or future pressures and management challenges associated with them, and the specific circumstances will need to be taken into account in any listing process.

In addition to the guidance provided to the proponent(s), it is the long-term aim that this document will contribute a degree of consistency within and comparability between assessment processes (while recognising that each potential HSM will have its own requirements and dynamics), and ensure that the process is sufficiently documented for future reference.

The following materials are relevant reference and framework documents for these guidelines:

- Annex V to the Environment Protocol (specifically Article 8);
- Annex III to the Environment Protocol;
- Resolution 3 (2009) on *Guidelines for the designation and protection of Historic Sites and Monuments;*
- Resolution 5 (2001) on handling of pre-1958 historic remains; and Resolution 5 (2011) providing a revised Guide to the presentation of Working Papers containing proposals for Antarctic Specially Protected Areas, Antarctic Specially Managed Areas or Historic Sites and Monuments;
- Current list of Historic Sites and Monuments: *http://ats.aq/documents/recatt/ att596_e.pdf*
- Annex I to the Environment Protocol

An overview of other relevant background material and documents is included in Chapter 11.

2. Aim of guidelines

These guidelines constitute an element in the CEP's effort to reach the overarching vision of *recognizing, managing, conserving and promoting Antarctic heritage for the benefit of current and future generations.*

The aim of the material contained in these guidelines is to assist both those making an initial assessment of a potential heritage site/object, both in the context of Annex III and Annex V, and the CEP in evaluating submissions/proposals for new HSMs. The twin objectives of the guidance are:

- Objective 1: Provide guidance to decide whether a site/object should be managed as heritage, including whether it merits/requires /needs HSM listing.
- Objective 2: Provide guidance as to management options for HSMs and other heritage sites/objects.

Figure 1 provides an overview of the process described in this document, consisting of the following steps:

1. Consider whether an object/site has heritage value as specified in Resolution 3 (2009);[1]

2. Determine whether to list as HSM, preserve *ex situ* or plan for retaining for different reasons/removing;

3. All sites/objects listed as HSMs, should consider options for management, including additional protection through Treaty system mechanisms;

4. For listed HSMs and site/objects with other heritage values including any preserved *ex situ*, consider appropriate outreach/dissemination activities.

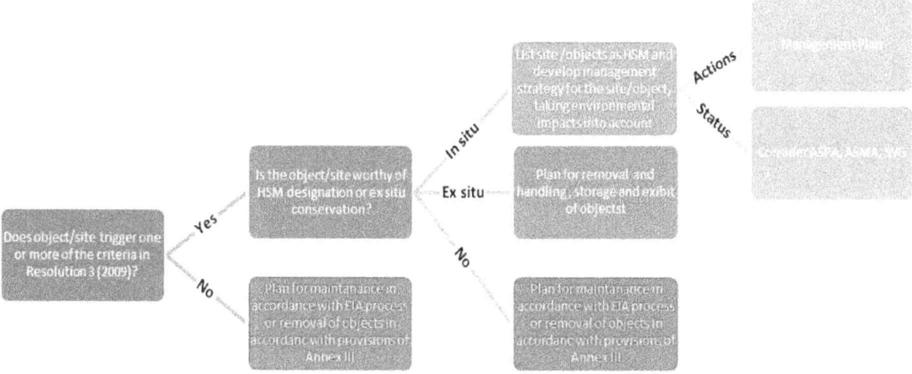

Figure 1

3. Heritage and historic values in the Antarctic context

Humans' presence in Antarctica is, seen in the global context, extremely short. Since the first sighting of the continent in 1820, the extent to which humans have left their mark here is relatively limited. In such a context, the limited historical evidence of a connection between man and land becomes extremely visible and special.

Parties gave full recognition to the historic sites, structures and objects as part of humankind's cultural heritage already at the first Antarctic Treaty Consultative Meeting in 1961.

The Environment Protocol makes the Historic Sites and Monuments (HSM) list[2] the key mechanism for the protection of historic values in Antarctica. The Environment Protocol provisions state that sites and monuments on the HSM list are to be protected from damage, removal or destruction.

---

[1] This document touches on the principles of considering heritage values, but does not attempt to provide full and comprehensive guidance to this complex and nationally/culturally framed issue.

[2] The HSM list was first introduced and agreed to at the fifth Antarctic Treaty Consultative Meeting (ATCM) in 1968-

Resolution 3 (2009) provides Parties with more detailed guidance on designation, protection and preservation of HSMs. Section 4.2 provides a further description and consideration of these guidelines. Resolution 3 (2009) remains key for determining whether a site meets the criteria for being listed an HSM.

In addition, Resolution 5 (2001) provides Parties with a mechanism for interim protection of pre-1958 historic artefacts/sites until they have had due time to consider their inclusion into HSM list.

The terms "site" and "monument" are fundamental terms in the framework provided by the Environment Protocol. These terms depend largely on national contexts and national legal frameworks, but the following basic definitions and descriptions, drawn on definitions supplied by the ICOMOS International Polar Heritage Committee (IPHC), are relevant to inform our understanding:

- **Site**: the setting in which a monument(s) occur(s) or where artefact(s) are located and which is directly related to the monument(s) or the artefact(s).

- **Object and artefacts**: Every item that is taken to Antarctica is an 'object' (a neutral term), but it may be formally ascribed with significance as an 'artefact' which gives it a heritage value.

- **Monument**: all standing structures over the ground that have cultural heritage values.

- **Memorials or commemorative objects**: Memorials are established with the aim of ascribing significance to people, events or cultural traditions and include endeavours associated with achievement, loss and sacrifice. Memorials range from plaques and artworks to philanthropic trusts, which fund ongoing research. They may also be associated with a research institute, community facility or religious structure. An existing artefact or structure can be ascribed memorial status.

4. Determining and assessing heritage and historical values

4.1. Determining whether an object or site has heritage value as specified in Resolution 3 (2009)

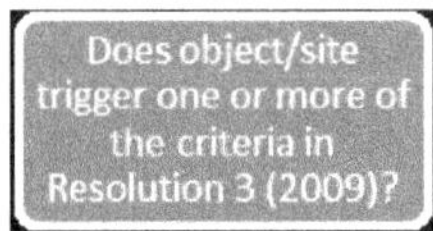

Figure 2

Ahead of assessing any object/site for HSM listing it is assumed that the proposing Party will have made a preliminary assessment to determine whether an object or site has potential heritage value, and should thus be further considered in line with guidance provided in this document, or whether it is simply material with no heritage value remaining from past activities that therefore requires removal from Antarctica in accordance with Annex III to the Environment Protocol.

In many cases this will be obvious, with a clear difference between objects/sites that should be considered worthy of management as heritage versus what can essentially be considered waste. It is to be assumed that the vast majority of objects present in Antarctica should fall under the latter, and thus be removed when their utility in Antarctica has expired.

In a small number of cases the object or site may have heritage value, connoting a product, place, or such that evokes a nostalgic sense of tradition or history, informing us about the past in general terms, and providing tangible evidence of the continuity between past, present, and future.

In making such a preliminary assessment, the process would greatly benefit by drawing on appropriate expertise and stakeholder engagement. See Chapter 11 for information about potential relevant expert resources.

If it is determined that the object/site merits further consideration then Parties should look to Article 8 of Annex V to the Environment Protocol, which very broadly identifies "recognised historic value" as the criterion for listing an HSM. However, Parties have agreed that an object or site having a "recognised historic value" should meet at least one of the criteria[3] listed in Annex to Resolution 3 (2009). The criteria listed in Resolution 3 (2009) are further described and explored below in order to provide guidance in the assessment process. For heritage dating before 1958, Resolution 5 (2001) should be noted and considered.

If the assessment process determines that an object/site does not require consideration for further protection, then these objects should be considered and handled in light of the clean-up provisions of Annex III to the Environment Protocol and supporting documents such as the Antarctic Clean-up Manual (adopted through Resolution 2 [2013]).

4.2. Guidance to the evaluation criteria contained in Resolution 3 (2009)

The ATCM has, through Resolution 3 (2009), adopted a set of criteria, which provide an indication as to whether an object or site has a "recognised historic value." These are described and explored here in order to aid Parties in their assessment process.

1. A particular event of importance in the history of science or exploration of Antarctica

Determining the importance of an event in history is both difficult and to a certain degree controversial due to the subjective nature of the issue. As a starting point, one should note that events could be considered those points in history when an act, decision or natural phenomenon altered or informed the direction of a community's evolution, in this case the human occupation of Antarctica being the community evolution. Events are typically not spread over a long time – they are rather sharp and discrete moments. To guide assessment against this criterion it is relevant to consider the following:

- Can the event be defined as a single, discrete event that can also be seen as the inaugural moment of events and activities that follow – and that can be seen as describing the history of that particular theme?

[3] Cf. Annex to Resolution 3 (2009): *Guidelines for the designation and protection of Historic Sites and Monuments.*

- Does this event have relevance for many people or nations?
- Can the event be connected to a specific site or place?

Historic Site and Monument No. 80 (Amundsen's Tent) is an example from the current list of HSMs that trigger this "event" criterion.

2. A particular association with a person who played an important role in the history of science or exploration in Antarctica

Individuals of historical significance can typically be either those whose life's work helped define and guide the course of Antarctic history or those whose lives stand as examples for the community. To guide assessment against this criterion it is relevant to consider the following:

- Did the person make, invent or devise an idea or product that was and has continued to be used in the Antarctic context (and possibly outside) that had an impact on the evolution of Antarctica?
- Can the person be said to be representative of an Antarctic activity?

In doing the assessment, the following should also be considered:

- The length of the person or group's influence on/in the Antarctic context.
- The number of people or nation having a connection to the activities of the individual or group.
- Connections to extant site, that is, are there major extant site connections that still exist where the person lived and worked, or is the person buried at an Antarctic site?

Historic Site and Monument No. 3 (Mawson's Rock Cairn) is an example from the current list of HSMs that trigger this "person" criterion.

3. A particular association with a notable feat of endurance or achievement

This criterion is similar in nature to criterion 1 and the same factors should be considered, although firmly in the context of a notable feat of endurance:

- Feat: an achievement that requires great courage, skill, or strength
- Endurance: the ability to endure an unpleasant or difficult process or situation without giving way

Historic Site and Monument No. 53 (Endurance Memorial Site) is an example from the current list of HSMs that trigger this "feat" criterion.

4. Representative of, or forms part of, some wide-ranging activity that has been important in the development and knowledge of Antarctica

This criterion is similar in nature to criterion 2 and the same factors should be considered, although firmly in the context of increasing knowledge about Antarctica or the wider world. This could for example be a site/object linked to or representative of a particular scientific discovery.

Historic Site and Monument No. 42 (Scotia Bay huts) is an example from the current list of HSMs that trigger this "activity" criterion.

5. Particular technical, historical, cultural or architectural value in its materials, design or method of construction

This criterion aims to consider whether the place or object demonstrates innovative or important methods of construction or design, whether it contains unusual construction materials, is an early example of the use of a particular construction technique or has the potential to contribute information about technological or engineering history. Questions that can help clarify and inform assessments in this regard include:

- Is the place significant because of its design, form, scale, materials, style, ornamentation, period, craftsmanship or other architectural element?

- Does the place demonstrate innovative or important methods of construction or design, does it contain unusual construction materials, is it an early example of the use of a particular construction technique, or does it have the potential to contribute information about technological or engineering history?

- Does the place have integrity, retaining significant features from its time of construction, or later periods when important modifications or additions were carried out?

- Is the site or area a good example of its class, for example, in terms of design, type, features, use, technology or time period?

Historic Site and Monument No. 83 (Base "W", Detaille Island, Lallemand Fjord, Loubet Coast) is an example from the current list of HSMs that trigger this "construction" criterion.

6. Potential, through study, to reveal information or has the potential to educate people about significant human activities in Antarctica

Artefacts and sites can offer an insight into technological processes, economic development and social structure, etc, and thereby provide a broader understanding of both the times that were as well as the present:

- Does the area or place (where the artefact/s is/are located) have the potential to provide scientific information about the history of Antarctica?

- Is the object/site of high real or potential interest to scholars and/or archaeologists?

- Does the object/site hold the potential for new scholarship in a field of study?

- Does the object/site have the potential to make a significant and lasting contribution to a field of study?

- Could the place contribute, through public education, to people's awareness, understanding and appreciation of Antarctica, including exploration and scientific achievement?

Historic Site and Monument No. 4 (Pole of Inaccessibility Station building) is an example from the current list of HSMs that trigger this "study" criterion.

7. Symbolic or commemorative value for people of many nations

With all the other criteria discussed above in mind it is useful to consider the extent to which the values identified are most relevant to the broader Antarctic community. As mentioned above the importance of national heritage should be evaluated in the context of broader significance, considering its importance in the wider history of humankind's activities in Antarctica and/or relevance to several nation states.

Historic Site and Monument No. 82 (Antarctic Treaty Monument) is an example from the current list of HSMs that trigger this "symbolic for many" criterion.

4.3. Determining whether values merit Historic Site and Monument Listing

Having assessed the various heritage values attached to the site/object against the criteria set out in Resolution 3 (2009) the proponents will have a clear view on whether the site/object should be conserved.

If it is not clear whether it should be conserved then parties responsible for the site/object will need to consider whether it should i) be maintained in Antarctica for a different purpose with the environmental impacts of doing so appropriately assessed; or ii) removed from the continent under the terms of Annex III.

Where it is determined that the site/object should be conserved the next step is to consider whether to seek HSM listing for protection *in situ* in Antarctica or whether is more suited to being preserved *ex situ*.

5. Consider *in situ* or *ex situ* conservation

5.1. *In situ* vs. *ex situ* preservation

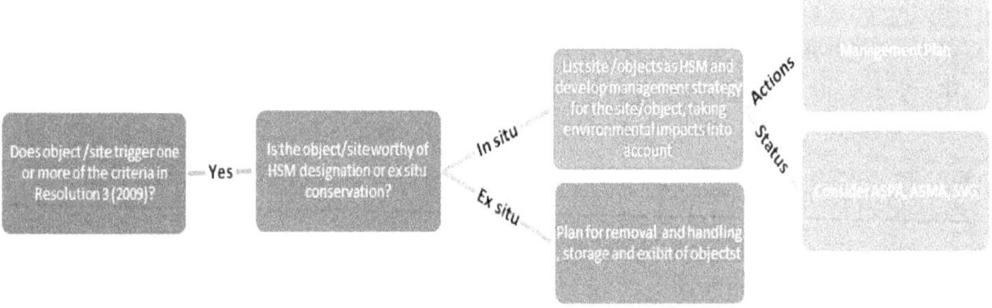

Figure 3

When it has been determined that an object or site has heritage and/or historic value it is time to consider appropriate approaches and needs for protection. First in line in this regard is to consider whether the value is best maintained by leaving it in place in Antarctica or by moving it or by other means maintain the value outside of Antarctica.

The potential environmental impacts must be considered appropriately both when assessing whether to maintain the object *in situ* and when to maintain *ex situ*, this to ensure that the environmental principles set out in Article 3 (2) of the Environment Protocol are respected. It may often be appropriate to do so through an environmental impact assessment (EIA) process as set out in Article 8 (and Annex I) of the Environment Protocol. See "Section 12 – Resources" for examples of EIAs related to HSMs.

Most often it is natural to maintain any fixed objects (such as infrastructure) associated with the site *in situ*, although in some instances it may be more appropriate and relevant to remove and restructure such objects *ex situ* (for example by relocating to a museum).

Any movable objects, on the other hand, can be maintained both *in situ* and *ex situ*. There can be both advantages and disadvantages to both approaches.

- *Relevance to the setting*: The object can best/only be understood and appreciated in full in its original setting (e.g. coldness, isolation, and wilderness).

- *Local interest and enthusiasm for protection*: Heritage belonging to or 'adopted' by a local population (i.e. a nearby Station) will normally be adequately cared for.

- *Long-term maintenance expenditure and resource usage*: Although there could be short term saving of resources by not moving the object, adequate maintenance over time will normally be costly (logistics and conservation resources).

- *A smaller audience*: The visitation potential for sites and objects in remote locations will never match more central locations.

- *Local interest (and therefore care) may be less than interest shown from outside*: No or limited number of people in the area will make heritage maintenance dependent on continued high interest from temporary populations.

Considerations that may guide a decision as to whether *ex situ* conservation or *in situ* protection of fixed and movable objects would be most appropriate include:

- *Ex situ* conservation may be relevant and appropriate if the objects are at risk from natural degradation processes.

- *Ex situ* conservation may be relevant and appropriate if it is obvious that it will be too costly or difficult to maintain the objects *in situ* over time.

- An assessment of how important it is that the object can be seen and appreciated by a large number of people could be useful in considering *ex situ* vs. *in situ*.

- *Ex situ* conservation may be relevant and appropriate if the objects are located in a particularly sensitive environment where protection of this environment may be a higher priority. Preserving *in situ* may be relevant and appropriate if there is a high risk of damage were objects to be removed.

- The ability (logistically and financially) to maintain objects *in situ* will have bearings on the decision.

- If an object cannot be portrayed appropriately in a contextual setting and the object loses its value by being removed from its surroundings, it may be more appropriate to consider protection *in situ* rather than removal for *ex situ* conservation.

- If it has been shown through an appropriate assessment that the existing suite of Antarctic HSMs already adequately covers the value of the object in question, it may be useful to consider *ex situ*. However, if the object/site is considered representative (e.g. examples of an important class of significant items) or rare (unusual aspect of Antarctic history or heritage), where no similar object/site is listed, it may be more appropriate to consider *in situ* maintenance.

In cases where highly important heritage objects are in danger, copies may be made while the original is inaccessible. A foreign *ex situ* setting may be partly alleviated by using various effects to give an impression of the original setting.

Removal of objects for *ex situ* conservation should only occur after having consulted and agreed with all Parties that have or may have a connection to or interest in the object at hand, as well as on basis of assessment and advice from heritage expertise. This is particularly important as legal and other related issues may arise in terms of the origin or ownership of an object or artefact.

5.2. Documentation

If it is determined that *ex situ* conservation may be most appropriate, a thorough documentation of the site is advisable for it to be available in archive form. Rigorous documentation provides a means by which scholars and the public comprehend a site that has since changed radically or disappeared.

New technologies have opened up new opportunities in the process of documenting historic heritage. Filming, 3D scanning, photography, interviews and storage of archival records are all accepted recording methods.

With modern technology it is possible to create virtual realities, used *inter alia* to avoid impacts or to provide "access" to remote and inaccessible sites.

6. Historic Site or Monument Listing

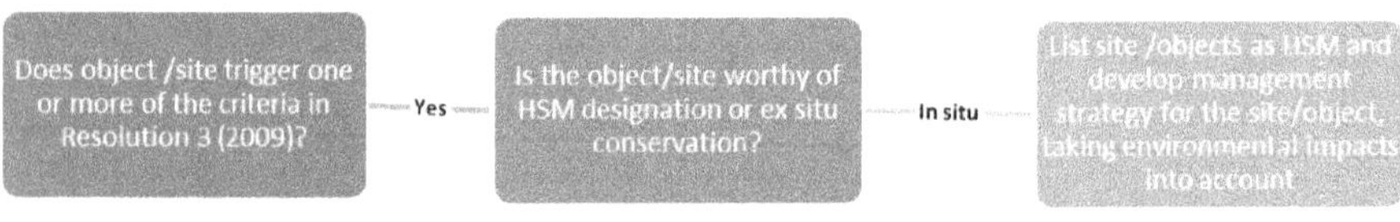

Figure 4

Once a site/object has been determined to trigger one or more of the criteria of Resolution 3 (2009) a decision must be made as to whether the object should be managed as a heritage value associated with national operations or whether it merits listing as a HSM. The strength of the value (against the HSM criteria in Resolution 3 [2009]) will likely have provided substantial basis for making this decision. Some details regarding how the assessment and potential listing process is achieved are provided below.

Article 8 (2) of Annex V to the Environment Protocol stipulates that any Party may propose a site or monument of recognised historic value for listing as a HSM, to be approved by the ATCM.

The following steps are useful to follow to determine and propose an object or site as an HSM:

- **Step 1**: Assess site/object – cf. Section 3 and 4.

- **Step 2**: Decide whether HSM listing is appropriate.

- **Step 3**: Consult with Parties with an interest in the site/object in question in accordance with Resolution 4 (1996) and reiterated in Resolution 3 (2009), which stipulates that during the preparations for the Listing of a HSM, adequate liaison is accorded by the proposing Party with the originator of the HSM and other Parties, as appropriate.

- **Step 4**: In cooperation with interested Parties, develop management framework.

- **Step 5**: Prepare and submit proposal to the CEP. The following information should be included in the proposal in a format that can be easily moved into the formal HSM list:[4]

  Introduction

  - *HSM name*

  - *Original proposing Party:* List proponent(s)

  - *Party undertaking management:* Name the country/countries which are committed to following-up (with management approach specified for the object/site)

  - *Type:* Building (hut, station, other building remains etc.), site, other remains (expedition cairn, tent, lighthouse, etc.) or monument/commemorative (plaque, bust)

  Description and documentation of the site

  - *Site Location*: Provide both place name and coordinates (where known) relevant for site/object. Describe materials, construction, function, use. Physical Features & Local/cultural landscape. Provide pictures showing the site, monument and the location in the surroundings.

  Historical / Cultural features

  - *Description of the historical context*: Overview of the site in question. It would be useful if the information also clearly indicates which primary evaluation criteria contained in Resolution 3 (2009) the object/site in question triggers.

---

[4] The items here listed are in large part based on requirements contained in Resolution 3 (2009).

Management

- *Describe management and/or monitoring actions planned for the object/site in question – cf. Section 6 and 7, as well as pt. 5 in Annex to Resolution 3 (2009)*, as well as measures, which will be taken to limit any environmental impacts that the management of the HSM may cause.

- **Step 6**: In cooperation with interested Parties, implement management framework (cf. Section 7).

7. Determining management actions for an HSM

7.1. Methods of management

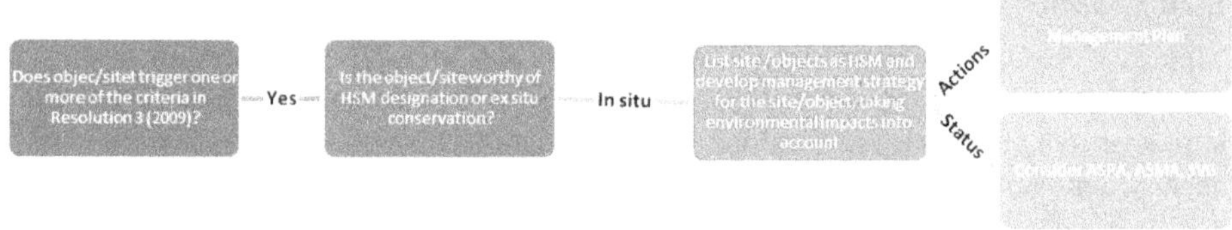

Figure 5

Once it has been determined that an object or site should be maintained *in situ* as an HSM, an assessment of its particular challenges and sensitivities is advisable, along with consideration of the options available for its management. In considering management approaches, it is also necessary to take into account the requirements of Annex I related to EIA as well as monitoring and mitigation measures. These elements are relevant as basis a for the development of any management and/or conservation plan for the object or site.

"Minimal intervention" is an overarching aim in global heritage conservation. The decision that has to be made with regard to the site or object in question is whether a non-intervention approach or active management (some intervention) is to be the guiding light, balancing the need to protect the HSM with the environmental protection principles of the Environment Protocol.

In certain instances, it may be appropriate to allow a site, even though recognised as an important site, to be managed according to the principle of controlled deterioration, which is allowing natural decay to proceed with only limited protection. However, health, safety and environmental considerations usually make this impractical and some minimal maintenance is usually required in order to ensure a site is not dangerous for either humans or wildlife.

Active management involves people managing change to a significant place in its setting, in ways that sustain, reveal or reinforce its cultural and natural heritage values. Conservation is not limited to physical intervention, for it includes such activities as the interpretation and sustainable use of places. It may simply involve maintaining the status quo, intervening only as necessary to counter the effects of growth and decay, but equally may be achieved through major interventions; it can be active as well as reactive. Change to a significant place is inevitable, if only as a result of the passage of time, but can be neutral or beneficial in its effect on heritage values. It is only harmful if (and to the extent that) significance is eroded.

Issues to consider when determining what level and type of management action is required and desired include the following:

- Identification of the current use of the object and site and consideration of any need for an appropriate change of use;

- The condition of the object and any need for repair: Repair is work beyond the scope of normal maintenance, to remedy defects caused by decay, damage or use, and is normally carried out to sustain the significance of the building or place. Repairs should normally be done with minimal or no changes to the original fabric of the structure and in like materials, and if possible using the same methods as first created. Such work would greatly benefit by drawing on appropriate expertise.

- Actions needed to conserve or restore the object: Restoration indicates bringing an object back to a former position or condition. Focusing on conservation, the absolute maximum amount of the original material, in as unaltered a condition as possible, is preserved. Any repairs or additions must not remove, alter or permanently bond/cross-link to any original material. Such work would greatly benefit by drawing on appropriate expertise.

- Potential impacts on the environment that may arise from the deterioration of the object.

- Servicing needs.

- The costs of the various recommended measures.

- The likely resources available for the asset, both immediately and in the future.

- Education and outreach. Note, further guidance and examples provided in Section 9.

7.2. Supplementary management approaches

When considering how best to manage/maintain a site/object of historic heritage value there are a number of formal approaches that could be considered, some of which have formal status within the Treaty system and which afford various degrees of protection.

7.2.1. Management plans

A management plan can provide a useful guiding document for the conservation and management of a heritage site or object. Through such a plan it will be possible to identify what policies are required to ensure the heritage values of the site/object are retained in its future use and development. A management plan will also provide an important framework for ensuring that the management of the heritage site or object has the least possible impacts on the environment. Each plan will vary and will need to be tailored to each site/object, based on the type and size of its place, heritage attributes and needs. A conservation management plan provides guidance in managing change in the heritage site or object without compromising the heritage significance of its place.

7.2.2. Site Guidelines for Visitors (SGV)

The Antarctic Treaty Parties have since 2005 developed and utilised Site Guidelines for Visitors as a management tool. The aim of the guidelines is to provide specific instructions on the conduct of activities at the most frequently visited Antarctic sites. This includes practical guidance for tour operators and guides on how they should conduct visits in those sites, taking into account their environmental values and sensitivities. SGV are developed based on the current levels and types of visits at each specific site, and such SGV would require review if there were any significant changes to the levels or types of visits to a site. Heritage and historic values at highly visited areas may benefit from the development of specific SGVs, whether formally adopted as HSMs or not, and in this manner guide visitors' activities in this area to reduce potential for negative impact, damage and destruction.

Relevant examples of such SGV include:

- SGV No. 8: Paulet Island[5]
- SGV No. 14: Snow Hill[6]
- SGV No. 17: Whalers Bay[7]

7.2.3. Antarctic Specially Protected Areas (ASPA)

Article 3 (1) of Annex V to the Environment Protocol specifies that any area may be designated as an ASPA to protect *inter alia* outstanding historic values. According to Article 8 of Annex V sites or monuments that are designated as ASPAs shall also be listed as HSMs. Managing the site as an ASPA would give added value through the development and adoption of a formal management plan for the area, as well as requiring permits for entry into the area. Such a management approach may be particularly useful in situations where it is important to regulate, limit or control visitor pressure.

Guidance material is already available for the designation process for ASPAs:

- ASPA No. 155: Cape Evans, Ross Island[8]
- ASPA No. 158: Hut Point, Ross Island[9]
- ASPA No. 162: Mawson's Huts, Cape Denison, Commonwealth Bay, George V Land, East Antarctica[10]

---

[5] *https://www.ats.aq/devAS/ats_other_template.aspx?lang=e&id=c0ed3255-ee8c-4839-b1d5-e105957f7c74*
[6] *https://www.ats.aq/devAS/ats_other_template.aspx?lang=e&id=98fdfcd3-4883-49d6-9ef1-b60f2d1e005d*
[7] *https://www.ats.aq/devAS/ats_other_template.aspx?lang=e&id=e36c1a8f-3ae7-4187-9b24-194c8cf5e780*
[8] *http://www.ats.aq/documents/recatt/att572_e.pdf*
[9] *http://www.ats.aq/documents/recatt/att574_e.pdf*
[10] *http://www.ats.aq/documents/recatt/att549_e.pdf*

7.2.4. Antarctic Specially Managed Areas (ASMA)

Article 3 (1) in Annex V to the Environment Protocol specifies that any area may be designated as an ASMA to protect *inter alia* outstanding historic values. According to Article 8 of Annex V sites or monuments which are designated as ASMAs shall also be listed as HSMs. Managing the site as an ASMA would give added value through the development and adoption of a formal management plan for the area. Such a management approach may be particularly useful in situations where there are a number of ongoing, potentially competing activities and interests, where coordination is required to ensure appropriate control of activities in order not to put the historic values of the area at risk.

Guidance material is already available for the designation process for ASMAs:

* ASMA No. 4: Deception Island[11]
* ASMA No. 5: Amundsen-Scott South Pole Station, South Pole[12]

8. Environmental Considerations

It is important to take environmental issues into account throughout the process for assessing a potential heritage site/object; indeed environmental considerations should be at the forefront of thinking on how to handle a site/object.

As noted, assessment of environmental impacts of actions and decisions taken are needed throughout the assessment process, and it is likely that the relevant member will find it necessary to complete an EIA at some point in the process. Not only is an EIA likely to be a formal requirement for many actions described in these guidelines but it can also be a useful tool.

Clearly the impact on wildlife (and the wider ecosystem) will need to be seriously considered under all scenarios. Clean up, which will be the primary outcome for most sites of human activity, and indeed *ex situ* preservation (which will require objects to be removed from a site) will both require careful environmental assessment and planning.

Meanwhile different conservation options will also require varying degrees of environmental assessment, with the option of natural decay for example needing particularly careful appraisal.

The decision on when and to what level an EIA is required will need to be determined on a case by case basis but this decision should be done in the context of the continual review of the environmental impacts.

When initiating and conducting an EIA process, reference should as appropriate be made to and guidance taken from Annex I of the Environment Protocol and the Guidelines for Environmental Impact Assessment in Antarctica (as adopted by Resolution 1 [2016]).

---

[11] *http://www.ats.aq/documents/recatt/Att512_e.pdf*
[12] *http://www.ats.aq/documents/recatt/Att357_e.pdf*

If and when an EIA has been completed as part of an assessment process leading to an HSM proposal, it would be helpful to the CEP if proponents were to reference the conclusions of the EIA in the Working Paper presenting the proposal for consideration by the CEP.

9. Education and outreach

Whatever the form of protection determined necessary for individual sites/objects it is essential that appropriate methods of outreach are considered. Given that only around 40,000 tourists currently visit Antarctica every year, it is clear that Antarctic heritage is not and will not be accessible to the wider public. While protecting heritage is important for its own sake, its value can diminish somewhat if it cannot be seen. This is partly why *ex situ* conservation in some instances should be given serious consideration, allowing people to view Antarctic heritage in a museum or some other form of public display. Likewise, this is also why *in situ* objects should form part of wider outreach and education process, considering that most people will not be able to experience the heritage on site. Many methods can be used to help alleviate the fact that not everyone can visit or see everything in person.

Some of the tools described in Chapter 5.2 make this process easier than it was in the past, with the details of HSMs now potentially available online to anyone who wishes to see them in the form of photos, video tours or digital maps, alongside more traditional approaches such as literature. It should also be possible to draw together records of the sites together with archival material and testimonials.

Proponents should consider building education and outreach into their management plans, making it an integral part of managing a heritage site/object. Parties should also consider outreach within their own countries, especially with children, to ensure the Antarctic heritage is shared and appreciated as widely as possible. Central to heritage management are ongoing outreach and education endeavours that inform and inspire the public about the values the specific Antarctic heritage carries with it. This enhancement is important when engaging the public with Antarctic heritage.

10. Terms/Acronyms

ATCM: Antarctic Treaty Consultative Meeting

CEP: Committee for Environmental Protection

HSM: Historic Site and Monument

Memorials or commemorative objects: Memorials are established with the aim of ascribing significance to people, events or cultural traditions and include endeavours associated with achievement, loss and sacrifice. Memorials range from plaques and artworks to philanthropic trusts, which fund ongoing research. They may also be associated with a research institute, community facility or religious structure. An existing artefact or structure can be ascribed memorial status.

Monument: all standing structures over the ground that have cultural heritage values.

Object and artefacts: Every item that is taken to Antarctica is an 'object' (a neutral term), but it may be formally ascribed with significance as an 'artefact' which gives it a heritage value.

Site: the setting in which a monument(s) occur(s) and which is directly related to the monuments.

11. References

11.1. ATCM decisions

* Resolution 4 (1996): *https://www.ats.aq/devAS/info_measures_listitem.aspx?lang=e&id=237*
* Resolution 3 (2009): *https://www.ats.aq/devAS/info_measures_listitem.aspx?lang=e&id=444*
* Measure 3 (2003): *https://www.ats.aq/devAS/info_measures_listitem.aspx?lang=e&id=296*
* Resolution 1 (2016): *https://www.ats.aq/documents/recatt/Att605_e.pdf*
* Resolution 2 (2013) Antarctic Clean-up Manual: *https://www.ats.aq/documents/recatt/att540_e.pdf*

11.2. ATCM/CEP Documents

* ATCM XXXIII WP 47 (Argentina): Proposal for the discussion of aspects related to the management of Historic Sites and Monuments
* ATCM XXXIV WP 27 (Argentina): Report of the Informal Discussions on Historic Sites and Monuments
* ATCM XXXV WP 46 (Argentina): Final Report of the Informal Discussions on Historic Sites and Monuments
* ATCM XXXIX WP 12 (UK): Managing Antarctic Heritage: British Historic Bases in the Antarctic Peninsula
* ATCM XXXIX WP 30 (Norway): Consideration of protection approaches for historic heritage in Antarctica
* ATCM XXXIII IP 22 (Argentina): Additional information for the discussion of aspects related to the management of Historic Sites and Monuments

12. Resources

12.1. Organizations

* International Council on Monuments and Sites (ICOMOS): *www.icomos.org/en*
    - ICOMOS Australia. Burra Charter, 2013. *http://australia.icomos.org/publications/burra-charter-practice-notes/*

- ICOMOS. The Nara Document on Authenticity, 1994. *https://www.icomos. org/charters/nara-e.pdf*

- ICOMOS. Xi'an Declaration, 2005. *https://www.icomos.org/xian2005/ xian-declaration.pdf*

- ICOMOS. Charter for the Protection and Management of Archaeological Heritage, 1990. *http://wp.icahm.icomos.org/wp-content/uploads/2017/01/1990-Lausanne-Charter-for-Protection-and-Management-of-Archaeological-Heritage.pdf*

- ICOMOS' International Polar Heritage Committee (IPHC)

   - ICOMOS: IPHC Statutes. *http://iphc.icomos.org/index.php/statutes/*

12.2. International agreements

- The UNESCO Convention on the Protection of the Underwater Cultural Heritage, 2001. *http://www.unesco.org/new/en/culture/themes/underwater-cultural-heritage/2001-convention/*

- The UNESCO Convention concerning the Protection of the World Cultural and Natural Heritage, 1972

12.3. General heritage literature

- Logan, W., M.C. Craith, and U. Kockel, eds. 2015. A Companion to Heritage Studies. Chichester. Wiley-Blackwell.

12.4. Case studies

- New Zealand. 2015. Ross Sea Heritage Restoration Project, Historic Huts at Cape Adare
- Russia. 2016. Restoration of the Buromsky Island Cemetery (HSM 9) within the programme of the Russian Antarctic Expedition activities.

12.5. Environmental Impact Assessments

- New Zealand. 2009. IEE. Removal of artefacts from historic sites in Antarctica for the purpose of restoration and protection.
- New Zealand. 2012. Initial Environmental Assessment Ross Sea Heritage Restoration

Revised Guide to the presentation of Working Papers containing proposals for Antarctic Specially Protected Areas, Antarctic Specially Managed Areas or Historic Sites and Monuments

The Representatives,

Noting that Annex V to the Protocol on Environmental Protection to the Antarctic Treaty provides for the Antarctic Treaty Consultative Meeting ("ATCM") to adopt proposals to designate an Antarctic Specially Protected Area ("ASPA") or an Antarctic Specially Managed Area ("ASMA"), to adopt or amend a Management Plan for such an area, or to designate an Historic Site and Monument ("HSM"), by a measure in accordance with Article IX(1) of the Antarctic Treaty;

Conscious of the need to ensure clarity concerning the current status of each ASPA and ASMA and its Management Plan, and each HSM;

Recalling Resolution 1 (2008), which recommended that the Guide to the presentation of Working Papers containing proposals for Antarctic Specially Protected Areas, Antarctic Specially Managed Areas or Historic Sites and Monuments ("the Guide"), annexed to it, be used by those engaged in the preparation of such Working Papers;

Recalling also Resolution 5 (2011), which updated the Guide to facilitate the collection of information to assist with the assessment and further development of the Antarctic protected areas system, and Resolution 5 (2016), which further updated the Guide to reflect further tools that could be used to identify protected areas within a systematic environmental-geographical framework;

Noting Resolution 2 (2018) which recommended the use of Guidelines for the assessment and management of Heritage in Antarctica, which provides guidance with regard to required information for the purpose of HSM-listings;

Desiring to update Template B of the Guide, to reflect the further guidance provided with regard to assessment of heritage in Antarctica;

Recommend to their Governments that:

1. the revised Guide to the presentation of Working Papers containing proposals for Antarctic Specially Protected Areas, Antarctic Specially Managed Areas or Historic Sites and Monuments annexed to this Resolution be used by those engaged in the preparation of such Working Papers; and

2. the Secretariat of the Antarctic Treaty post the text of Resolution 5 (2016) on its website in a way that makes clear that it is no longer current.

Guide to the presentation of Working Papers containing proposals for Antarctic Specially Protected Areas, Antarctic Specially Managed Areas or Historic Sites and Monuments

A. Working Papers on ASPA or ASMA

It is recommended that the Working Paper contain two parts:

(i)   a **COVER SHEET** explaining the intended effects of the proposal and the history of the ASPA/ASMA, using Template A as a guide. **This cover sheet will NOT form part of the Measure** adopted by the ATCM, so will not be published in the Final Report nor on the ATS website. Its sole purpose is to facilitate consideration of the proposal and the drafting of the Measures by the ATCM.

and

(ii)   a **MANAGEMENT PLAN,** written as a final version as it is intended to be published. **This will be annexed to the Measure and published** in the Final Report and on the ATS website.

It would be helpful if the plan is written *as final*, ready for publication. Of course, when it is first submitted to the CEP it is a draft and may be amended by the CEP or ATCM. However, the version adopted by the ATCM should be in final form for publication, and should not require further editing by the Secretariat, other than to insert cross-references to other instruments adopted at the same meeting.

For example, in its final form, the plan should not contain expressions such as:

- "this *proposed* area";
- "this *draft* plan";
- "this plan, *if adopted*, would…";
- accounts of discussions in the CEP or ATCM or details of intersessional work (unless this covers important information, *eg*, about the consultation process or activities that have occurred within the Area since the last review);
- views of individual delegations on the draft or intermediate versions of it;
- references to other protected areas using their pre-Annex V designations.

Please use the "Guide to the Preparation of Management Plans for Antarctic Specially Protected Areas" if the proposal concerns an ASPA. (The current version of this Guide is appended to Resolution 2 [2011] and is contained in the CEP Handbook.)

There are several high quality management plans, including that for ASPA No. 109: Moe Island, that could be used as a model for the preparation of new and revised plans.

B. Working Papers on Historic Sites and Monuments (HSM)

HSMs do not have management plans, unless they are also designated as ASPAs or ASMAs. All essential information about the HSM is included in the Measure. The rest of the Working Paper will not be annexed to the Measure; if it is desired to keep any additional background information on the record, this material may be annexed to the report of the CEP for inclusion in the Final Report of the ATCM. To ensure that all the information required for inclusion in the Measure is provided, it is recommended that Template B below is used as a guide when drafting the Working Paper.

C. The tabling of draft Measures on ASPA, ASMA and HSM to the ATCM

When a draft Measure to give effect to the advice of the CEP on an ASPA, ASMA or HSM is submitted to the Secretariat for tabling at the ATCM, the Secretariat is requested also to provide to the ATCM copies of the cover sheet from the original Working Paper setting out the proposal, subject to any revisions made by the CEP.

The sequence of events is as follows:

- A Working Paper consisting of a draft management plan and an explanatory cover sheet is prepared and submitted by the proponent;
- The Secretariat prepares a draft Measure before the ATCM;
- Draft Management Plan is discussed by CEP and any revisions made (by the proponent in liaison with the Secretariat);
- If CEP recommends adoption, the Management Plan (as agreed) plus the cover sheet (as agreed) are passed from the CEP Chair to the Chair of the Legal and Institutional Working Group;
- Legal and Institutional Working Group reviews the draft Measure;
- Secretariat formally tables the draft measure plus the agreed cover sheet;
- ATCM considers and makes decision.

TEMPLATE A: COVER SHEET FOR A WORKING PAPER ON AN ASPA OR ASMA

Please ensure that the following information is provided on the cover sheet:

1) Is a new ASPA proposed? Yes/No
2) Is a new ASMA proposed? Yes/No
3) Does the proposal relate to an existing ASPA or ASMA?

If so, list all Recommendations, Measures, Resolutions and Decisions pertaining to this ASPA/ASMA, including any previous designations of this area as an SPA, SSSI or other type of protected area:

In particular, please include the date and relevant Recommendation/Measure for the following:

- First designation:
- First adoption of management plan:
- Any revisions to management plan:
- Current management plan:
- Any extensions of expiry dates of management plan:
- Renaming and renumbering as ………….. by Decision 1 (2002).

(Note: this information may be found on the ATS website in the Documents database by searching under the name of the area. While the ATS has made every effort to ensure the completeness and accuracy of the information in the database, occasional errors or omissions may occur. The proponents of any revision to a protected area are best placed to know the history of that area, and are kindly requested to contact the Secretariat if they notice any apparent discrepancy between the regulatory history as they understand it and that displayed on the ATS database.)

4)   If the proposal contains a revision of an existing management plan, please indicate the types of amendment:

   (i)   Major or minor?

   (ii)   any changes to the boundaries or coordinates?

   (iii)   any changes to the maps? If yes, are the changes in the captions only or also in the graphics?

   (iv)   any change to the description of the area that is relevant to identifying its location or its boundaries?

   (v)   any changes that affect any other ASPA, ASMA or HSM within this area or adjacent to it? In particular, please explain any merger with, incorporation of or abolition of any existing area or site.

   (vi)   Other - brief summary of other types of changes, indicating the paragraphs of the management plan in which these are located (especially helpful if the plan is long).

5)   If a new ASPA or ASMA is proposed, does it contain any marine area? Yes/No

6)   If yes, does the proposal require the prior approval of CCAMLR in accordance with Decision 9 (2005)? Yes/No

7)   If yes, has the prior approval of CCAMLR been obtained? Yes/No (If yes, the reference to the relevant paragraph of the relevant CCAMLR Final Report should be given).

8)   If the proposal relates to an ASPA, what is the primary reason for designation (*ie*, which part under Article 3.2 of Annex V)?

9) If relevant, have you identified the main Environmental Domain represented by the ASPA/ASMA (refer to the 'Environmental Domains Analysis for the Antarctic Continent' appended to Resolution 3 [2008])? Yes/No (If yes, the main Environmental Domain should be noted here.)

10) If relevant, have you identified the main Antarctic Conservation Biogeographic Region represented by the ASPA/ASMA (refer to the 'Antarctic Conservation Biogeographic Regions' appended to Resolution 6 [2012])? Yes/No (If yes, the main Antarctic Conservation Biogeographic Region should be noted here.)

11) If relevant, have you identified any Antarctic Important Bird Areas (Resolution 5 [2015]) represented by the ASPA/ASMA (refer to the 'Important Bird Areas in Antarctica 2015 Summary' appended to ATCM XXXVIII - IP 27 and the full report available at: *http://www.era.gs/resources/iba/*)? Yes/No (If yes, the Important Bird Area[s] should be noted here.)

The above format may be used as a template or as a check-list for the cover sheet, to ensure that all the requested information is provided.

TEMPLATE B: COVER SHEET FOR A WORKING PAPER ON A HISTORIC SITE OR MONUMENT

Please ensure that the following information is provided on the cover sheet:

1) Has this site or monument been designated by a previous ATCM as a Historic Site or Monument? Yes/No (If yes, please list the relevant Recommendations and Measures.)

2) If the proposal is for a new Historic Site or Monument, please include the following information, worded for inclusion in the Measure:

Introduction

(i)   Name of the proposed HSM, to be added to the list annexed to Measure 2 (2003);

(ii) *Original proposing Party;* List proponent(s);

(iii) Party undertaking management: Name the country/countries which are committed to following-up (with management approach specified for the object/site);

(iv) *Type:* Building (hut, station, other building remains etc.), site, other remains (expedition cairn, tent, lighthouse, etc.) or monument/commemorative (plaque, bust)

Description and documentation of the site

(v)   Site Location: Provide both place name and coordinates (where known) relevant for site/object. Describe materials, construction, function, use. Physical Features & Local/cultural landscape. Provide pictures showing the site, monument and the location in the surrounding.

Historical / cultural features

(vi) Description of the historical context: Overview of the site in question. It would be useful if the information also clearly indicates which primary evaluation criteria contained in Resolution 3 (2009) the object/site in question triggers.

Management

(vii) Describe management and/or monitoring actions planned for the object/site in question – cf. Section 6 and 7, as well as pt. 5 in Annex to Resolution 3 (2009), as well as measures which will be taken to limit any environmental impacts that the management of the HSM may cause. It will not always be appropriate to have a formal management plan but this can be noted in the proposal.

3) If the proposal is to revise an existing designation of an HSM, please list the relevant past Recommendations and Measures.

The above format may be used as a template or as a check-list for the cover sheet, to ensure that all the requested information is provided.

Resolution 4 (2018)

Environmental Guidelines for operation of Remotely Piloted Aircraft Systems (RPAS) in Antarctica

The Representatives,

Recalling Article 3 of the Protocol on Environmental Protection to the Antarctic Treaty ("the Protocol"), which requires that activities in the Antarctic Treaty area shall be planned and conducted so as to limit adverse impacts on the Antarctic environment and dependent and associated ecosystems;

Recognising that increasing use of Remotely Piloted Aircraft Systems ("RPAS") is being made in the Antarctic Treaty area and that the technology offers many benefits, including for science and operations, and also has the potential to reduce environmental impacts in some circumstances;

Recognising also that RPAS have the potential to cause environmental impacts, and that there is benefit to adopting best practice environmental guidelines for RPAS based on the precautionary principle in order to help minimize those impacts and to assist users in meeting their obligations under the Protocol;

Welcoming the development through broad consultation amongst members and the science community, including with the Scientific Committee on Antarctic Research ("SCAR") and the Council of Managers of National Antarctic Programs ("COMNAP"), of the Environmental Guidelines for operation of Remotely Piloted Aircraft Systems (RPAS) in Antarctica ("Environmental Guidelines for operation of RPAS") that Parties can apply and use, as appropriate;

Recommend that their Governments:

1. endorse the non-mandatory Environmental Guidelines for operation of RPAS, annexed to this Resolution, as representing current environmental

best practice for planning and undertaking RPAS activities, as appropriate, in Antarctica;

2. consider when appropriate the Environmental Guidelines for operation of RPAS during the environmental impact assessment process for RPAS activities within Antarctica;

3. encourage all those authorised to use RPAS to plan and undertake RPAS activities to abide, to the best of their ability by the Environmental Guidelines for operation of RPAS;

4. encourage SCAR and the scientific community to develop research on the environmental impacts of RPAS in order to reduce current uncertainties; and

5. encourage the Committee for Environmental Protection to continue to develop these guidelines as both the technology and scientific understanding of the potential impacts of RPAS are advanced.

Environmental Guidelines for operation of Remotely Piloted Aircraft Systems (RPAS)[1] in Antarctica[2]

Introduction

Deployment of Remotely Piloted Aircraft Systems (RPAS) can, in some circumstances, reduce or avoid environmental impacts that might otherwise occur. Their use may also be safer and require less logistical support than other means of deployment for the same purpose.

These Environmental Guidelines for operation of RPAS in Antarctica aim to assist implementation of Environmental Impact Assessment (EIA) requirements and aid decision-making for use of RPAS through provision of guidance based on current best available knowledge.

System failures and/or RPA loss in Antarctica may release waste into the environment. The short and long-term impacts of RPAS, including of noise and visual intrusion on Antarctic wildlife, are presently not well understood, and there remain uncertainties about the extent to which RPAS have the potential to cause environmental impacts. As such, there is a recommendation to proceed with a precautionary approach to use of RPAS in Antarctica at the same time as seeking to maximise the many potential scientific, logistic and other benefits of RPAS technology.

It is recognised that in some cases it may be desirable deliberately to operate close to fauna or flora to meet specific scientific or other objectives that have been assessed in the EIA or permitting process. Scientific understanding of the impacts of RPAS on Antarctic wildlife is currently not well developed, with limited knowledge of physiological or long-term demographic effects. Species vary widely in the extent to which they appear to be affected by RPAS operations, and this may also vary by many other factors such as breeding stage, local conditions, etc. Behavioural displays, or their lack, are not necessarily clear indicators of the level of disturbance occurring to wildlife. RPAS operations over or near wildlife should be sufficiently justified taking into account potential for disturbance through the EIA or permitting process.

Guidelines to address aspects of RPAS in Antarctica are available from the Council of Managers of National Antarctic Programs (COMNAP), and a number of competent authorities have also prepared practical manuals for RPAS use within national programmes.

---

[1] A Remotely Piloted Aircraft System (RPAS) is defined by the International Civil Aviation Authority (ICAO) (2015) as "A remotely piloted aircraft, its associated remote pilot station(s), the required command and control links and any other components as specified in the type design". A Remotely Piloted Aircraft (RPA) is "An unmanned aircraft which is piloted from a remote pilot station". RPAS are one class of Unmanned Aerial System (UAS), and they are often referred to as Unmanned Aerial Vehicles (UAVs), Unmanned Aircraft Systems (UAS) or 'drones'. In these guidelines RPAS is used for all types of remotely piloted drone systems and RPA is used to refer specifically to the aircraft itself.

[2] These guidelines are intended primarily for application to RPAS of small to medium size ($\leq$25 kg in weight). While many of the principles and guidelines also apply to use of large RPAS (>25 kg in weight), these operations may present additional potential risks in need of specific management procedures that should be addressed in project-specific EIAs.

RPAS users are referred to these guidelines for essential additional information, particularly related to operational and safety aspects (see Appendix 1).

Pre-deployment Planning and Environmental Impact Assessment (EIA)

1. Requirements of the Madrid Protocol and its Annexes

1.1   Any proposed activities undertaken in the Antarctic Treaty area shall be subject to the procedures set out in Annex I of the Madrid Protocol[3] for prior assessment of the impacts of those activities on the Antarctic environment.

1.2   Flying or landing an aircraft in a manner that disturbs concentrations of birds and seals is prohibited in Antarctica, except in accordance with a permit issued by an appropriate authority under Annex II to the Madrid Protocol.[4]

1.3   Removal of wastes from Antarctica, including electrical batteries, fuels, plastics, etc. is required by Annex III,[5] which should be considered in contingency plans for lost or damaged RPAS as part of the Environmental Impact Assessment (EIA).

1.4   A permit issued by an appropriate national authority is required to enter an Antarctic Specially Protected Area (ASPA),[6] and special requirements to operate RPAS may apply within an ASPA or an Antarctic Specially Managed Area (ASMA): any planned RPAS operation within ASPAs or ASMAs, including any overflight of these areas, must be in accordance with the respective ASPA or ASMA Management Plan.

2. General considerations

2.1   When planning RPAS use in Antarctica, the current approved versions of the documents listed in Appendix 1, which include, *inter alia*, recommendations, guidelines, Codes of Conduct and manuals prepared by the Antarctic Treaty Parties, SCAR and COMNAP and also recent published scientific papers such as those listed in Appendix 2 may be helpful additional considerations to these guidelines.

2.2   Consider the relative environmental advantages and disadvantages of RPAS and other alternatives, and consider the environmental characteristics of the RPAS and the values present at the proposed location(s) of operation, weighing up both the benefits and environmental impacts of RPAS use.

2.3   Undertake detailed pre-flight planning, including thoroughly assessing the particularities of the operational site in advance of deployment, to ensure an appropriate understanding of its topography, weather and any hazards that may impact upon an environmentally sound operation. Where possible, carry out simulated flights using software tools.

---

[3] As required by Art. 8 of the Madrid Protocol.
[4] As required by Art. 3 Annex II to the Protocol. This permit can only be granted under certain conditions.
[5] As required by Art. 2 Annex III to the Protocol.
[6] As required by Annex V to the Protocol.

2.4   Map out flight plans, prepare contingency plans for incidents or malfunctions, including alternative landing sites and plans for RPA retrieval should there be a crash.

2.5   Assess the particularities and dynamics of the values that could be affected at the site, including the species of fauna and flora present, their numbers and/or extent, and where they are located to assess their concentrations, as part of the environmental impact assessment process and mission planning. Where appropriate, adjust flight plans, including the timing of the mission to avoid sensitive breeding periods (including for all species that may be present in addition to any study species), so that potential disturbance is minimised.

2.6   Identify any specially protected sites (*eg,* ASPAs, ASMAs, Historic Sites and Monuments (HSMs) and any special zones within these areas), or sites subject to Antarctic Treaty Visitor Site Guidelines, in the vicinity of planned RPAS operations and ensure any overflight restrictions specified in their management plans or site guidelines are followed.

2.7   Consider options and contingencies carefully in the EIA before planning to operate in and over potentially environmentally sensitive areas (*eg,* wildlife colony, or extensive vegetation cover that could be impacted by trampling), or where retrieval of a lost RPA would be difficult or impossible, while recognising that such areas may also be of particular interest for RPAS surveys.

2.8   If you plan to operate RPAS from boats or ships, be aware of elevated risks of collisions with flying birds that often follow ships.

2.9   Where multiple RPAS operations are anticipated to occur in the same area or repeatedly over time, consider in the EIA the potential for cumulative environmental impacts.

3. RPAS Characteristics

3.1   Carefully select the type of RPAS and sensors that will be most appropriate for fulfilling the objectives of planned air operations and where possible use Best Available Technology to minimise environmental impacts. Carry out test flights outside Antarctica to verify your choice (*eg,* testing sensor capabilities at different flight altitudes, and where practicable selecting sensors or lenses that allow greater separation distances from wildlife).

3.2   Consider selecting RPA models with the lowest practicable noise levels, and models with non-threatening shapes, sizes and/or colours, for example that do not closely resemble aerial predators likely to be present at the site of operation to minimise stress on prey species and/or attacks by territorial species.

3.3   Ensure the RPAS is well-maintained and operates reliably before deployment to reduce risk of failure and loss. The use of RPAS equipped with a Return To Home (RTH) feature is recommended. Ensure sufficient power or fuel to accomplish missions. For electric RPAS closely monitor battery capacity and performance, which varies with conditions. For combustion RPAS, check there are no fuel leaks, that fuel caps are secure, use best practice when handling fuel and refuelling and ensure that fuel spillage counter-measures are in place.

3.4　To reduce the risk of non-native species introductions, ensure that the RPAS and all associated equipment and carrying cases are clean and free of soil, vegetation, seeds, propagules or invertebrates prior to shipment to Antarctica. To reduce the risk of species transfer within Antarctica, carefully clean RPAS and associated equipment after use and prior to use at another site.

4. Operator Characteristics

4.1　RPAS pilots should be well-trained and experienced before undertaking operations on-site in Antarctica.

4.2　Before operating in Antarctica, RPAS test flights should be undertaken in a variety of conditions by the pilot that will be operating in Antarctica with the specific type, model and payload of RPAS that will be deployed.

4.3　RPAS operations should comprise a pilot and, as appropriate, at least one observer. Pilots should have good knowledge of the environmental requirements as listed in Section 1, and all aspects of the planned site of operations before deployment to the field, including site sensitivities and potential hazards.

On-site and In-flight Operations

5. General considerations

5.1　Pilots and any designated observers should operate within Visual Line Of Sight (VLOS) with the RPA at all times, unless the operation is approved by a competent authority to operate "Beyond Visual Line Of Sight (BVLOS)".

5.2　Pilots and any designated observers should be vigilant during operations and maintain good communications with each other throughout operations, watching for wildlife moving into the area of operations.

5.3　Complete flight operations with number and duration of flights as practicable, while still achieving mission objectives.

6. Operations over or near wildlife

6.1　Select RPAS launch/landing site(s) carefully, considering topography and other factors (*eg*, prevailing wind direction) that may influence selection of the optimal distance from wildlife. Where practicable, consider locating RPAS launch/landing sites out of sight (bearing in mind any requirements to operate within VLOS) and downwind from concentrations of wildlife, and as far away from wildlife as possible.

6.2 Consider the noise level emitted by the RPA during launch and flight to inform decisions about the location of launch/landing site and flight altitude, taking into account the influence of wind conditions on noise at ground level.

6.3 Where practicable, consider attaining flight altitude while avoiding unnecessary overflight of wildlife.

6.4 Where practicable, consider operating RPAS at times of the day or year when the risk of disturbance to species present is minimised.

6.5 During VLOS operations, pilots and any designated observers should be aware of and monitor the proximity and behaviour of predators that could attack animals or their young within the area of RPAS operations, or attack the RPA to present significant risk of collision. Should proximity of predators be observed and if their behaviour is observed to exceed levels of disturbance deemed acceptable in approvals for the activity, RPAS operations should be modified or ceased.

6.6 To the extent practicable, consider avoiding unnecessary or sudden RPA manoeuvres over wildlife, or flying RPA directly at or from above wildlife, and if possible fly in a grid flight pattern while still achieving mission objectives.

6.7 Fly as high as practicable and not lower than necessary when operating near or over wildlife. Where operation of RPA near wildlife is necessary, exercise minimum wildlife disturbance flight practices, maintaining a precautionary distance from wildlife at all times during flight which ensures that no visible disturbance occurs. Wildlife reactions to RPA vary extensively, for example depending on the species, their breeding status, the flight altitude and whether flight approaches are either horizontal or vertical.

Where multiple species are present, follow the most precautionary approach and if wildlife disturbance is observed at any separation distance, a greater distance should be maintained.

6.8 Pilots and any designated observers should operate with special care near cliffs where birds may be nesting, and where practicable maintain the horizontal separation distance. During VLOS operations, pilots and any designated observers should watch for, and inform each other of, signs of wildlife disturbance. They should be mindful that outward behavioural displays may not be a good indicator of the actual level of stress being experienced by wildlife, which should also be taken into account in the EIA and planning phase. Should wildlife disturbance be observed to exceed levels deemed acceptable in approvals for the activity, pilots should adopt a precautionary approach by considering increasing RPA distances from animals if safe to do so, and considering ceasing operations if disturbance persists.

6.9 When BVLOS operations over or near wildlife concentrations are planned, consider the practicality of placing an observer nearby to note potential behavioural changes and inform the pilot.

7. Operations over terrestrial & freshwater ecosystems

7.1 Pilots and observers should take care to minimise disturbance to sensitive geological or geomorphological features (*eg*, geothermal environments, fragile surface features such as crusts or sedimentary deposits), soils, rivers, lakes and vegetation in the area of RPAS operations, and conduct their activities, including walking over the site, so as to avoid sensitive sites to the maximum extent practicable.

7.2 Should it be necessary to make an unplanned landing and/or retrieve an RPA from an unfamiliar area, the pilot and/or observer should be especially careful to minimise disturbance to site features that may be sensitive, such as wildlife, vegetation or soils.

8. Human considerations

8.1 To the extent practicable, avoid operating RPAS over Historic Sites or Monuments (HSMs) to minimise the risk of RPA loss at these sites. Should retrieval of a failed RPA within an HSM be necessary, notify the appropriate authority and receive advice before undertaking any action.

8.2 RPAS operators should be aware that many people value Antarctica for its remoteness, isolation and aesthetic and wilderness values. Respect the rights of others to experience and appreciate these values, and where practicable adjust flight operations (*eg*, timing, duration, distance) to avoid or minimise intrusion.

Post-flight Actions and Reporting

9. Actions

9.1 In the event of an unplanned forced landing or crash, and mindful of the obligations for removal of waste from Antarctica in accordance with the Madrid Protocol (see Item 1.3), retrieve the RPA if:

- It is safe to do so;
- There is a risk that human life, wildlife or important environmental values are endangered, in which case notify the competent authority and as appropriate emergency procedures should be taken to neutralise the risk;
- The environmental impact of removal is not likely to be greater than that of leaving the RPA *in situ*;
- The RPA does not lie within an ASPA for which you do not have a Permit for entry, unless the RPA poses a significant threat to the values of the ASPA in which case notify the competent authority and as appropriate emergency procedures should be taken to neutralise the risk.

9.2 If a lost RPA cannot be retrieved, notify the competent authority, providing details of the last known position (GPS coordinates) and the potential for any environmental impacts.

10. Reporting and updating these Guidelines

10.1 Observe and record animal reactions before, during and after RPAS flights, preferably by a dedicated observer rather than the pilot who should be principally focused on RPA systems and control.

10.2 Post-activity reporting should be completed in accordance with the EIA and/ or permitting associated with the activity. Consider including details of any environmental impacts and consider how such impacts may be avoided in the future. Where practicable, consider using a standard format to report this information (*eg*, see forms provided in the COMNAP RPAS Operator's Handbook), and consider making the information accessible in order to improve RPAS environmental best practices in the future.

10.3 RPAS operators are encouraged to carry out further research into the environmental impacts of RPAS to help minimise uncertainties, undertake regular reviews of the research, and publish observations in the literature to help refine and improve these Best Practice Environmental Guidelines for the operation of RPAS in Antarctica.

Appendix 1

Selected technical documents relevant to environmental guidelines for Remotely Piloted Aircraft Systems (RPAS) in Antarctica

Antarctic Treaty Parties, Resolution 2 (2004) *Guidelines for the Operation of Aircraft Near Concentrations of Birds in Antarctica.*

Antarctic Treaty Parties, Committee for Environmental Protection *Non-Native Species Manual* (Version 2017).

COMNAP (Council of Managers of National Antarctic Programs) 2017. Antarctic Remotely Piloted Aircraft Systems (RPAS) Operator's Handbook. Version 7, 27 November 2017.

IAATO (International Association of Antarctica Tour Operators) 2016. IAATO Policies on the use of Unmanned Aerial Vehicles (UAVs) in Antarctica: update for the 2016/17 season. Information Paper 120, XXXVIII ATCM held in Santiago, Chile, 23 May - 01 Jun 2016.

ICAO (International Civil Aviation Organisation) 2015. *Manual on Remotely Piloted Aircraft Systems (RPAS)* First Edition. International Civil Aviation Organization Document 10019. Montréal, Canada.

SCAR *Code of Conduct for Terrestrial Scientific Field Research in Antarctica* (2009).

SCAR *Code of Conduct for Activity within Terrestrial Geothermal Environments in Antarctica* (2016).

Appendix 2

Selected peer reviewed scientific papers on the environmental impacts of Remotely Piloted Aircraft Systems (RPAS)

Acevedo-Whitehouse, K. Rocha-Gosselin, A. & Gendron, D. 2010. A novel non-invasive tool for disease surveillance of freeranging whales and its relevance to conservation programs. *Animal Conservation* 13: 217–225.

Borrelle, S.B. & Fletcher, A.T. 2017. Will drones reduce investigator disturbance to surface-nesting seabirds? *Marine Ornithology* 45: 89–94.

Christiansen F, Rojano-Doñate L, Madsen PT and Bejder L. 2016. Noise levels of multirotor Unmanned Aerial Vehicles with implications for potential underwater impacts on marine mammals. *Frontiers in Marine Science* 3: 277. doi: *10.3389/fmars.2016.00277*

Erbe, C., Parsons, M., Duncan, A., Osterrieder, S.K. & Allen, K. 2017. Aerial and underwater sound of unmanned aerial vehicles (UAV). *Journal of Unmanned Vehicle Systems* 5: 92–101. *dx.doi.org/10.1139/juvs-2016-0018*

Goebel M.E., Perryman W.L., Hinke J.T., Krause D.J., Hann N.A., Gardner S. & LeRoi D.J. 2015. A small unmanned aerial system for estimating abundance and size of Antarctic predators. *Polar Biology* 38: 619-630 doi:*10.1007/s00300-014-1625-4*

Hodgson, J.C. & Koh, L.P. 2016. Best practice for minimising unmanned aerial vehicle disturbance to wildlife in biological field research. *Current Biology* 26: R404-R405 doi:*http://dx.doi.org/10.1016/j.cub.2016.04.001*

Korczak-Abshire, M., Kidawa, A., Zmarz, A., Storvold, R., Karlsen, S.R., Rodzewicz, M., Chwedorzewska, K., & Znoj, A. 2016. Preliminary study on nesting Adélie penguins disturbance by unmanned aerial vehicles. *CCAMLR Science* 23: 1-16.

McClelland, G.T.W., Bond, A.L., Sardana, A. & Glass, T. 2016. Rapid population estimate of a surface-nesting seabird on a remote island using a low-cost unmanned aerial vehicle. *Marine Ornithology* 44: 215–220.

McEvoy, J.F., Hall, G.P. & McDonald, P.G. 2016. Evaluation of unmanned aerial vehicle shape, flight path and camera type for waterfowl surveys: disturbance effects and species recognition. *PeerJ* 4: e1831. doi: *10.7717/peerj.1831*

Moreland, E.E., Cameron, M.F., Angliss, R.P. & Boveng, P.L. 2015. Evaluation of a ship-based unoccupied aircraft system (UAS) for surveys of spotted and ribbon seals in the Bering Sea pack ice. *Journal of Unmanned Vehicle Systems* 3: 114–22. *dx.doi. org/10.1139/juvs-2015-0012*

Mulero-Pázmány, M., Jenni-Eiermann, S., Strebel, N., Sattler, T., Negro, J.J. & Tablado, Z. 2017. Unmanned aircraft systems as a new source of disturbance for wildlife: A systematic review. *PLoS ONE* 12 (6): e0178448. doi:*10.1371/journal.pone.0178448*

Mustafa, O., Esefeld, J., Grämer, H., Maercker, J., Rümmler, M-C., Senf, M., Pfeifer, C., & Peter, H-U. 2017. Monitoring penguin colonies in the Antarctic using remote sensing data. Umweltbundesamt, Dessau-Roßlau.

Pomeroy, P., O'Connor, L. & Davies, P. 2015. Assessing use of and reaction to unmanned aerial systems in gray and harbor seals during breeding and molt in the UK. *Journal of Unmanned Vehicle Systems* 3: 102–13. *dx.doi.org/10.1139/juvs-2015-0013*

Rümmler, M-C., Mustafa, O., Maercker, J., Peter, H-U. & Esefeld, J. 2016. Measuring the influence of unmanned aerial vehicles on Adélie penguins. *Polar Biology* **39** (7): 1329–34. doi:*10.1007/s00300-015-1838-1.*

Smith, C.E., Sykora-Bodie, S.T., Bloodworth, B., Pack, S.M., Spradlin, T.R. & LeBoeuf, N.R. 2016. Assessment of known impacts of unmanned aerial systems (UAS) on marine mammals: data gaps and recommendations for researchers in the United States. *Journal of Unmanned Vehicle Systems* 4: 1–14. *dx.doi.org/10.1139/juvs-2015-0017.*

Vas, E., Lescroël, A., Duriez, O., Boguszewski, G. & Grémillet, D. 2015 Approaching birds with drones: first experiments and ethical guidelines. *Biology Letters* 11: 20140754. *dx.doi.org/10.1098/rsbl.2014.0754.*

Weimerskirch, H., Prudor, A. & Schull, Q. 2017. Flights of drones over sub-Antarctic seabirds show species and status-specific behavioural and physiological responses. *Polar Biology* (online). DOI *10.1007/s00300-017-2187-z.*

SCAR's Environmental Code of Conduct
for Terrestrial Scientific Field Research in Antarctica

The Representatives,

Recalling Article 3 of the Protocol on Environmental Protection to the Antarctic Treaty ("the Protocol"), which requires that activities in the Antarctic Treaty area shall be planned and conducted so as to limit adverse impacts on the Antarctic environment and dependent and associated ecosystems;

Recognising the diversity of terrestrial environments, which include intrinsic and scientific values;

Acknowledging that these environments may be at risk from impacts associated with research activities, including through the introduction of non-native species, transfer of native species between locations, or the accidental release of contaminants;

Welcoming the development by the Scientific Committee on Antarctic Research ("SCAR") through broad consultation, including with the input of the Council of Managers of National Antarctic Programs ("COMNAP"), of SCAR's Environmental Code of Conduct for Terrestrial Scientific Field Research in Antarctica ("the Code of Conduct") that Parties can apply and use, as appropriate, to assist with meeting their obligations under the Protocol;

Recommend that their Governments:

1. endorse the non-mandatory Code of Conduct as representing current best practice for planning and undertaking activities in terrestrial Antarctic environments; and

2. encourage the consideration of the Code of Conduct during the environmental impact assessment process for activities to be conducted within terrestrial environments and encourage their researchers to abide, to the best of their ability by the contents of the Code of Conduct in conducting research activities in terrestrial environments.

SCAR's Environmental Code of Conduct for Terrestrial Scientific Field Research in Antarctica

Background

This Scientific Committee on Antarctic Research (SCAR) Code of Conduct (CoC) provides guidance for scientists undertaking terrestrial scientific field research in Antarctica. Reference was made to the need for this CoC during CEP IX (CEP IX Final Report; para. 132). A CoC was approved by the XXX SCAR Delegates Meeting in Moscow July 2008. SCAR presented the CoC to the CEP XII (2009) as IP 4. A further review of the CoC was coordinated by SCAR in 2017, through experts and the broader SCAR community, and the revised version submitted for consideration at CEP XX (WP 18). Further consultation was carried out in the 2017/18 intersessional period, including with COMNAP.

This CoC has its origins in the 2006 CEP discussions on avoiding the introduction of propagules[1] of non-native species. Since those discussions, the CoC has been broadened to provide guidance to design and conduct terrestrial scientific field research in a way that minimises environmental impacts, including, but not limited to, the transfer of non-native species.

Introduction

Antarctica contains many unique geological, paleontological, glaciological, and biological features. This landscape and its biological communities often have limited natural ability to recover from disturbance. Many features could be easily and irreversibly damaged. This CoC provides recommendations on how scientists and associated personnel can undertake scientific field activities while protecting the Antarctic environment for future generations, as well as not compromising future scientific research. These protocols ensure that human presence will have as little impact as possible. All personnel undertaking scientific research in Antarctica should be familiar with this CoC and field activities in Antarctica should be designed to have as little environmental impact as possible.

The Protocol on Environmental Protection to the Antarctic Treaty (also known as the Madrid Protocol or Environmental Protocol) provides a basis for environmental protection and management in the Antarctic. Climate change and increasing pressure from human activities suggest that comprehensive guidelines are needed to protect the unique features of Antarctica. This CoC complements the relevant sections of the Protocol and provides guidance for researchers conducting land-based field research (including, but not limited to - limnological, terrestrial, coastal/littoral, glaciological, biological, paleontological, sociological, historical, archaeological, climatological and geological research). A 'field'

---

[1] Propagule: means of propagation, *eg*, seed, spore, egg, live insect (including microbes in non-sterile soil).

activity is defined here as any scientific activity, and the logistics to support this activity, which is conducted in the natural environment, irrespective of its duration.

All countries with researchers that undertake terrestrial field research in Antarctica are encouraged to include this CoC within their operational procedures and to ensure that personnel undertaking or supporting scientific field research follow this CoC.

It is recommended that this CoC be followed by all personnel undertaking scientific research to the maximum extent possible and as long as it does not affect the safety of the expedition.

General Guidelines

Antarctic scientists potentially have a higher likelihood of carrying non-native propagules to Antarctic [and sub-Antarctic] ecosystems than other Antarctic travellers because their field of study often takes them to alpine or northern polar habitats. Moreover, Antarctic scientists also move between the Antarctic Conservation Biogeographic Regions (ACBRs)[2][3][4] which can differ substantially in biodiversity and geodiversity. In the process of conducting research within these habitats, Antarctic scientists can inadvertently entrain propagules and/or soil on clothing, equipment and equipment cases. If these items are then taken to the Antarctic, or among ACBRs, and they have not been cleaned/sterilised to remove or kill the propagules, an opportunity to transfer such material to and around Antarctica is created. Equipment should be properly cleaned before it enters the Antarctic, or moves between regions within Antarctica.

The implications of human transfer of taxa between locations can range from the modification of the genetic structure of populations to changes in local biodiversity and subsequent effects on community dynamics. Human transfer may involve species (or their propagules) from sites outside Antarctica, and such species would in most cases be considered non-native. However, given the differences between regions, intra-regional transfer of indigenous species also needs to be minimised. Such accidental movement of indigenous biota could compromise scientific studies of molecular adaptation, regional evolution and biogeography and reduce the inherent value that Antarctica offers as a system with very limited anthropogenic influence.

Before going into the field

Report planned activities to the appropriate national authority as thoroughly as possible and well in advance, in order to allow an assessment of the environmental impact that may be

[2] Terauds A, Chown SL, Morgan F, Peat HJ, Watts DJ, Keys H, Convey P & Bergstrom DM (2012) Conservation biogeography of the Antarctic. *Diversity and Distributions* 18:726-741.
[3] Terauds A & Lee JR (2016) Antarctic biogeography revisited: updating the Antarctic Conservation Biogeographic Regions. *Diversity and Distributions* 22:836-840.
[4] Resolution 6 (2012) - ATCM XXXV Hobart; Resolution 3 (2017) - ATCM XL Beijing.

caused on the field site(s) visited, as required by Annex I to the Protocol on Environmental Protection to the Antarctic Treaty.

Prior to conducting any scientific activity, it is essential to consider and clearly define the scope of the planned activity, including its area, duration, and intensity.

Be aware of the cumulative impacts of the activity, both by itself and in combination with other activities within the region. Consider lower impact alternatives to the activity and re-use of existing facilities wherever possible.

In order to minimise environmental impacts of field activities:

(i)   Choose sites as close as possible to research stations and use existing pathways.

(ii)   Limit the number of visitors to field sites to the people required to carry out the fieldwork.

(iii)   Where possible avoid areas that are especially vulnerable to disturbance such as vegetated areas, breeding sites, patterned ground, and water bodies.

(iv)   Re-use existing sites wherever possible.

(v)   Consider the capacity required to prevent and respond promptly and effectively to any environmental accident or incident.

Everything taken into the field must be cleaned before being taken into the field, and returned to the main station for proper cleaning, where it is feasible and safe to do so.

Precautions should be taken to avoid introduction of non-native species, or of chemical contamination, and transfer of materials between sites:

(i)   Ensure that all equipment and clothing, including footwear, is thoroughly cleaned.

(ii)   Avoid taking unnecessary packaging and materials into the field. Note that several products used for packaging are prohibited in Antarctica, such as polystyrene beads or chips.

Once in the field

Particular care should be taken in areas with sensitive biological, geological, paleontological, historical, archaeological and geomorphological features such as bird and seal colonies, roosting areas, vegetated areas, freshwater lakes and ponds, sand dunes, screes, fluvial terraces, fossil beds, fragile or vulnerable landforms (*eg*, patterned ground, unconsolidated or poorly consolidated sediments, biological soil crusts, weathering pits, water-saturated soils during summer melt periods, etc.), ice core pyramids and ventifacts.

Avoid unnecessary disturbance of Antarctic flora and fauna. Avoid areas where wildlife is easily disturbed, especially during the breeding season.

When taking samples (*ie*, geological, paleontological, biological, ice, etc.) take as small a sample as possible to minimise environmental impacts. Only take samples in accordance with the Environmental Impact Assessment undertaken for the activity and, where appropriate, any permits issued by an appropriate national authority.

The location of any spill, camp site, soil pit, drilling site, sampling site, experimental site, or any other disturbance should be recorded (preferably using a GPS), and reported to the appropriate national authority, for the benefit of future researchers.

Minimise impacts when moving around in the environment:

(i)   Stay on established trails where available.

(ii)   Avoid walking on vegetated areas, streambeds, lake margins, and delicate rock, landforms and soil formations.

(iii)   Restrict ground vehicle usage to snow and ice surfaces, or designated tracks, wherever possible.

(iv)   Where feasible, use recognized helicopter landing sites and ensure that markers for helicopter pads are clearly visible from the air.

(v)   Minimise the disturbance to wildlife by following the ATCM guidelines for operations of aircraft near concentrations of birds.[5]

(vi)   Restore any disturbances caused by activities, as long as such restoration does not cause any further environmental impacts.

(vii)   Algae and invertebrates live beneath stones. Moving rocks and stones should therefore be minimised to the extent required for the work being undertaken.

(viii) Do not build cairns.

Management of scientific field sites

Minimise environmental impacts of field sites:

(i)   Make sites no larger than needed for the proposed scientific activities.

(ii)   Keep sites tidy during use.

(iii)   Avoid activities which could result in the dispersal of foreign materials into the environment. In particular, avoid the use of spray paint, wooden post markers, etc., and, where feasible, conduct activities such as sawing or unpacking inside a tent or hut.

(iv)   Secure equipment from being blown away or stolen by inquisitive birds (*eg*, skuas, penguins).

(v)   Wherever possible, all precautionary measures should be taken to ensure collection and removal of human waste and grey water.

---

[5] ATCM Resolution 2 (2004) Antarctic Treaty Consultative Meeting XXVII – Cape Town.

When the work is complete, restore sites as far as feasible without creating further environmental impact. Remember that sites may require subsequent monitoring to comply with the Protocol for Environmental Protection to the Antarctic Treaty.

As it is important to prevent the introduction of foreign materials and contaminants into the environment:

(i)   Avoid materials liable to shatter at low temperatures, *eg*, polyethylene-based plastics.

(ii)   Take care when handling fuel, chemicals and isotopes (stable or radioactive) to avoid spills or unintentional release into the environment. Consider the recommendations in the CEP Clean-up Manual.[6]

(iii)   Store and handle fuel and chemicals using appropriate containers.

(iv)   Use drip trays where possible when handling fuels or other liquids and take special care when handling fuel in high winds.

Report any environmental accident or incident to the appropriate national authority.

If equipment is planned to be installed in the field in the longer term:

(i)   Ensure an Environmental Impact Assessment is undertaken prior to any installation, as required by Annex I to the Protocol for Environmental Protection to the Antarctic Treaty.

(ii)   Clearly identify any equipment by country, name of the principal investigator and year of installation, and state the duration of the deployment.

(iii)   Make sure installations can be retrieved and removed when no longer required, unless it is impractical, or would result in a higher environmental impact, or have been identified as useful for long-term monitoring and/or research.

Do not displace materials or collect samples of any kind, except in accordance with the associated Environmental Impact Assessment and any required permits.

When undertaking research with live animals, consider the legal requirements of national authorities and those set out in *SCAR's Code of Conduct for the Use of Animals for Scientific Purposes in Antarctica*.

Field camps

Camping and scientific equipment should be cleaned before being brought into the Antarctic or before being transferred between sites.

Minimise the environmental footprint of field camps by:

(i)   Camping on permanent snow or glaciers where possible and only if safe to do so.

(ii)   Locating camps as far as feasible from lake margins, stream beds and associated fans, and vegetated areas, to avoid damage or contamination.

[6] Committee for Environmental Protection Clean-up Manual *(http://www.ats.aq/documents/recatt/att540_e.pdf)*.

(iii) Taking special care to ensure that no food or wastes are accessible to animals.

(iv) Re-using campsites whenever possible.

(v) Keeping camps tidy during use and restore, as far as is feasible and without causing any further environmental damage, after use.

(vi) Using solar and wind power as much as possible to minimise fuel usage.

Ensure that equipment and supplies are properly secured at all times to avoid dispersion by high winds or helicopter downdrafts. Remember that in some locations high velocity katabatic winds can arrive suddenly and with little warning.

Remember that when working in an ASPA or ASMA, the area management plan may have additional requirements for field camps. Follow any conditions contained in the entry permit required for access to an ASPA. Visitor report forms[7] should be submitted to the appropriate national authority as soon as practicable.

Location-specific guidelines

Lakes and streams

Choose sampling equipment that is the least destructive to the aquatic or coastal environment. Sample carefully and avoid excessive and unnecessary sampling. Minimise cumulative impact if sampling repeatedly at a location over a long period or several field seasons. Use of dredges, trawls and box corers should be minimised.

Aquatic ecosystems in Antarctica are typically extremely poor in nutrients (except those with animal influence) and thus are sensitive to anthropogenic pollution. Measures should be put in place to minimise, as far as possible, release of human waste into the environment.

Avoid walking in streams and lake beds or too close to their margins as this may disturb biota and affect bank stability and water flow patterns. When a crossing must be made, use designated crossing points if available, otherwise walk on rocks if possible.

Minimise the use of vehicles on lake ice if possible. If access to the water body is required for scientific research, use non-motorised boats whenever possible.

Ensure that all sampling equipment is tethered or otherwise secured and does not contaminate the water body.

Clean all sampling equipment before using it in another water body in order to avoid cross-contamination. Alternatively, use separate equipment at different sites.

Wherever possible use flumes, not weirs, when monitoring streams to minimise any potential impacts of the study.

---

[7] See Appendix 2 of the Committee for Environmental Protection Guide to the Preparation of Management Plans for Antarctic Specially Protected Areas. Resolution 2 – ATCM XXXIV CEP XIV – Buenos Aires (2011)

To the maximum extent practicable, avoid the use of stable isotope tracers at the complete ecosystem level, but rather use them in closed vessels. Consider the use of naturally occurring tracers in experiments. Radioactive isotope tracers should only be used in closed vessels or in *ex situ* experiments. No stable or radioactive isotope tracer waste should be disposed into ecosystems. Document all tracer use (location, type of tracer, amount) and report this information to the appropriate national authority.

To avoid introduction of contaminants or disturbance of the stratification of the water body and its sediments:

(i)   Do not swim or dive in lakes, unless it is required for scientific purposes.

(ii)   Remove all unwanted water and sediment materials from the site, even on permanently ice-covered lakes, rather than discharging them back into the lake.

(iii) Ensure that nothing is left frozen into the lake ice that may ablate out.

(iv)   Consider using a remotely operated underwater vehicle (ROV) as a tool for underwater and under-ice research in lakes and coastal/littoral habitats.

Ice-free environments

Terrestrial vegetation includes very slow growing species and fragile growth forms. Damage by trampling may remain visible for years or even decades and further impact upon the many terrestrial invertebrate species that live in soils and feed on soil algae.

In high use areas, use existing trails where possible in order to avoid disturbing large areas of vegetation and/or soil or surface material. In lower use areas, consider whether trails or a dispersed pattern of travel would have least impact and implement accordingly. Local knowledge will often be a useful guide.

Clean all equipment and footwear, as far as is feasible, between sites to avoid transfer of soil and propagules among sites.

When sampling in vegetated areas, ensure that the site is restored as far as is feasible without causing any further environmental impact.

Limit the use of mechanical equipment for sample collection, whenever possible.

When sampling soil in desert areas, use groundsheets to contain excavated material to minimise the extent of damage to the desert pavement. Backfill soil pits and, as far as feasible, replace the desert pavement materials at the soil surface to restore the site appearance.

Do not disturb or remove rocks, minerals, fossils, meteorites or ventifacts unless it is necessary for the permitted research.

For specific guidance on undertaking scientific activities in terrestrial geothermally heated areas, please consult the *SCAR Code of Conduct for Activity within Terrestrial Geothermal Environments in Antarctica*.

Glaciers and ice fields

Remember that the use of water in hot water drills, and the use of other drilling fluids, could contaminate the isotopic and chemical record within the glacier ice.

Given that the hydrological systems under glaciers and ice sheets are connected to the wider environment and downstream contamination could occur, exercise caution when using chemical-based fluids to drill to the base of an ice sheet. Similar caution is necessary when drilling is made through ice shelves to ocean beneath. For further information on activities in subglacial environments, please consult *SCAR's Code of Conduct for the Exploration and Research of Subglacial Aquatic Environments*.

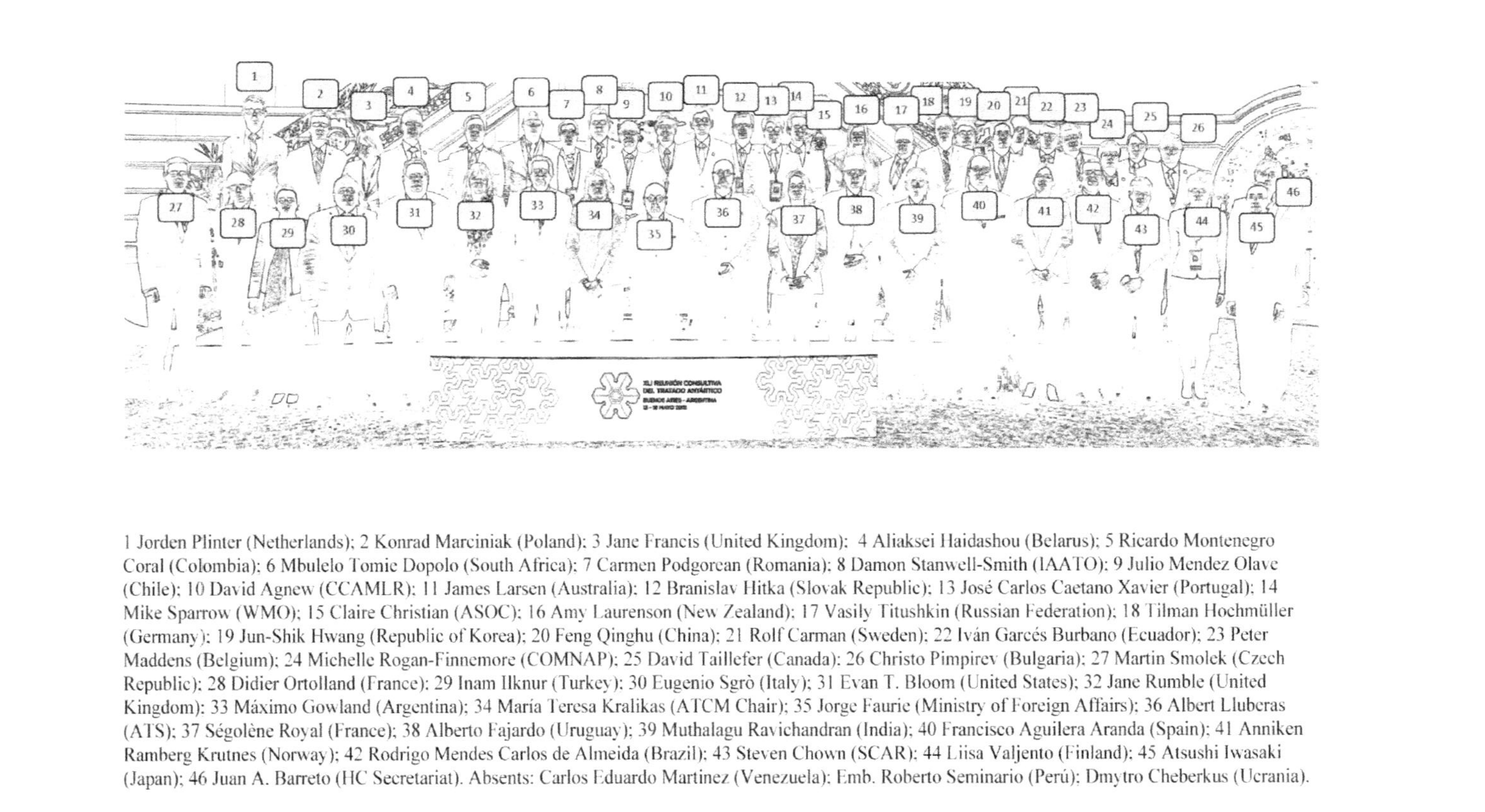

1 Jorden Plinter (Netherlands); 2 Konrad Marciniak (Poland); 3 Jane Francis (United Kingdom); 4 Aliaksei Haidashou (Belarus); 5 Ricardo Montenegro Coral (Colombia); 6 Mbulelo Tomie Dopolo (South Africa); 7 Carmen Podgorean (Romania); 8 Damon Stanwell-Smith (IAATO); 9 Julio Mendez Olave (Chile); 10 David Agnew (CCAMLR); 11 James Larsen (Australia); 12 Branislav Hitka (Slovak Republic); 13 José Carlos Caetano Xavier (Portugal); 14 Mike Sparrow (WMO); 15 Claire Christian (ASOC); 16 Amy Laurenson (New Zealand); 17 Vasily Titushkin (Russian Federation); 18 Tilman Hochmüller (Germany); 19 Jun-Shik Hwang (Republic of Korea); 20 Feng Qinghu (China); 21 Rolf Carman (Sweden); 22 Iván Garcés Burbano (Ecuador); 23 Peter Maddens (Belgium); 24 Michelle Rogan-Finnemore (COMNAP); 25 David Taillefer (Canada); 26 Christo Pimpirev (Bulgaria); 27 Martin Smolek (Czech Republic); 28 Didier Ortolland (France); 29 Inam Ilknur (Turkey); 30 Eugenio Sgrò (Italy); 31 Evan T. Bloom (United States); 32 Jane Rumble (United Kingdom); 33 Máximo Gowland (Argentina); 34 María Teresa Kralikas (ATCM Chair); 35 Jorge Faurie (Ministry of Foreign Affairs); 36 Albert Lluberas (ATS); 37 Ségolène Royal (France); 38 Alberto Fajardo (Uruguay); 39 Muthalagu Ravichandran (India); 40 Francisco Aguilera Aranda (Spain); 41 Anniken Ramberg Krutnes (Norway); 42 Rodrigo Mendes Carlos de Almeida (Brazil); 43 Steven Chown (SCAR); 44 Liisa Valjento (Finland); 45 Atsushi Iwasaki (Japan); 46 Juan A. Barreto (HC Secretariat). Absents: Carlos Eduardo Martinez (Venezuela); Emb. Roberto Seminario (Perú); Dmytro Cheberkus (Ucrania).

XLI REUNIÓN CONSULTIVA
DEL TRATADO ANTÁRTICO
BUENOS AIRES - ARGENTINA